NEW LEADERSHIP INTO THE 21ST CENTURY

Yahya ibn Shabazz

New Leadership into the 21ˢᵗ Century
Copyright © 2023 by Yahya ibn Shabazz

All rights reserved. No part of this publication may be reproduced, distributed, or transmitted in any form or by any means, including photocopying, recording, or other electronic or mechanical methods, without the prior written permission of the publisher or author, except in the case of brief quotations embodied in critical reviews and certain other noncommercial uses permitted by copyright law.

Library of Congress Control Number: 2023910677

ISBN:

Paperback: 978-1639450558

e-book: 978-1639456789

The views expressed in this book are solely those of the author and do not necessarily reflect the views of the publisher, and the publisher hereby disclaims any responsibility for them.

Writers' Branding
1-800-608-6550
www.writersbranding.com
media@writersbranding.com

Contents

Acknowledgements..v
Foreword..vii
Introduction...xv

Chapter 1:   Moral Intellectualism and its Purpose 1
Chapter 2:   Reconstruction..22
Chapter 3:   Civil Rights or Human Rights? 62
Chapter 4:   Why we Regressed an Imposed Culture 108
Chapter 5:   "Up you Mighty Nation, you can
             Accomplish What you Will"—Solutions...............178
Chapter 6:   New Leadership 230
Chapter 7:   Spiritual Application: A Summary........................253
Chapter 8:   The Rise of Moral Intellectualism.........................277

References 293
Dedication 297
Bibliography..299

Acknowledgements

The people I wish to thank for their help, without which this project would have been almost impossible for me to do, are as follows

Bro. Tariq Abdul Mu'min
Sis. Dorita McCarty
Sis. Tracy Hicks
Sis. Zubaydah N. Madyun
Sis. Peggy Van Devender
Sis. Vicki Brown
Sis. Jewell Williams
Sis. Majeedah Shabazz
Sis. Amirah Salaam
Sis. Shana Cohagan

Editors:
Sis. Daisey McKenzie,
Sis. Jamillia Lott
Sis. Fahizah Alim

Cover Design: Malik Seneferu. We pray for Allah's blessings upon us all for our sincere efforts. Any mistakes that may be found in this work belong to me alone.

Note: The reason that we omit the "o" in our spelling of G-d is because of its derogatory connotations in its reversed spelling.

Foreword

This book by Imam Yahya Shabbazz is an important addition to the small but growing body of literature written by native-born African-American Muslim leaders. There are a number of reasons why this book deserves the attention of Muslims and non-Muslims living in the United States of America and beyond. First, to the best of my knowledge, this is the first book written by an African-American imam who combines historical analysis with theological considerations in the presentation of the African-American Muslim experience. To put it in another way, one could argue that the Imam Yahya has pressed into service these intellectual resources in the articulation of Muslim American hopes to a larger audience. What I mean here is that the author tries to bring to the attention of his readers the unique situation of the African-American Muslim as he or she relates to the problems and challenges of the human condition. Certainly, many of the African-American imams have preached about the points of convergence and divergence between the black experience seen through the lens of Christianity and the black experience seen through the prism of the old Nation of Islam philosophy. What is remarkable about this work is the manner in which Imam Shabbazz negotiates two important terrains in the black experience in America. On the one hand, he is writing about the black experience from a historical perspective; on the other, he is trying to understand and interpret that historical experience through the lens of the Quran. This is to say, he locates the African-American Muslim experience in the field of black studies while at the same time drawing on biblical and Quranic narratives to underscore some of the points he wishes to emphasize to his audience. Here he follows closely the works of a number of black writers who wrote profusely about ante and post bellum America.

It is indeed against this background that I now take this opportunity to share with you some of the major highlights of the work. Imam Shabbazz opens his book with a historical recounting of events before the arrival of the slaves to America. Here he follows very closely the familiar accounts written by men and women like W.E.B. Dubois, John Hope Franklin. Leronne Bennett and countless others in and out of the academy. The main reason for this recounting is to show that black people had a glorious and honorable past and that the slave trade was a tragic moment in the history of people of African descent living in the Americas. Drawing heavily on these historical materials the imam from Mississippi bring back to our memory the glorious days of African peoples before the advent of the slavers who not only violated African peoples and their lands, but also in their vicious and rapacious ways reduced millions of them into property who were bought and sold at will until the Civil War of the United States of America.

Not being a historian but conscious of timelines and periods in the historical narratives of the professional historians, the imam implicitly identifies four stages in his narration of the black experience in the United States of America. As I stated above, the first stage in the history of the African slaves in the US goes to the pre-Columbian era in African history. These were the days when the human experience in Africa revolved around cities, towns and villages of Ancient Ghana, Mali, Songhai and other centers of civilization. My reading of Imam Shabbazz text leads me to the conclusion that, as far as he is concerned, the cultural and civilizational achievements of the individual slaves who ended in colonial and post colonial America depended heavily on what part of the continent these fortunate and unfortunate slaves came from. By fortunate slave we referred to the case of the Muslim princes, Ayub Ibn Sulayman Diallo and Abdur Rahman Ibn Ibrahima

Sori. The former came to Annapolis, Maryland where he served as a slave for a short time and managed to get his freedom through the intervention of a member of the British Admiralty sometime before the eruption of the American Revolution. The latter worked as a slave for forty years in Natchez, Mississippi before he was manumitted thanks to the intervention of a U.S. President who asked his Secretary of State, Henry Clay, to secure his freedom from Thomas Forster, the slave owner. The story of Abdur Rahman Ibn Ibrahim Sori linked fragments of American and African history by way of Morocco, for it was the Sultan of Morocco who brought the plight of this royal slave to the attention of the American president. This and other historical nuggets are part of the narrative about these fortunate slaves whose stories are being discovered and revisited almost on a daily basis among Muslims in the United States of America and beyond. Yet, while calling attention to these historical fragments which are now part of the African-American Muslim claims of historicity and authenticity of their modern day Islam, Knowing fully well that not all slaves had royal pedigree and not all were of the Islamic faith, the imam recounts the story of Africa before the slave trade very much in the manner Ali A. Mazrui called Africana Gloriana. But if there is a tinge of gloriana a la Mazrui, the imam is not fixated with this part of his heritage. Rather he recounts this story to accomplish his goal of making Americans realized that the African-American Muslims indeed shared a common heritage with other blacks in the Diaspora. Not only did they shared the agony of slavery, but they also went through both the process of deracination and of inferiorization under slavery, that institution American historians described as the Peculiar Institution. This point is very significant to the imam because his book is written with certain objectives in mind. By refreshing the memory of fellow Americans about the dignified African origins of the black man in America, the imam feels that he could move on to tackle some of the thorniest problems of American history. Not only did he examine the period of slavery but he also looked at the historical events in light of biblical and Quranic understanding. To the imam the present situation in black-white relations in the United States of America cannot be sufficiently understood by anyone if attention is not paid to the atrocities and ugliness of the period of slavery. Slavery, in his view, dehumanized the black man and women who went through this agony. Not only did they lose their humanity, but also their oppressors did everything within their power to cut them off from their religious and historical roots. This aspect of the slave trade captured the attention of the imam and he tries to relate it to the religious and political history of the black man in America,

In examining the different threads that go into the making of his tapestry of African-American history, one notices the Imam's attempt to demonstrate the convergence of early Islamic history in America and the tradition of resistance and struggle for freedom and justice among African-Americans. For example, he writes:" I believe that they(African slaves) were speaking from their Islamic heritage. It was their devotion to Allah that made them refuse to bow to another man and I believe that same spirit existed in those leaders who came along in later years to set the example for true leadership. It is only in these latter times that we hear the voices of dependency and willing submission." To back up his claim, he not only list the names of Muslim slaves that are now fully documented in the works of Allan Austin, Terry Alford, Phillip D. Curtin and Sylvain Diouf, but he also add new names that were unknown to me. Adding to the pantheon of black heroes of the War of Independence, Imam Yahya brings to our attention Saleem Poor and Peter Saleem, two black soldiers who won distinction in the battle of Bunker Hill. In this new historiography of black American history, we see the Imam listed two Muslim soldiers in the company of the better-known figure, Crispus Attucks.

Indeed the imam's discussion of the African-American historical experience suggests that for him the Nation of Islam philosophy, no matter how far it now looks removed from orthodox Islam of Prophet Muhammad of Arabia, is an historical movement that has embodied the fighting spirit of Professor Diouf called servants of Allah who were enslaved in the New World. Throughout his narrative, Imam Yahya has tried to emphasize the claim of Muslims that their religion empowers themselves psychologically to the point that they would never surrender to any human force. Their belief in Tawhid(Unity of Allah) and their unflagging faith in the reality of life beyond the grave, have always inspired them to maintain a tradition of resistance to oppression and injustice.

Chronologically, the imam's story about the black religious experience led him to the examination of the black encounter with Christianity. Knowing fully well that the black church played an important role in the black experience in America, and recognizing the relationship between black leadership training in the church and the history of black leadership in African past, he makes a number of arguments for greater achievements in this area of life. In the opinion of the imam, the leaders and the led in the Christian churches had interpreted their faith to justify and defend slavery. Yet, he is not oblivious to the pro-abolitionist activities of another set of Christian leaders who collaborated fully with black heroes and heroines of the anti-slavery movement. To those immigrant Muslims whose knowledge of the black struggle for freedom in America is pitiful, and to those African-Americans who are not sufficiently schooled about their history and heritage, this book has a lot to offer in terms of how, when and why black leaders in and out of the church championed the cause of black freedom in America. It was in this context that the imam came to the third phase in his narrative on the black struggle for freedom in America. This is the post civil war and reconstruction era in American history.

In analyzing this moment in black history, the imam acknowledges how Christianity was used by the guardians of the plantation economy to tamper both with the minds and bodies of black people. In his view, the mental transformation of the black man from his dignified self of earlier times before the Middle Passage, created the conditions and the psychological climate of white superiority, an aberration that has not only poisoned the waters of interracial relations but has also damaged the minds and bodies of many a black man and woman in American society. In this recounting of the record the imam argues that white racism in America, especially in the South, was not only a sublunary phenomenon, but it also has metaphysical implications. What the imam is saying to his readers is that the Christian concept of incarnation, which taught the slaves that God (he chooses to spell it G-D) came to us in the person of Jesus of Nazareth, is an abstract concept that predated American slavery. Yet, while conceding this fact, the imam still argues that the slave trader's portrayal of Jesus the Christ as a white man compounded what was originally an historical and sociological human problem by elevating it to a metaphysical one. How? To the imam, the theological manipulation of scriptures and the self-serving association of Church portraits of Jesus with the white race led almost all slaves to believe that their plight in America was not only historically determined but providentially decreed. It was this kind of logic and thinking that led one African-American theologian to write a book entitled, Is God A White Racist? Both the black Christian theologian and the imam in their separate ways have come to the same conclusion that there is no theodicy that could attribute to God human follies of tribalism, racism, sexism and class struggle.

Since the imam's main focus is on black leadership and the sad state of affairs in the contemporary period, he skillfully builds an ideological bridge linking the achievements of the first generation of black leadership after slavery to the present era. In his view, the achievements of the founding fathers and mothers of emancipated African-Americans society in the USA have not been sufficiently appreciated and imitated by those who are its inheritors. Against tremendous odds, the imam argues, these men and women built institutions and structures that are carrying many of us living in America today. In this part of his narrative, the imam goes to the quality of political and economic leaders that emerged during the difficult times of Reconstruction. His research led him to the list of prominent African-Americans who served in various capacities in the legislative assemblies of the post civil war south. Some of the individuals named in his list of black political leaders may not be familiar to Muslims and non-Muslims living today. However, it is an exercise in the restoration of black historical memories. Such acts of recollections made it clear to young blacks and Muslims that black leadership was evident even under trying times such as the early days of emancipation.

In his examination of these historical fragments, Imam Yahya talks about Booker T. Washington and W.E.B. Dubois as two sides of the same coin of black liberation. Like many who wrote before him, Imam Yahya too feels that the two leaders of Afro-America disagreed not on goals for the black man in America, but on tactics. Drawing heavily from the works on the most famous black leader since Frederick Douglas, Imam Yahya tells us how Booker T. Washington worked energetically to build himself up in Reconstruction America. Recalling the Washington saga with pride and admiration, Imam Yahya tells both African-American Muslims and Christians to learn from his life experiences as well as from the wisdom contained in his Up From Slavery. Apart from the political and civic leadership of the likes of Dubois and Washington, Imam Yahya also examines the contribution of black entrepreneurs in the development of the black community. Madam C.J. Walker, Maggie Lena Walker, and Ida B. Wells are celebrated as black women who by dint of hard work and character won the admiration of many in the black community. He narrates their stories with pride and joy and challenges his contemporaries to draw upon that heritage of leadership and to fertilize those achievements with modern scientific and technological knowledge and with the reclaimed knowledge of Islam that has once again entered black consciousness in America.

It is indeed against this background that the imam entered the last and final phase in his analysis. After having shown that the black man and woman of the United States of America has dignified African origins, and after having traced the historical and theological roots of white racism in the American south, the imam moves on to show how the late Honorable Elijah Muhammad contributed to the transformation of the mental estate of the African-American. In his view, the creation of the Nation of Islam by Farad Muhammad and his faithful disciple, Elijah Muhammad, was a major development in the history of the black man in America. Not only did the NOI change the way many African-American men and women looked at themselves, but also it impacted tremendously on American society. Evidences for this claim are the changed lives of thousands of men and women who were trapped in all the ills and vices of the dominant society. The movement changed lives, improved material condition, brought about new patterns and forms of leadership, and gave an immeasurable sense of pride to blacks in the USA and beyond. While tracing the history of the NOI and the kind of leadership it brought to African-Americans, The imam from Mississippi draws a picture of the black struggle of the sixties and seventies that shows how the activities of Dr. Martin Luther King and the Civil Rights Movement dovetailed and reinforced those of the Honorable Elijah Muhammad and his disciple, Malcolm X. Other scholars and commentators of the black struggle for freedom in the United States of America have presented the story in almost the same way. According to Imam Yahya Shabbazz, the reunification of blacks with Islam has an empowering effect to those who recognized that all humans are created equal and the absence of any anthropomorphism in Islam helps eliminate from the African-American Muslim mind all feelings of inferiority by virtue of the incarnation concept that elevates and privileges whiteness in the churches and beyond. The imam dwells on this issue in parts of his text and he quotes Quranic verses to support his arguments.

Imam Yahya has shown in his book that leadership in the black community could benefit a great deal from the example, teachings and activities of Imam W.D. Muhammad. Towards the end of the book Imam Shabbazz calls attention to the Post Elijahian era and the kind and quality of leadership identified with Imam Muhammad and his associates. Being the inheritors of the Honorable Elijah Muhammad and having made their contributions to the restoration of black honor and pride, blacks who are adherents of Islam should strived hard to balance the Islamic call of duty through faith in Tawhid (Unity of Alllah) and fear of the hereafter with the demands of modernity in civil society. Imam Yahya's book is that of a spiritual and civic leader among American Muslims who are very conscious of the challenges and realities of modern American life. He follows not only the teachings of Imam W. D. Mohammed but he also celebrates his leadership so that all human beings, American or not, Muslim or non-Muslim, who are genuinely committed to both Islam and the positive advancement of human society can profit from it. The book will certainly add to our knowledge about African-American Muslims and their efforts to locate themselves on the map of American religious and social history.

Sulayman S. Nyang, Ph. D.
Howard University
Washington, D. C.

Introduction

By Yahya ibn Shabazz

Imam W. Deen Mohammed said in a public address, **"Words make people."** I believe that a word can be anything that leaves an impression on the minds of human society, be it spoken, acted out, or whatever form it may take; all creation is to be seen as a word. According to scripture, all creation is here as a result of a word spoken by G-d, so again we say, "Words make people." If we can go deeper and look at the mind of the human being and look at what kinds of words go into the mental makeup of a person, we then can get a better picture of what forms the character of that person. We must understand that our physical construction only acts as a vehicle that transports the mind, which is the real person. So just to view the physical makeup of a person is not really seeing that person at all. It is the ideas, the activities, the words, etc., that come from that person's mind that help us to see the real person.

So now we can see the importance of understanding a word like "leader." **Leader:** a person that leads or has commanding influence or authority over others. The director, conductor, or guide or one who has the genuine well-being of the people as his primary concern. **Ship:** the state, condition, or quality of something. **Art:** skill of office. So now, we see that not only do we still need leaders, but also we must have leaders that have the best interest of the people at heart. Leaders with the vision, the wisdom, knowledge, and the integrity to know when to stay or change courses so that not only will they be able to get the people to the next level, but will also give the people the knowledge so that they may guide themselves through the rough waters of society. When we talk about leadership, we should understand that for the subject to even come up, there has to be something lacking in the minds of the people in terms of where we, as a people or as a society, want to go, and how we are going to reach the goals we have set for ourselves.

Leadership is a word that is part of our everyday vocabulary. We use it, however, without understanding its significance, as we do with many of the words in the English language, some of which are very important and carry with them profound meanings. Unfortunately, we use them so loosely, and in many cases, the true meanings have faded completely out of our everyday use. Words like *honor, dignity, respect, integrity,* etc., for the masses, for the most part, are rarely incorporated into our everyday language. These types of words can mold and shape the character of a person in terms of their positive development. However, when they are not used or understood or have been lost or stolen, then the whole society loses.

In today's society, we hear some foolish people make the statement, "I don't need a leader," or "I follow myself, I make my own decisions." We must understand that there's not a thought or an idea that we can think of that is our very own. We are influenced by the environment that we live in. We should also realize that this society is not "haphazard," but rather, very orchestrated. Therefore, many decisions that we make become life-determining.

In today's society, we are led to think that all accomplishments have to be material. With this kind of thinking, we can easily see how a person can become so limited in terms of growth and development, and a non contributor to the positive development of human society as a whole. Many are influenced by the pervasiveness of the media which, contrary to what those in the media would have us believe, is not art mimicking life, but rather, it helps to set the trends in life. We see many people with lots of money but with little or no vision, especially those in the field of entertainment, reach their peak in the early stages of their development, and then suddenly crash as a result of the trials of life. Still, others who desire to have these material accomplishments, although they never rise to that level, still see it as their life's goal, and in their quest for it, use illegal methods, which eventually leaves them dead, in the streets, or locked up behind bars for a good deal of their young lives. Then, there are those who continue to struggle to make ends meet and those who do manage to make it up the higher end of the economic ladder. Too many of these tend to lose their identity because they have been led to believe that the goal for the African-American community is voting rights, integration or material acquisitions. Once these goals are achieved, then the struggle is over. As a consequence of this kind of thinking, we still see ourselves, as African-Americans, at the bottom of society, not only here in America but wherever we are.

It is unfortunate that here in the twenty-first century, we are still addressing the same problems we were addressing in both the nineteenth and twentieth centuries. What is even more tragic is that we're still using the same language and the same tactics as well. If one would step outside the situation and look at the moral and mental state of the African-American community and see the old, worn-out tactics our so-called leaders are using, one would conclude that for those who are sincere but just don't know any better, it's a tragedy, but for those who do know better and continue to use their position and celebrity to keep themselves in the limelight, thereby keeping the masses under the control of others, it's a crime against the human family. Hence, the need for "New Leadership."

In no way do we mean to imply that the achievements made by the African-American community from the beginning of the twentieth century through the early periods of that era, and then on up through the Civil Rights Movement, did not have a dynamic and positive effect on the African-American community and on the whole society as well. When we reflect back on the thinking of the African-American community prior to the Civil Rights, we find great achievements, both personal and societal as well. I'm sure many of us can look back over our history during the early periods of the twentieth century and recall the personal goals that were set and accomplished by our relatives and family friends. These personal accomplishments within themselves left a lasting positive impression, not only on those of us who were close to these individuals, but their successes uplifted the entire community as well. We don't know the names of these people for they were just ordinary folks who were a part of the fabric of their respective communities, and they came from all over the country. They were not well-known heroes, nor were they national leaders. They were just common people who wanted something from life and set out to realize the goals they had set for themselves. Some of these people were schoolteachers, some became doctors and nurses. Some set up small, mom-and-pop stores in the community, and some were just fine, upstanding role models that looked after their children and had something positive to impart to the people they lived around with. As stated before, these were not nationally known individuals, but they set the tone for positive community life. Those who were in the professions made us stand and be proud as a community because of the accomplishments they made. We looked to them as representatives of the best we had to offer. Today, we might wonder what is it that made these accomplishments so wonderful and so great. We say to ourselves, these are just regular professions that anybody can just learn any time, anywhere. As a people, we should never forget our history and the struggles of our people because these accomplishments, however small they may seem to us today, were major accomplishments back in those day. We realize that just at the turn of the century, we were just coming up from physical slavery, where it was capital law for an African-American to even read a book or anything, not to mention teach others of the race to read. Most of us lived in abject poverty, and in most cases, it took everything we could make and scrape just to make ends meet. But nevertheless, we had a sense of value, and we still possessed a sense of pride and dignity that was brought over with us from the Motherland, so with that kind of thinking, we sacrificed and saved a portion of whatever money we had and made sure that someone in the family went on to get higher education, and once that person made it, he then reached back and helped other family members. This was also the period of Jim Crowism, the unwritten law that allowed white people to murder and torture blacks whenever they thought the blacks might be making some progress.

A white lynch mob would make frequent raids throughout the black community for the sole purpose of intimidation. They would drag a black man or woman from their homes and take them out and kill them. Not because these people had committed a crime or done any wrong at all; but this terrible act was done many times for the sole purpose of striking fear into the hearts of other blacks so they would think twice before trying to climb the ladder of human dignity. Even in the courts, properties owned by blacks were taken for little or no reason. In many cases, African-American businesses were burned to the ground, without even so much as an investigation from law enforcement. These examples are just the tip of the iceberg in terms of the obstacles faced by African-Americans here in America. So when our people were able to succeed in those days, we considered it a success for the whole community. Even though we had less in terms of material goods to work with, we were not lacking in spirit or the knowledge of our human worth, and these are what propelled us on to succeed against great odds.

As we reflect back upon that era, we also see people who were great leaders shoulder the task of responsibility to help keep that spirit of courage and dignity alive in the minds of the people. With the memory of physical slavery still fresh in our minds, our people could still hear the far-reaching voice of the great Frederick Douglass calling upon America to release the yoke of slavery that was holding our people back from the life of human dignity that Allah had meant for all people to have. Then there was Marcus Garvey, Mary McLeod Bethune, Carter G. Woodson, and the African-American press that helped to set the climate for positive thinking in the black community. Perhaps the two major voices that came along at that time were the voices of Booker T. Washington and W. E. B. DuBois. These two giants stood front and foremost in the African-American community, pointing in the direction of the progress of life. While Booker T. Washington favored academic, agriculture, and industrial training as the methods to bring us to a level of equal footing with others, W. E. B. DuBois chose the philosophy of agitation to bring America face to face with the injustices faced by her black citizens at the hands of white Americans.

As we came to the era of Civil Rights, most of us who were directly involved knew that period as the struggle for human rights. As African-Americans, we have always been aware of our civic responsibility. We fought America's wars, we paid taxes, in some parts of the country, we even served in political positions, and the list goes on. But when it came time to be respected as a member of the human family, America fell short. Floyd McKissick, Brother Kwame Toure, Rev. Ralph Albernathy, John Lewis, and the rest of those who led the masses stepped up to the plate of responsibility. At this time again, we see two great leaders whose voices were heard above the others pointing the direction for the African-American community. Dr. Martin Luther King, with his philosophy of agitation and his call on the conscience of America to give fair treatment to her black citizens, and the Honorable Elijah Muhammad, with his philosophy of dignity and self-respect through doing for self. It was through their leadership that the world found out about the unjust treatment the African-American community was receiving at the hands of white America. It was through the use of protest marches, demonstrations led by Dr. King, and the help of the news media that the eyes of the world came to be focused on America and the cruel and inhuman treatment of black Americans. So we, as African-Americans, were denied our civil rights, not because we didn't serve America, but because we were looked on as lesser human beings. So the struggle was for our human respectability. Somehow, as the movement progressed, this message got lost and our vision of the goal got blurred. Suddenly, we found ourselves marching to be able to sit next to someone at a lunch counter, or live in a neighborhood next door to white people, or force someone to hire us for their business. We forgot that everything we were asking others to do for us, we had already been doing for ourselves just a very few years before. Originally, all we wanted as a people was that the laws that were already on the books protect us the same way as they protected others, and the rest we could do for ourselves. As new laws were written for minorities and put on the books, it seem that every one has benefited from them, except us as a people. Others have taken these laws, used them to improve their lives and the lives of their loved ones, while we, as a people, are just like the lame man in Biblical scripture, waiting by the pool for the water to be troubled so that someone can help us so that we may be healed. Water in this scriptural sense represents the human sentiments of society that we depend on to do for us what we can do for ourselves. Or we are like Lazarus, who sat by the rich man's table waiting for the crumbs to fall. Or even Jonas, who stole away on the ship and went to sleep next to all the cargo or material wealth on the ship. The ship is symbolic of America. While others have taken advantage of the laws that we were responsible for bringing into existence, we seem to be stuck in the period of protest and demonstrations, and instead of using those laws to improve ourselves, we have made begging and protesting a way of life. Our so-called leaders have seized on our tragic situation and have used it to keep themselves gainfully employed. I do not believe that this was the vision of Dr. King. In fact, I believe that he would be quite disturbed if he was here to witness the outrageous activities of those who claim to carry on his leadership. I believe that the work that was accomplished by Dr. King was his contribution to the progress of the African-American community, and ultimately, to the total society, because his life was a benefit to the world. However, we are not to view him as the ultimate leader, as we were led to believe. Dr. King had a part to play. He did his work, and now its time for us to move on to the next level. We always want to remember his contributions and the contributions of all our ancestors, but we don't want to get caught up in sentimental memory, for then, our progress stops.

The Honorable Elijah Muhammad, with his program of dignity, self-respect and doing for self, was also at that time a very powerful and influential leader. While the media gave the praise to Dr. King for his stand on non-violent tactics and highlighted integration more so than human rights, which was the real goal of the movement, they presented the Honorable Elijah Muhammad as a teacher of hate, thereby turning the attitude of many blacks against him. The Honorable Elijah Muhammad was taught by Fard Muhammad, who introduced him to the Islamic faith, although this was not the true religion of Al-Islam. The Marcus Garvey Movement also influenced the Honorable Elijah Muhammad as well. So with this philosophy of pride, dignity and independent thinking he had for black America, it is little wonder why the powers that be sought to turn blacks away from Elijah Muhammad by misrepresenting his teachings. Ironically, this idea of doing for self was put in the atmosphere by the Honorable Elijah Muhammad, and today, we see it, alive and well in use by many of those who rejected his philosophy back in the day.

With the assassination of Dr. Martin Luther King and the passing of the Honorable Elijah Muhammad, the world looked on in wonder and pondered the question, "Who will they turn to now? Who will pick up the banner of leadership for the Black man now?" Suddenly, in stepped Imam W. Deen Mohammed, with a new language and a new vision for progress. This progress is not only for the African-American community, but it's to be an example for world progress.

Imam W. Deen Mohammed is the only leader on the scene today that uses obedience to G-d, along with the example of Prophet Muhammad and the courage of the Ancestors to advance the whole of mankind. He is the only leader we see on the national scene today that is calling on African America to reach deep within ourselves and tap our own human potential and use it to improve ourselves and our loved ones. It is then when we have accomplishments, as do others, that we will garner the respect of others. His leadership is not based so much on the tangibles, such as focusing on issues like black and white, as was done back in the sixties. Rather, his method is to teach us how to identify this new and more powerful kind of slavery that gives the appearance of freedom, but in reality, it's the worse kind of slavery. It is the kind of slavery that we enjoy and rush headlong into, but in the end, it breeds apathy, ignorance, destruction, and destitution. So a leader would not only have to have vision, but moral vision, and possess a deep and genuine concern for the well-being of the people. Also, that leader has to see all people as his people. Above all, that leader has to be a servant of G-d. A study of the pattern of conduct, both private and public, will identify such a leader.

A true leader has to be able to read the signs or the abstracts in the society, and also teach those who follow him to be able to do the same. A true leader does not want to lord it over the people and have them focus on him as their savior; but rather, he teaches them as much as he can, holding back nothing, thereby giving the people the power and the mastery over themselves, the wisdom and the knowledge to be able to guide themselves, their families, and their communities to true freedom. With this method, we can see why he cannot be bought and sold, or intimidated by this society. Imam Mohammed is the leader of the American Society of Muslims, and is respected as a renowned leader around the world. It is this leadership that is setting the pace for human society. New Leadership into the 21st Century gives direction to not only finding the answer to true Freedom, Justice, and Equality, but it points to the real goal that we all should be striving for. That goal is "Human Excellence."

Chapter 1

Moral Intellectualism and its Purpose

This topic is so important, that it required a review of some of the giant scholars and thinkers of the past, and their views on the responsibilities of intellectuals, for it is and was always the intellectuals who spoke out in defense of high standards, concerns, and fair play for the citizenry. Much of what is presented in the following pages of this writing on the intellect will give us a better understanding from a moral, social, and spiritual perspective, so as to understand not only its purpose, but why some see it as a duty to use their minds against injustice. They also recognize why it is so important to those who seek to undermine the thinking capacity of the masses for control over them, to use every tool to suppress their ability to think and reason. In the history of our world, all kinds of methods have been used to elevate the wealthy and powerful, while keeping the common people subordinated. We have the Dark Ages of kingdoms, Lords and Nobels, who ruled over the serfs, on through the times of slaves and plantation owners here in America. During those times the people were ruled over through brute strength. The king ruled at will. In today's society we have a whole lot of intelligent people, but we don't have many intellectuals. These intelligent people are from the high institutions of education, but their minds are bought off by the corporations to be used to speak for them not the public. The great poet Publius Vergilius Maro usually called Virgil, October, 70 BC-September19 BC, wrote, "The Noblest Motive is the Public Good." 1. Internet, accessed October 5th, 2021. These kinds of writings act to give us a view on the thinking of the thinkers of times gone by, and why it is so very important to resurrect that kind of thinking today. Virgil lived at a time in Rome of high literacy and was considered the most influential poet in his time. He is known primarily for his poem Aeneid about the founding of Roman after the Trojan war. There is no known outcry from Virgil regarding political and social issues, but in spite of this though, my own opinion is that because his origin was from meager beginnings, his sympathies leaned in that direction, hence the statement on "The Noblest Motive." We hear the term "Commonwealth," meaning a state or nation united based on laws and united in agreement of the people for the common good. I view the commonwealth as the source of humanity for the society. The human wealth within the common person. They are the ones who identify with the folk who carry the weight of the government on their shoulders and maintain human concerns for the masses of the people. That is our wealth, our humanity. We are wealthy in human concerns; hence we are the "commonwealth." The common people. Our common identity that we all share is our humanity. That is the identity all humans share, those of us who have not allowed this society to destroy us as human beings. We are, or should be rich in our humanity, that is our common bond. When these kinds of concerns begin to fade from the society, intellectuals are usually those who recognize the evil pattern. It is no accident that society get derailed as time passes, but there are always those who have been blessed by Allah to watch over the people are point out these evils and their dangers to humanity.

When the world was less evil than we see it today, there were great thinkers who used their minds to make sense of creation and connect it to human life. Most were of Greek origin and made real contributions to getting the thought process in motion.

The direct influence of Ancient Egyptian literature on Archaic Greece has never been fully acknowledged. Greek philosophy (in particular of the Classical Period) has -especially since the Renaissance- been understood as an excellent standard sprung out of the genius of the Greeks, the Greek miracle. Hellenocentrism was and still is a powerful view, underlining the intellectual superiority of the Greeks and hence of all cultures immediately linked with this Graeco-Roman heritage, such as (Alexandrian) Judaism, (Eastern) Christianity but also Islam (via Harran and the translators). Only recently, and thanks to the critical- historical approach, have scholars reconsidered Greek Antiquity, to discover the "other" side of the Greek spirit, with its popular Dionysian and elitist Orphic mysteries, mystical schools (Pythagoras), chorals, lyric poetric, drama, proze and tragedies.

What exactly did the Greeks incorporate when visiting Egypt? They surely witnessed (at the earliest in ca. 570 BCE, when Naukratis became the channel through which all Greek trade was required to flow by law) the extremely wealthy Egyptian state at work and may have participated, in particular in the areas they were allowed to travel, in the popular festivals and feasts happening everywhere in Egypt (the Egyptians found good religious reasons to feast with an average of once every five days).

In his Timaeus (21-23), Plato (428/427 - 348/347 BCE) testified the Egyptian priests of Sais of Pharaoh Amasis (570-526 BCE) saw the Greeks as young souls, children who had received language only recently and who did not keep written records of any of their venerated (oral) traditions. In the same passage of the Timaeus, Plato acknowledges the Egyptians seem to speak in myth, "although there is truth in it." According to a story told by Diogenius Laertius (in his The Lives of the Philosophers, Book VIII), Plato bought a book from a Pythagorean called Philolaus when he visited Sicily for 40 Alexandrian Minae of silver. From it, he copied the contents of the Timaeus... The Greeks, and this is the hypothesis we are set to prove, linearized major parts of the Ancient Egyptian proto-rational mindset. Alexandrian Hermetism was a Hellenistic blend of Egyptian ink lore and Denali manth Dieteni bt Search 2. Internet. Last accessed February 9th, 2023. Wim Van Den Dungen. The Impact of Ancient Egypt on Greek Philosophy.

These were pre-Socratic philosophers, and their focus were primarily cosmology, the beginning of the substance of the universe, but their inquiries went well into the workings of the natural world as well as human society, ethics and religion. There was Thales, Anaximander and Anaximenes. They all attributed the origin of the world to water. There was also Pythagoras the mathematician who created the well-known Pythagoras Theorem. Pre-Socratics have had enormous impact on western society bringing such concepts as naturalism, rationalism and paved the way for scientific methodology.

3. Internet, Access October 20th, 2021.

While the pre-Socratics, or those who came before Socrates, were philosophers who focused primarily on the natural creation, Socrates was an intellectual and his attention was directed towards human conduct, the right and wrong of the human being. He maintained a very high regard for the human being and created the idea that 'No one does wrong intentionally.'

For Socrates (469–399 BC), intellectualism is the view that «one will do what is right or best just as soon as one truly understands what is right or best," that virtue is a purely intellectual matter, since virtue and knowledge are cerebral relatives, which a person accrues and improves with dedication to reason. So defined, **Socratic intellectualism** became a key philosophic doctrine of Stoicism. The Stoics are well known for their teaching that the good is to be identified with virtue.

Typically, Stoic accounts of care for the self-required specific ascetic exercises meant to ensure that not only was knowledge of truth memorized, but learned, and then integrated to the self, in the course of transforming oneself into a good person. Therefore, to understand truth meant «intellectual knowledge», requiring one›s integration to the (universal) truth, and authentically living it in one›s speech, heart, and conduct. Achieving that difficult task required continual care of the self, but also meant being someone who embodies truth, and so can readily practice the Classical-era rhetorical device of parrhesia: "to speak candidly, and to ask forgiveness for so speaking"; and, by extension, practice the moral obligation to speak the truth for the common good, even at personal risk. This ancient, Socratic moral philosophic perspective contradicts the contemporary understanding of truth and knowledge as rational undertakings. 4. Internet, Accessed October 12th, 2021.

It can correctly be said that Socrates was among the first to use the intellect to rationalize and address issues that impacted human society which is how the term Moral Intellectualism came to be seen as part of the language. He started us to think and use our minds and rationale for how we related to each other as human beings. The intellect is that part of our human makeup that guides us, causing us to stop and think about the various influences that impact the society. It causes us to think and investigate, to question and sometimes oppose the actions of government or any influence that could impact society adversely. All humans are born virtuous meaning that we were all born with good character. Therefore, virtue doesn't have to be integrated or built into us, it is inherently who we are and what makes us human. We do however have to be mindful and prevent the negative influences in the environment that causes us to be other than what Allah created us to be not to control us. As stated earlier, some people desire to have power and authority over others and once in position of that authority they become oppressors. This is where moral intellectualism appears, not just merely to identify the difference between the right and wrong of a thing, but to raise the conversation to a much higher level, for now we're dealing with moral logic, ethics, integrity, etc;.

Please allow me to pause here to add that all the afore mentioned thinkers and philosophers although of Greek origin, their wisdom and thought process were derived from their interactions with the Egyptian schools of thought. Plato, Pythagoras, Heracleitous, etc.; Imam W. Deen Mohammed, son of the Honorable Elijah Mohammed, leader of the Nation of Islam, said, 'morality graduates, it evolves from the elementary definitions of just knowing what's right and what's wrong, or pretty and ugly. Morality graduates to moral logic, moral vision, ethics, security, and so on.' That is to say that when we evolve into understanding morality in the higher levels of the society, it becomes the duty of the higher mind, the intellect that's under the influence of moral judgement to call society back to the path of moral consciousness sometimes even at great harm or loss of life to themselves.

To be clear, while Socrates saw virtue as purely intellectual, and the Stoics saw it as something that had to be learned and then added to the human makeup, these were excellent beginnings to get the thinking process started and improve upon this already laid foundation. Let us understand that virtue is an innate part of our human makeup. Although virtue or our moral character, does evolve into the intellectual realm, it starts out as our basic moral principle, but it cannot remain on the elementary level and be able to move the society forward. That is to say that morality must graduate to the intellectual realm as we see the world in intellectual warfare today. Allah created us with a moral nature, and a conscience to let us know when we are about to commit a wrong act.

In the Holy Quran, 30:30, Allah says to us, "So set thy face truly to the religion, being upright, the nature in which Allah has created mankind: no change (there is) in the work wrought by Allah. This is the true religion, but most men understand not." Since the Quran was revealed in the Arabic language, it is important to translate some of the words for the purpose of clarity. The Arabic word for face in the above verse is "wajh," and it means the reason or purpose for something, the intent or design, the face or purpose of an act. What is being said here is the witness to the words of Socrates in his saying that people will do what is right or best just as soon as one understands what is right or best. To expand on these words, let us also look at the term "being upright," also the phrase, "the nature in which Allah has made mankind." The term "being upright" from the Arabic word "hanif" meaning the true believer, that one who through reflecting on their past life, has evolved to the level of the true believer, and sees the foolishness, and wrongs happening in the environment as the influences to be shunned, and also abolished. The phrase that says, the nature in which Allah has made mankind is from the Arabic word fitr, and it means that which is natural, the natural nature of mankind. That which is innate. That is to say that the nature of the human being was created by Allah, in obedience to Allah with a mind to think and make decisions for self. We must understand that in the creation of human nature, there is also the conscience acting as a guide for human conduct. The Holy Quran calls it the self-accusing spirit. Socrates omits the God element in his dissertations and in doing so, his views are limited. However, this is not to be seen as a fault, for we evolve in our thinking as human beings and add more clarity to the valuable information already available, and I do believe that he was a believer in a higher power.

Allah! There is no God but He, the Living, the Self-subsisting, Eternal. No slumber can seize Him nor sleep. His are all things in the heavens and on earth. Who is there can intercede in His presence except as He permits? He knows what (appears to His creatures as) before or after or behind them. Nor shall they compass aught of His knowledge except as He wills. His Throne doth extend over the heavens and the earth, and He feel no fatigue in guarding and preserving them for He is the Highest, the Supreme (in glory). Let there be no compulsion in religion: Truth stands out clear from error: whoever rejects evil and believes in Allah hath grasped the most trustworthy handhold, that never breaks. And Allah heareth and know all things. 5. Holy Quran. 2: 255-256. Yusuf Ali's Translation

We should understand the mind, or the intellect is created by Allah to obey Allah. As God's crown of creation, he has invested within the genes of the human being the wisdom of using the intellect to create, to imagine, fantasize and advance human society by using the creation given to us by God to make life better for the world. And even though the intellect was created to obey the Creator, it is the environment we live in that we act otherwise, because the powerful and rich gain control of the natural resources of creation and use them to control and manipulate the masses. In His mercy Allah doesn't require that we obey Him. In the above ayat God tells us there's no compulsion in religion, not even from Him to His subjects. This tells us the intellect has the freedom to move with at least limited will. What is so wonderful about this is that the human being who is the highest of Allah's creation has the freedom to make choices about our lives. God gives us the freedom to believe in Him or not, but He also lets us know that our downfall is at our own disobedience. But at the same time, we see the intellectuals rise to oppose those who would bring humanity under their rule so they can continue to exercise material and political dominance over the people. Although we may not think of them in this manner, but the prophets were some of the first intellectuals, hence we see the meaning of "Moral Intellectualism." Although they were men who had to eat their daily bread, they married and had families while at the same time, speaking for the good of the people. All the prophet from Adam, Noah, Abraham, Moses, Jesus, Mohammed the last Prophet, all were men of one faith, and all came with the same truth from the same God.

All these prophets are mentioned in both Bible and Holy Quran, however there are other prophet in Quran that aren't in the Bible, but they bring the same message. Allah sent the Prophet Hud to the Ad people to warn them against fabricating falsehood. The people whom Hud was sent to was so steeped in lies, falsehood, calumny that Allah saw need to wipe them from the earth. Another Prophet named Salih was sent to the Thamud people. Salih told the people not to ham-string the she-camel. The she camel is symbolic of a community of people that if left to themselves, can be self-supportive and very productive. The term hamstring is from the Arabic word "'aqara" meaning to be given to drinking, to be sterile, or barren. We see evidence of this today in the masses as we are confronted with a bombardment of negative issues that leaves us so confused that we continue to stumble in darkness. This is especially true in the African American community where resources are wasted on foolishness such as drugs, alcohol, fads and other destructive lifestyles that hinder progress. etc, which is promoted through media and other sources. The words barren and sterile refers to the absence of the ability to find answers for guidance and direction. The Prophet Shuaib was sent to the Madyan people to admonish them against withholding from the people what was rightfully theirs, thus causing oppression and hardship on the people.

Allah didn't only give men the ability of the intellect, there were also women who were great thinkers of the day. One such was Mary the mother of Jesus. We find in surah 21:91 entitled, The Prophets where Allah is blessing the Prophets He sent to mankind, and she is mentioned among them, not as a prophet, but great in character as were the prophets. She is also mentioned in 3:37 where her caretaker Zakariyah would enter her chamber to give her wisdom, but found she was already blessed by Allah. Then there was Queen Asiya, the wife of Pharaoh the ruler of Egypt during the times of Prophet Moses. It was Asiya who saved Moses' life when he was but a babe, and she stood against her husband the Pharaoh because of her faith for which she was tortured. She is also mentioned in 66:11. There is also Hagar one of the wives of Prophet Abraham. It was Hagar through which Allah blessed us with the well of Zam Zam that sprung up at her heels while she was in childbirth with her son the Prophet Ishmeal son of Abraham who he helped to build the Ka'abah the First House for the worship of the one God. There is so much that can be said about all these great men and women of God and of the people that to elaborate on their lives would take never ending volumes based on new understanding we have about their lives today. However, I think the most important point is that many of these people have been elevated to spiritual levels so high that we the common people are unable to identify with them. We see them as unreachable because of that high level they're placed on when they're people just like us, but Allah saw something in their character that set them apart from the larger society and He called them to Prophethood and service to humankind. But they were mortal beings with needs and desires as all people possess. Allah addresses this in the Holy Quran in the following ayats as well as other places in His Holy Book. 3:144 and 21:7-8, and they all represented different nations at different times. Moses went right to Pharoah and addressed him about the inhumane treatment of the people, and Abraham became the unifying force of all the great religions, while Lot the nephew of Abraham preached hard to the people of Sodom and Gomorrah on a lifestyle so abominable that God referred to it as something never practiced before in history. Jesus was not only persecuted by the government but also by the religious leadership among his own people for waking up the minds of the people, speaking truth to the power of government and condemning the religious leadership for keeping the minds of the people in slavery. Prophet Mohammed, known as the universal and the last Prophet, received revelation of the Holy Quran condemning racism, slavery, mistreatment of women, and reawakened the sciences again after Europe had gone into the Darkness Ages. With the Quran he brought intellectualism, science, philosophy, agriculture, medicine and all that advances mankind stimulating the minds of men for the good of all humanity. He is that prophet mentioned in Old and New Testaments of the Bible. That one Jesus referred to as the Comforter and the one who will come and lead us into all truths. So, although most of society may not regard prophets as intellectuals and freedom fighters, we can see that this is exactly what they were.

Centuries after Socrates, there arose another great thinker by the name of Renee Descartes (1596-1650). He was really among some of the world's greatest thinkers, in my opinion. I believe his greatest contribution was to encourage the stimulation of thought for the expressed purpose of realizing that one actually exists. Descartes' idea of being, depended on the activity of thought. His idea of himself as a physical entity meant nothing unless his mind was busy. It was Descartes who coined the phrase, "Cogito, ergo sum." Which is Latin for, "I think, therefore I am." In one of his writings called Theory of Ideas. In his mind, Descartes saw ideas as the fuel for his reason for being. In other words, to have an idea is to say that the thinking process exist, therefore, he exists. In a letter to Guillaume Gibieuf, dated January 19, 1642, he says, "I am certain that I can have no knowledge of what is outside me except by means of the ideas I have within me," 6. Internet, Accessed November 29, 2021. Descartes' Theory of Ideas. Stanford Encyclopedia of Philosophy.

The term "Man means mind," again coming from the mind of the renowned modern-day scholar and thinker, Imam W. Deen Mohammed when he told his followers that the true person is the mind. This physical body just transports us around, so the real person is really the mind. He also said that in studying scripture, he found that the old scribes when using the term man or mankind, it referred to all humanity. So, what we're saying here is that these terms are not gender based but are meant to address the thought process of the people. Man means mind is speaking to that universal human mind.

Both men and women use their minds to help bring about progress in the society, and although these ideas are coming from either men or women, they're designed to advance humanity. So now, we realize a progression, or an evolutionary process here. Let us not forget that we're talking about moral intellectualism and its purpose of guiding humanity to enlightenment and progress. It is today and always has been the intellectuals who have recognized the dark forces of the satans or the satanic mentality in their effort to deceive the people for their own control. When we reflect on the pre-Socratic Era, those great philosophers like Thales, Anixamander and Anixamenes who saw water as the beginning of creation, Pythagoras who saw the universe as created from numbers. Leucippus and Democritus known for their atomism and for their opinions that only void, and matter exist, while the Sophist advanced critical thinking and philosophical relativism.

These pre-Socratic thinkers developed ideas that are central to western society today such as naturalism and rationalism and paved the way for scientific methodology. As we can see that although the primary focus at the time was cosmology, they were able to see all creation as one creation and that it worked in an orderly fashion presenting no confused ideas to human thought, and I would venture to say that it was for this reason that Socrates developed the idea that intellectualism means that people will do what is right or best as soon as they realize what is right or best, and that no one will intentionally do wrong. The perplexing and catastrophic events we see in today's world that causes stress and in too many instances, brings out the worst in all of us, just wasn't happening in that time period to the degree as we are witnessing today.

As mentioned earlier in this writing, the mind that is in tune with its natural self, and sees nobility in the human being, it is this mind that by its very nature, stand for the safeguard of the society, and it is that voice that is raised in defense of humanity. It is because of this self-imposed obligation that the morally based intellectuals can see and hear what the masses of the people can' hear or see, as they go about their daily tasks in the society. Those who lift their voices for the good of humanity aren't chosen by anyone, or group or organization to let their voices be heard, they are just people who see a great wrong and serious deceptions imposed on the people and they speak because God created the human being to obey Him alone, but those who seek dominion over the people create false desires and appetites unchecked by knowledge within the people and thus the masses become controlled by the evil forces in the world.

It should be noted here that not all intellectuals are from the higher institutions of learning. Some are and others are not. Dr. Mattin Luther King, and Booker T. Washington are examples of some who did come from academia, but the Honorable Elijah Mohammed who had only a third-grade education, and Fredrick Douglass who was tutored by the owners of the plantation he was on and taught himself as well. These were some of the most influential men in the history of the world and they all saw that, 'the good of the people is the noblest cause.' In reflecting on the history of the Prophets we know that Prophet Mohammed ibn Abdullah, 570 Mecca to 632 Medina, and was the last of the prophets sent to humanity really brought the knowledge of the importance of thought into full and complete view. It was his concern over the moral condition of the people that burden him. Although he was a businessman, he was not versed in the high science we of language. It has been said that Mohammed could not read but we know this is an incorrect statement because as was just stated, we know he was a very successful businessman which requires some literacy. So, what is meant by saying he could not read is that he was not educated in the sciences and symbolic teachings as was just stated above. It was because of his upright character and concern for the people that Allah blessed him with the revelation of the Holy Quran which through the diligent study and application of those who followed him, not only improved upon the knowledge of the pre-Socratic philosophers of centuries past, also opened up an entire new world of enlightenment in science, medicine, astronomy, and all aspects of human growth and development. Therefore, much emphasis is placed on the intellect because it is the place where ideas for human development is born. Everything we have comes from the minds of human beings by the grace of God.

The first surah or chapter of the Quran revealed to Prophet Mohammed was "Iqraa" or "Read," again, addressing thought, the mind of humanity. The first five ayats or verses of that surah are as followers. "Proclaim! (or Read!) with the name of thy Lord and Cherisher, who created. Created man out of a leech like clot. Proclaim, and thy Lord is most bountiful. He who taught (the use of the pen.). Taught man that which he knew not.

In the second verse of this chapter the term "leech-like clot" from the Arabic word "alaq," refers to the mind. It means to cling, to adhere or stick to something. A thing of value. This describes the functions of the mind as it absorbs the knowledge of the environment associated with it. Also, the term "Most Bountiful," in the third verse refers to the great blessings Allah has placed upon us as humans. It is from the Arabic term " 'Akram" meaning that which is more nobler, precious, valuable. To be high minded, generous, noble hearted. This definition is really the definition of the person, because the mind is the true person. So, we see that Mohammed the Prophet was an intellectual, and through the Quran, he addressed us through the intellect, the best of our human makeup.

Some centuries later, Abu Hamid Al – Ghazali, 1056-111, was born in Iran. He was a follower of Prophet Mohammed and was a Persian polymath. He was from the Shafi'I school of Islamic thought and was one of the most prominent and influential figures of his time. Known as Imam Muhammad -I Ghazali, he was the author of many books, one of which is known as Ihya 'ulum al-din which made Sufism (Islamic mysticism) part of orthodox Islam. 7. Internet Accessed December 12th, 2021. Here we want to address his great work on; "On the Intellect, its Noble Nature, its Definition, and its Divisions." The Noble Nature of the Intellect: It will be superfluous to show the noble nature of the intellect (al'aql) especially because through it the noble nature of knowledge has been revealed. Intellect is the source and fountainhead of knowledge as well as its foundation. Knowledge springs from it as the fruit from the tree and the light from the sun and vision from the eye. How then could that which is the means of happiness in this world and the next not be noble or how could it ever be doubted? 7.
Imam Ghazali. On the Intellect, its Noble Nature, its Definition, and its Divisions. Section vii.

A further explanation of the nobility of the intellect and the knowledge that springs from it, is to realize that the reason or purpose for the creation of the mind is for the service of Allah. It was Allah's first creation as it relates to the human being, and as such, surah 96, Iqraa, Read, or Proclaim, an appeal to the intellect by Allah is the first surah revealed to Prophet Mohammed in the Revelation of the Holy Quran. This is because as mentioned earlier in this writing, there are always those who seek dominance over others and will use the mind and their limited free will to rob God of the allegiance of mankind that belongs to Allah. So, when Allah says to us to Read or Proclaim, we are to understand that the nobility of the intellect lies in the effort we put forth to dispel the darkness thus opening the society up to light, or intelligent thinking.

The terms 'nur' and 'nari,' both refer to the mind, the thinking of man. Nur means to seek enlightenment, to be illuminated, to have insight, while nari means fire, gun fire, satan, to be fiery, etc;. We must keep in mind that we're talking about the intellect, a state of mind. One that builds up, another that tares down. Nur, light or knowledge never changes at its base or foundation. Allah tells us in HQ 24:35, "Allah is the light of the heavens and the earth." God's word, or light never change, but what does change is our understanding of its application from generation to generation, but the foundational aspect stays the same. An example of this is the fact that Allah has created us human, and regardless of the troubles we find in the world at any given time or place, the best way to deal with it is from the point of our humanity. The term nari also means light but it's a different kind of light. It refers to the super ego, the fiery mind puffed up with pride and self-importance refusing to obey Allah. In HQ: 7:11-13 Allah commands the angles to prostrate before Adam, but Iblis refused and was haughty, because of his fiery intellect, or mentality. Although this is light, it's not the kind of light that gives direction that allow us to grow and evolve because it destroys rather than build up.

Just to clarify, when Imam Ghazali says to us on this same page of this book, "To be sure the noble nature of the intellect is perceived instinctively," we should not mistake this to mean that humans move on instinct, but rather the intellect is part of our natural human makeup, in fact, we are mind and mind is us. As humans we do not operate on instinct, we operate on intelligence. However, we should understand that if we want to evolve into a greater knowledge of who we are and our relationship with God, we must give ourselves to that which lifts us up. Study the attributes of Allah and strive in that direction. If we give ourselves to the mundane and profane influences of the society, then we do become animals, and we will follow instincts as opposed to intelligence. Further explanation on surah HQ: 24:35, where God tells us in his Holy Book, "Allah is the light of the heavens and the earth. The parable of his light is as if there were a niche and within it a lamp: the lamp enclosed in a glass: the glass as if it were a brilliant star: lit from a blessed tree, an olive, neither of the East or of the West, whose oil is well – nigh luminous, though fire scarce touched it. Light upon light! Allah doth guide whom he will to his light: Allah doth set forth parables for men: and Allah doth know all things."

In this ayat we see all truth and knowledge is from Allah and its available to humanity if we avail ourselves to it. Before the age of the electric light, people used an oil lamp to light their homes with. The base of the lamp had an opening or a niche in the center of it. The base of the lamp would then be filled with oil and a wick would extend from within the oil filled base of the lamp up through the niche, an inch or so above it. The wick has absorbed the oil so when lit, it burns like a candle. When first lit it only lights a small portion of the room, but when the glass globe is placed over the flame, the entire room as well as other portions of the house becomes lighted.

The niche for the human being is our willingness to submit to God's will. Sometimes the negative influences of society pull at us drawing us away from obedience to Allah leaving just a small amount of will power in us. That small amount of will power or resolve is like the niche and the more oil, God's pure truth we absorb the stronger we become as believers and the more our light will shine for the good of humanity just as Prophet Mohammed did upon receiving Qur'anic Revelation. Our minds become the source of wisdom and knowledge which extends throughout our entire being and people can see the presence of the light through our character. How wonderful is the word of Allah! This light from a blessed tree neither from East or West is talking about centers of influence and domination, as we know the dominant forces of the world try to control mankind from these perspectives. But Allah is telling us that he controls all, his throne or authority extends over all creation, and none can lay claim to it but Allah. He alone is God!

The light of Allah that illuminates the mind and develops us as human beings won't allow us to see injustice in the society and not raise our hand against it. This is what Moses, Jesus, Mohammed and all the prophets did. This is what Socrates and those who followed him spoke about pointing direction for human society.

Allah never leaves the society without light for its guidance. When society leaves the Straight Way or gets off the Right Path, there is always someone to call it back to its humanity. There will never be an excuse for man in his wrongdoing to his fellow man to say to Allah, "I didn't know, or there was no warner that came to us." We use our minds for all the wrong reasons not realizing that God created the mind is our true self. The mind is where ideas for human development originate. The structure we call flesh, or our bodies is the transport for the true person. So, when the ayat in the above passage from Allah's Holy Book bids us to "read," it's referring not only just the ink on the page but God's entire creation. Again, in the words of Imam W. Deen Mohammed, "man means mind," and its what we allow to enter our minds that determines the person we will be.

> The Prophet also said, *"The first thing that Allah created was the intellect. On creating it Allah ordered it saying, 'Come forth', and it came forth. He then ordered it saying, 'Return', and it returned. Thereupon Allah said, 'By My power and glory I have created nothing more reverent towards Me than thee. Through thee I take through thee I give; through thee I reward and through thee I punish."*

The intellect being the first part of our human makeup created by Allah tells us that it has to be used for the proper advancement of human society. We degrade ourselves when we place things of lesser value above who we really are. Greed, lust, worldly passions, material gains, etc; when we make these our priorities, we misuse the purpose our minds/we were created for in the beginning. So then we see the rise of the intellectuals calling society back to its true purpose, to wit, the service of God through serving our fellow human being.

It has also been related on the authority of Hadrat 'Umar that the Apostle of Allah said, "Man doth not gain anything like a worthy intellect which leadeth him to righteousness and dissuades him from sin; nor doth his belief become complete and his religion upright until his intellect matures." And again, "Verily man will attain the rank of the fasting worshipper through his good character; but no man will be blessed with good character until his intellect matures. Then and only then will his belief become complete, and not until then will he obey Allah and disobey the Devil."

It was also related on the authority of Hadrat Abu-Sa'id al-Khudri that the Apostle of Allah said, "For everything there is a support, and the support of the believer is his intellect; in proportion to his intellect will his worship be." For have you not heard the words of the sinners in Hell: "Had we but hearkened or understood, we would not have been among the dwellers of the flames." [67:10] It has also been related on the authority of Hadrat 'Umar that he himself once asked Tamim al-Dari [3] saying, "What holds the supreme authority among you?" Tamim replied, "The intellect." Thereupon 'Umar said, "Thou hast said the truth. I have asked the Apostle of God the same question and he gave me the same reply saying, "I have asked Gabriel what the supreme authority is and he answered, 'The intellect.'" 8. Imam Ghazali. On the Intellect, its Noble Nature, its Definition, and its Divisions. Section vii. The ferocious, and strongest among them, fear the very sight of man, because they sense his superiority over them, which is the result of his native resourcefulness. For this reason the Prophet said, "The position of the chief (shaykh) in his tribal organization is like unto that of the Prophet among his people." [1] This however, is not because of the abundant wealth of the shaykh, nor because of his great person, or his enormous power, but rather because of his rich experience, which is the fruit if his intellect ('aql). For this reason you find that the Turks and the Kurds as well as the ruffians among the Arabs and all other people, despite the fact that they are so close in their lives to the beasts, respect their shaykhs instinctively. Similarly, when several of the rebellious Arabs, who had made up their minds to kill the Prophet, saw him and beheld his noble countenance, they feared him, and there shone on them through his face The beasts, despite their weak understanding, respect the intellect, so that the largest; most the radiant light of prophecy, although it was only latent in his soul in the same manner as the intellect.

To be sure the noble nature of the intellect is perceived instinctively. It is our purpose, however, to relate what the tradition and the Qur'an say concerning its noble nature. Thus we find in the Qur'an that Allah called it light when He said, "Allah is the Light of the Heavens and Earth. His Light is like a niche in which is a lamp - the lamp encased in a glass - the glass, as it were, a glistening star." [24:35] The knowledge derived therefrom was called a spirit, a revelation, and a life. Said Allah, "Thus have We sent the Spirit to thee with a revelation, by Our command." [42:52] And again, "Shall the dead, whom We have quickened, and for whom We have ordained a light whereby he may walk among men, be like him, whose likeness is in the darkness, whence he will not come forth?" [6:122] Furthermore, whenever Allah mentions light and darkness He means thereby knowledge and ignorance respectively, as is evident in His words, "And He will bring them out of the darkness into light." [5:18]

It is important for us to understand that there is but one creation. In other words, the inanimate, the instinctive and the intelligent are all created by Allah with varying levels of existence. The inanimate meaning the sun, moon and stars, planets, trees, vegetation, etc; and then the instinctive, the animals, wild beasts, insects, etc; and then there are the homo sapiens, or the thinking part of God's creation known as the human being who moves on intellect. Imam W. Deen Mohammed called the human being "The Crown of Creation," meaning the highest part of the creation. To say that all creation is one is to say that none of the afore mentioned classes of the creation is made from a different material than the other, but whereas the inanimate only moves from the influence of an exterior force, the animals move only on instinct and the human being was given intelligence to move and improve our condition to make life better for ourselves. So the mind is the highest part of our human makeup and it is what Imam Al-Ghazali was referring to in his comments from Holy Quran 24:35. "Allah is the Light of the Heavens and Earth. His Light is like a niche in which is a lamp - the lamp encased in a glass - the glass, as it were, a glistening star."

The Prophet said, "O ye men! Know Allah and be ruled by intellect, then ye will know what ye have been enjoined and ye have been forbidden. Know ye that intellect is your glory before Allah. He who obeyeth Allah, although his looks may be ugly, his rank lowly, his station modest, and his appearance shabby, is intelligent; but he who disobeyeth Allah, although his looks may be good, his rank exalted, his station noble, his appearance fair, and his power of speech sharp and fluent, the same is ignorant. For the apes and the pigs are, in the sight of God, saner than he who disobeyeth. Therefore be not deceived by the honor which the men of this world receive: verily they are of those who are doomed."

The Prophet also said, "The first thing which Allah created was the intellect. On creating it Allah ordered it saying, 'Come forth', and it came forth. He then ordered it saying, 'Return', and it returned. Thereupon Allah said, 'By My power and glory I have created nothing more reverent towards Me than thee. Through thee I take through thee I give, through thee I reward and through thee I punish."

You may ask, if this intellect is an accident (*'arad*), how could it have been created before all other substances, and if it is an essence (*jawhar*), how could it be a self-existent (*qa'im binafsih*) essence and not be isolated? If you should ask such a question, then you should know that it belongs to the science of revelation (*'ilm al-mukashafah*), and, therefore, it is not proper to discuss it under the science of practical religion (*'ilm al-mu'amalah*) which is our present concern.

It has been related on the authority of Hadrat Anas that a group of people once commended a certain man in the presence of the Prophet and praised him excessively. Thereupon the Prophet said,

"What kind of an intellect hath that man?" But they replied saying, "We tell these about his diligence in prayer and about the various good works he doeth and thou inquirest from us concerning his intellect!" The Prophet answered and said. "The fool doeth more harm through his ignorance than doeth the wicked through his wickedness. Moreover, men will not advance to a higher degree of proximity to God except in proportion to their intellect."

It has also been related on the authority of Hadrat 'Umar that the Apostle of Allah said, "Man doth not gain anything like a worthy intellect which leadeth him to righteousness and dissuadeth him from sin; nor doth his belief become complete and his religion upright until his intellect matureth." And again, "Verily man will attain the rank of the fasting worshipper through his good character; but no man will be blessed with good character until his intellect matureth. Then and only then will his belief become complete, and not until then will he obey Allah and disobey the Devil."

It was also related on the authority of Hadrat Abu-Sa'id al-Khudri that the Apostle of Allah said, "For everything there is a support, and the support of the believer is his intellect; in proportion to his intellect will his worship be." For have you not heard the words of the sinners in Hell: "Had we but hearkened or understood, we would not have been among the dwellers of the flames." [67:10] It has also been related on the authority of Hadrat 'Umar that he himself once asked Tamim al-Dari [3] saying, "What holds the supreme authority among you?" Tamim replied, "The intellect." Thereupon 'Umar said, "Thou hast said the truth. I have asked the Apostle of God the same question and he gave me the same reply saying, "I have asked Gabriel what the supreme authority was, and he answered, "The intellect."

To speak on the purpose of the intellect today raises many questions, for never in the history of the world has there been a greater need than there is today. The world is in triple darkness in terms of guidance and vision. We have many great writers and historians that are well versed in the moral, social and political issues in the society, but none takes a stand to question the direction society is going. We don't hear the voice of Dr. Martin Luther King, or Malcolm X, whose name is El Hajj Malik Shabazz, Ralph Waldo

Emmerson, Paul Krugman, and many others both male and female who let their voices be heard against injustice and moral degradation. The best we can do today is listen to people who have great intellect. They are intelligent, but they represent a political party, or the views of big business, or some other entity that pays them. We don't see them speaking out against the true cause of racism, or homosexuality being forced on the people, or taking a stand against homelessness, worldwide poverty and its origins, etc.

Many of those who can speak out seem to settle for a tv interview, or funds for their organizations so they can continue to stay employed while they give the appearance of caring. The entertainment industry is the biggest slave master in the world today. Everything from greed and poverty to racism and the river of blood that have been left on the nation's school campuses can be deposited at the door of the entertainment industry. This is not to say that there is nothing good from that entity, its just that the bad is so bad that it overshadows any good that may come from that.

The term "Intellectual" has taken on a new meaning since the last time I looked up the definition. Today it carries a lot of vague meanings like intensive reasoning, or deep thinking on subjects such as literature or philosophy, and while this is true, it means literally nothing and has no use in dealing with the perplexing issues that weights so heavily on the minds of the people today. When I first looked it up a few years ago it meant someone who took a moral stand against issues that were harmful and sometimes deadly to human society. I'm using my own words here but this is the gist of what being an intellectual was about. No one ask them to be a leader but the causes they spoke out for or against was in line with the thinking of the general public, and the public saw them as unelected leaders and followed them. That was my understanding of "Moral Intellectualism and its Purpose."

Chapter 2

Reconstruction

Although this book is about leadership in the African-American community, its ramifications are for any that seek progress for themselves and others. To understand this statement properly, the context must be understood. An in-depth study of American history as it relates to the Institution of Slavery has to be undertaken. In fact, I would hope that a careful study of the historical events in general that went to make up this great country of ours will be revisited. My belief is that the history, the people involved with it, and the language they used, are so profound and such an integral part of what made the foundation of America so strong, I think it would be a mistake for us to allow that great wisdom to fade into oblivion. Now, I know that many people already keep the history, but too many of us don't, and this is to our own disadvantage. There are lessons to be learned and relearned by keeping in touch with the history. In a deeper study of the Institution of Slavery, I believe that we can then begin to realize its consequences on the minds of its victims, their descendants, the minds of those who established this dreaded institution, and their descendants as well.

My purpose here is not to continue to decry the era of slavery and the plantation days, certainly not to use it as an excuse for the regression of too large a part of the African-American community. Rather, it is to recognize the fact that in spite of the past, we must continue to grow as individuals and as a community. For in our growth, society will have hope. So this writing is not for the African-American community only, but rather for the general community, for in understanding the Institution of Slavery and how deeply it went into the very soul of the black community, and now, we are witnessing the rise of the descendants of those slaves to positions of leadership, without malice and hatred for the descendants of those responsible (though some of those descendants even today struggle to bring that dreaded institution back), and to understand the excellence of the human spirit.

The life and struggle of the African-American community is not to be seen as a victory for a race or ethnic group only, but more importantly, it is a victory for that entity that we all share, and that is the human spirit. This statement should not be misconstrued to mean that each of us is not proud of our ethnic makeup, indeed we all are, rather it is to say that along with the ethnic makeup given to us by G-d in order that we may distinguish each other physically, He has given us something even more precious: the sameness in spirit so that we may share the joys, the victories, the hurt and injustices of each other, thereby enabling us to see the need in working for the good of all mankind.

One of the most important characteristics of the human spirit is its resiliency. Even though man may try to destroy it or bring pressure to bear upon it through various means of manipulating the society, be it through economics, political, or social means, we find that the spirit always comes back strong, with new energy, and motivation. Man cannot destroy it because man did not create it. In the end, man is powerless, because the human spirit finds its origin in Allah. As we follow America's growth and development from the period of Reconstruction up to the present time, we will clearly be able to see the manifestation of that spirit personified in those who were responsible for bringing America back together again.

Reconstruction was that period of time in America right after the Civil War, from about 1867 to1878, when America was in the process of pulling itself back together again. There were lives lost and blood shed to keep this great country united under G-d. Congress had already decided that for each state to rejoin the Union, it must vote to rewrite its constitution. Along with this, for the first time, we see thousands of African-Americans becoming registered voters. The Republican Party and the Freedman's Bureau fueled participation of these newly registered voters, as it marked the first time African-Americans would vote in the South. Many of the names on the ballots were those of African-American convention delegates. The Republican Congress had also prohibited the old Confederate leaders from participating in the election, while others just refused to take part. So in effect, the old Southern aristocracy had died and would be powerless for the next few years.[1] (Wesley 2. 3)

So each of the Southern states held their constitutional convention, where both black and white Americans were represented among the delegates. During these conventions, there were educated as well as uneducated men of both races, but they all worked hard and in earnest to find solutions to the problems of their states. The South Carolina Daily *News* reported, "The best men in the convention are its colored members."[1](3) The primary concern of those African-Americans who came into political positions at that time was the well-being of the common man. It is my own belief that because of the effects of slavery, the voice of the African-American spoke loud and clear for the well-being of the common man. Laws were argued and debated at each state convention for public support of the welfare of the common citizen. These kinds of concerns were virtually unheard of in pre-Civil War days. The old Southern aristocracy concerned itself primarily with the well-being of those who were in affluent circles. So not only did they overlook the plight of the lowly slave to the point where it was considered a capital crime for a slave to read or even attempt to learn to read, the old Southern aristocracy had little or no regard for people of their own race.

The poor whites, with no other advantage than the color of their skin, found that the only way to elevate themselves in their own minds was to persecute blacks, while those in the aristocracy remained in control. So this idea of concern for the common citizen was new in the South, and it was the African-American delegates to the various state conventions that were leading the charge. It must also be noted that although African-Americans would not be able to take advantage of any of these services they helped to institute for many years to come, still, they led the way to put them in place.

If we look at the South Carolina legislature, we will see an example of the kinds of concerns the lawmakers were dealing with all over the South. As stated before, the laws passed by this body stood in stark contrast to those of pre-Civil War aristocratic government: The new government was concerned with the homes for the orphans, the poor, the blind, and a hospital for the mentally ill. Paramount to all other concerns, however, was that of free public education.1^). So if we look closely and study correctly, we will see that this period of Reconstruction was not only to bring the Southern states back into the Union again, but more importantly, to reconstruct the humanity of the human being. Of course we know that this monumental feat was never accomplished at that time, and in fact, we're still struggling with it today, but at least the idea was put into motion.

As I reflect back on the 1960s during the Civil Rights Movement, I remember talk circulating around the movement that white people were afraid that if black people came to power in this country, they would somehow retaliate for the treatment received by our ancestors during the days of slavery. If we look back over the history with just a little consideration, we will see that evidence will present itself concerning the great humanity of the African-American community. It was through their leadership and efforts at the constitutional conventions held in each state, that we can see that African-Americans supported, argued and fought for issues that would mean progress for every citizen of their state. In fact, they had to fight against white people in high political positions for the well-being of the common citizen, which also included the lowly, common white man. Ironically, as we shall see, it was the combination of those two constituents that led to the political demise of the African-Americans in the South.

In politics at that time, it was almost impossible to bring into the South any new ideas that provided public support and funding for relief measures that would benefit everyone. And as stated before, at the top of every state convention's concern was that of a free public education system. The battles fought were long and hard, because not only did the delegates have to deal with framing the issues discussed and debated in the legislature, but they also had to deal with prejudices and racism. For example, in Mississippi, there were eighteen African-American and eighty whites Americans, and framing a suitable constitution was next to impossible. When the convention opened, a white delegate stood and proposed that the word "colored" be placed by the name of each African-American on the rolls. John R. Lynch, an African-American delegate, proposed that the color of each delegate's hair be entered to show the silliness of such remarks by men whose purpose was lawmaking.1(3) On the subject of education, measures for integrated or segregated schools were left out all together.

In Louisiana, where half of the delegates were African-American, and many were freemen and landowners before the Civil War, black legislators objected to the disenfranchisement of the old Confederate leaders and proposed that they should be restricted only from holding office, but still maintain their voting rights. Even this idea was distasteful to the old confederacy. The idea of a black man being in position to lend them a helping hand seemed below them, and this made the struggle that much harder, but in the end, Louisiana's new constitution provided for equal rights, new labor laws, suffrage for men of both races, and public schools for everyone.

In South Carolina, an African-American tailor named Robert C. Deluge, who was also a Republican leader, led the charge for free public education. He argued that since the federal government had failed in their promise of land along with their freedom, the ex-slave needed an education to prepare for the future. So the delegates agreed upon the issue of education. Another African-American named Francis L. Cardozo spoke on the inevitability of segregation. "There can be separate schoolsfor white and colored," he stated, "and if any colored childwishes to go to a white school, he shall have the privilege of doing so. I have no doubt, in most localities, colored people will prefer separate schools, particularly until some of the prejudice against their race is removed."[1] **(4)**

So we have here in brief some history on the period of Reconstruction and some of the concerns contained in it. We can also see the struggle it took to bring some semblance of direction for progress to the conventions taking place throughout the South. These are examples of the struggles of all the state's conventions, and in spite of all the opposition, through difficulty, the task was achieved. So Congress, in order to reunify the union, required only a majority instead of a two-thirds vote for state constitutional ratification. Still, Mississippi had to have a presidential order and a special election to ratify her constitution.

In fact, it was 1870 before Mississippi, Florida, and Texas would rejoin the Union[1] (4) Massachusetts was the first state to send African-Americans to the state house. There was Edwin G. Walker, son of the great abolitionists David Walker, who was a frequent contributing writer to Freedom's Journal, an anti-slavery newspaper. He sold used clothes to seamen who traveled through the area. After starting his own newspaper, called Walker's Appeal, he would stuff copies in the pockets of the clothes he sold. Thus, he was able to get his anti-slavery publication circulated all over the country, including the South, where anti-slavery publications were outlawed. David Walker was also a proponent of education as well in that he saw it as an escape route to real freedom. He said in one of his writings: "I would crawl on my hands and knees through mud and mire to the feet of a learned man, where I would sit humbly and supplicate him to instill in me that which neither devils or tyrants could remove only with my life. For colored people to acquire learning in this country makes tyrants quake and tremble on their sandy foundations."[2] *(Bennett 30)*

Even after his death, Walker's Appeal continued to be circulated around the county, with its anti-slavery message that helped the conscience of the nation to continue to move in the direction of abolishing slavery. There were also others in the Massachusetts state house, such as John Smith, Joshua Smith, George L. Ruffin, and William Walker. John P. Green, a graduate of the Ohio Union Law School in Cleveland, was elected justice of the peace. In South Carolina, Louisiana, and Mississippi, African-Americans had considerable power and influence. Some were ex-slaves with crude manners, but they served as well or better than many of their white counterparts. In South Carolina, two speakers of the house were African-Americans, and three times, an African-American was chosen as president of the white-controlled Senate. An Englishman who had observed the African-Americans in action noted that they would have served credibly over any commonwealth assembly.1 (5)

The Mississippi House of Representatives of 1871 had thirty-eight African-Americans and seventy white Americans, with seven African-Americans serving in the Senate. John R. Lynch, a former slave freed during the Civil War in Louisiana, moved to Natchez, Mississippi, where he attended night classes. He also furthered his education through self-study. Governor Amos appointed him to justice of the peace. Lynch was later elected to the Lower House, and elected its speaker. He was given a testimonial and presented with a resolution commending his house leadership, and the impartial manner in which he had presided over its deliberations. Later, he was elected to the U.S. Congress. The Mississippi legislature set up a new school system, enacted civil rights laws, and rebuilt charitable and penal institutions.

In Louisiana, the varying shades of color made it difficult to determine the race of its members. The Senate was thought to include seven African-Americans out of its thirty-six members, and the house had nearly half. An African-American named R. H. Isbell was speaker of the house in 1868. The Ku Klux Klan worked within the legislature to weaken the Republican Party by intimidating both blacks and whites, and almost starting a civil war.1 (6)

The Alabama legislature in 1868 had twenty-six African-Americans in the state house, but only one senator. James T. Rapier, the noted African-American politician, served in the U.S. House of Representatives. The Ku Klux Klan was active in Alabama politics, especially during election time, which caused more conflict between whites and blacks. In Georgia, there were twenty-nine African-Americans elected to the state house, and three senators. The white legislature voted in 1868 not to seat its African-American members. Instead, they wanted to seat the whites with the next highest votes. The State Supreme Court sided with the African-Americans and they took their seats.

Two Georgians, Aaron A. Bradley, and Henry M. Turner, stood out from the rest of the black legislators. Bradley attacked discrimination fearlessly. He was defeated at the polls, but the voters rallied and he was returned to his seat in Atlanta. Henry Turner had studied law, history, and theology and was a preacher. President Lincoln appointed him as the first African-American chaplain in the Union army. He served on the education committee in the state legislature and helped to develop the public schools system. He was a Republican Party leader and was named postmaster general of Macon, Georgia by President Grant.1 (6). In Florida, the African-Americans sought alliances with poor whites, farmers, and carpetbaggers. The poor whites united to remove them from the lawmaking branch.

In North Carolina, the legislature had one hundred forty nine white Americans and twenty-one African-Americans. There were three African-Americans in the fifteen-man Senate. Two African-Americans served as speaker of the house. Just as in other Southern states, the old confederate leadership, the carpetbaggers, and the scalawags, struggled for power. The poor whites and blacks usually sided with one faction or the other. Eventually, the Southern whites united against the blacks and expelled them from the legislature. This same pattern took place all over the South 1(7). The African-Americans voted the Republican ticket, but also had a desire to work with the Southern Democratic planters, many of whom sought their cooperation. The poor whites became jealous of this continuous growth of political influence among the African-Americans and continually pushed them down. So, owing to intimidation, fraud, and their own lack of organization, African-Americans were eventually removed from the political scene[1] (8).

So we can see that despite the prejudices, bad attitudes, and resentments of the old Southern aristocracy, some form of governmental organization and direction was worked out, and once again, the nation was united as one. And although it would be years before they or their descendants could take advantage of them, it was the African-American politician who was primarily responsible for leading the charge of framing legislation that would create laws and institutions that would work for the benefit of the common citizen.

The seeds for these kinds of concerns were planted in the minds of leaders and laymen, and as a result, generations that followed are able to benefit from them. These same laws represent the foundation of the legislation that we see passed and improved upon today that respect the dignity of all people.

Reconstruction must also be seen from another angle, and that is the fact that while it was white people who wanted to divide the country for their own self-interest, it was a combination of both blacks and whites that stood up to the task of putting the country back together again. Without this period of Reconstruction, the nation would no doubt still lag behind in many of the social and racial ills we have today. Reconstruction was not only meant for rebuilding the nation, but more importantly, rebuilding the souls of men. Although we have come a long way, we still have a long way to go. The seeds for the journey have already been planted and we are now witnessing the progress made by the fruits of those seeds.

It has always been the desire and goal of the majority of the black community to build the government up so that America would be prepared for the long journey ahead of her for restoring dignity to all her citizens. The seed has already been planted and soon, we will witness the final fruit. The primary reason for this desire and goal of the black community to build the government up is so the concerns for human development can grow, to serve as a reminder to those past and to those to come, regardless of race, that if a people can be put down so low and still rise with the well-being of the whole at heart, and stand on top and reach back to help others, then this is a testimony to the power of G-d and the spirit given to man by G-d.

So we see the struggle of the African-American people not just for African-Americans alone, but for the life of the whole nation. Now let us consider the words of the great freedom-fighter, Sojourner Truth: "America owes to my people some of the dividends ... she can afford to pay, and she must pay. I shall make them understand that there is a debt to the Negro people they can never repay. At least then, they must make amends."[2] (28). So, just how do you pay a people back when you have tried to steal their souls? How do you really make amends? Since we all know that no amount of material wealth can even begin to compensate this debt, so then, we consider that which is most precious and valuable, and that is the mind of the human being. The minds of the people must be free to think for themselves and grow to their fullest potential. When we talk of freedom, we mean freedom in its true sense. Freedom in the way that G-d intended. This kind of freedom doesn't mean going shameless, nor does it mean doing whatever it is you think you're big enough to do. Freedom for the human being must mean maturity in responsibility; it must mean intelligence, progressiveness, lawfulness, compassion, rationale, all those things that go to improve the society of mankind. Freedom of the individual to be able to grow to his fullest potential, regardless of race or gender. Freedom to understand that this world belongs to all of us and that we all are responsible to the one G-d. When we begin to understand that we do not live in a haphazard world, then we will begin to take on our individual responsibility to be masters of our own destinies. Those who would seek to control the minds and the potential of the human being will no longer posses that ability. We must now begin to look at this new time as the time of righteousness. We are moving into a time when goodness will prevail, and we must work to be a part of the new day. So then, there is nothing that can be done to repay a people coming out of the doors of the Institution of Slavery, but if you want to attempt to make amends, stop hindering their progress for positive growth and development. Give the people, all the people, their minds back. This will go a long way in terms of patchwork, as it relates to the destructive history of mankind in this country. And if this attempt at amends is made, G-d will do the rest.

As we continue to move on through history, we see the emergence of two giants from the African-American community. The ideas and advice of these two great thinkers will dominate the landscape of African-American thought for the next century. Booker T. Washington and W. E. B. DuBois achieved much success and respect during their day, and their wisdom continues today. In order to understand their philosophies and the vast differences in their approach to solving the African-American problems, we must look at the backgrounds and the environments they came from.

Booker T. Washington was born somewhere around 1858 or 1859; he says himself he's not sure of the exact year, but it was near a post office crossing called Hales Ford. His family had no assets when he was born, as his birth took place on a plantation in the midst of the most miserable, desolate, and discouraging surroundings[3] (Washington 9). The lifestyle he and his family endured was barely a step above that of an animal. He knew nothing of his ancestors past his own mother. He had supposed that his ancestors on his mother's side had suffered in the middle passage on the slave ship from Africa to America. He does remember that his mother had a half-brother and a half-sister. In those days, not very much attention was given to keeping black family records. Since slaves were thought of on the same level as that of an animal, the arrival of new slaves to the plantation went virtually unnoticed.

Booker T. had heard reports that his father was a white man. He never knew his name. In fact, the only thing he did know about his father was that he never cared anything about him[3] (10). His mother was the plantation cook. The cabin they lived in not only had holes in the walls for light, but also for the cold air of winter. The door to their cabin also had large cracks in it, besides being too small for the doorway it was supposed to cover. The naked earth was their floor. There was no cooking stove, so all the cooking had to be done over an open fire, with pots and skillets. There was no time for his mother to spend with her children besides taking a few minutes with them before her work began in the early morning hours. He says he recalls his mother awakening him and his brother and sister late one night to feed them a chicken she had gotten from somewhere.

There were no pastimes or sports to take part in, as the life of the slave was nothing but work from his birth until his death. The only glimpse he got of school while he was a slave was when he would carry the books of one of his mistresses to the schoolhouse door[3] (12, 13, 14)

When it came time for the slaves to eat, there was no sitting around the table as family. It was more closely related to feeding the animals. You got what you could when you could, a scrap here and there. Some ate from pots while others ate from skillets, and all ate with their hands, scratching for the small morsels with their fingers, as would any other animal on the plantation.³ (16)

At the close of the war, Booker T's mother's husband sent for them. His stepfather had run off from the plantation he was on when the federal troops came through, and was living in the small town of Malden, West Virginia, where he worked in a salt furnace. It was here that the opportunity for him to secure an education for himself presented itself. After Booker T. and his family arrived in Malden, he found his stepfather had secured a job for him and his brother to work in the salt furnace as well. His workday usually started at around four o'clock in the morning. In the furnaces, the barrels of each packer was marked with a certain number, and his stepfather's number was "18." This was his first encounter with book learning.³ (33)

From his earliest recollection, Booker T. always had the burning desire to learn to read. Somehow, his mother was able to get an old copy of Webster's blue-back Spelling book for him. Although he had no one to teach him, he mastered the alphabet in a few weeks. His mother was right there with him to provide courage and moral support, and this, to a large degree, made the task much easier. After some time had gone by, a young black man from Ohio, who had been a soldier and was also educated, came to town. The people engaged him as a teacher, so the first school for black folks in that area was opened. Because of his work hours, he had to make arrangements with the teacher to give him night classes. After some time, Booker T. was able to go to school during the day by working earlier hours in the morning and coming back to work after school was done.³(36,38) The quest for an education was paramount in Booker T's mind and he allowed no obstacle to stand in the way of him securing one. His day schooling was soon cut short and he had to resume his night classes again. This time however, he had trouble getting a good instructor. Many times, he knew more than the instructor did.

Soon, he heard talk of the Hampton Institute. Booker T. secured a job at the home of Mrs. Viola Ruffner, wife of General Lewis Ruffner, owner of the salt furnace and coal mine. Several of the other boys had tried to serve her, but they all left with the same excuse. She was too strict. But Booker T. decided that he would much rather work for Mrs. Ruffner than stay in the furnace. So he went to work for her at $5 a month.3(43,49) Booker T. stayed with Mrs. Ruffner about a year and a half before going on to Hampton Institute. While there, he learned a great deal about the meaning of being responsible.

While he obviously already had many of these fine qualities that were more likely than not taken from his mother's personality, they were further enhanced by the time he spent working for Mrs. Ruffner. Her requirements were cleanliness, promptness, and organization. Above all, she wanted absolute honesty and frankness. Slackness was not tolerated.3(50) Soon, Booker T. was ready to leave for Hampton. The parting was a mixture of gladness and sadness. There was sadness because he hated leaving his mother and she was worried about the uncertain circumstances of the trip. To add to this, she was also in bad health. But he was glad to see the joy on the faces of the old people who had known nothing but slavery. They would come by to give him a nickel, a quarter, a handkerchief or some token of affection to show their appreciation that a member of their race was going off to boarding school. To them, this was a very, very proud day. After walking, riding in cars and wagons, Booker T. finally reached Richmond where by that time, he was completely out of money. He couldn't stay at the hotel even if he had money because he was black. So he walked the streets all night with no food, no money, but still more determined than ever to get to Hampton. Later, exhausted from walking and trying to keep warm, he went to sleep on the ground under the boardwalk. The next day, he found work unloading ships. Here he worked a few days until he had enough money to finish his trip to Hampton.3(52-55) When he reached Hampton, dirty and disheveled, the head teacher, Miss Mary F. Mackie, was undecided as to whether or not to admit him because of his appearance. So she asked him to clean the recitation room. He did such a good job at it that she gave him the job of janitor for the school.

By the end of his second year at Hampton, Booker T. was able to make the trip back home with the help of his mother and brother, John, as well as a small gift from his teachers at Hampton. It was during this trip home that his mother passed. What added to the sadness was the fact that he was not there when she died, as it had always been his desire to be right by her side when she died. He had no idea of her illness when he went to look for work, and it was during the time he was away that she died.

One of his main motivations was to get an education and take care of his mother. She had also expressed the desire to see her children educated and making their way in the world.3 (5759, 75) In June of 1875, Booker T. graduated from the Hampton Institute. He had also made the honor roll of commencement speakers. He then returned home, where he taught school for two years. He began his work at eight in the morning until ten at night. Not only did he teach book knowledge, but he also taught hygiene, as even these simple necessities were denied people on the slave plantation. The slave lived so close to the animal life that the slave master saw no need to have them clean. So Booker T. taught them simple things like combing their hair, brushing their teeth, keeping clean hands, faces, and clothes.

It was also during this time that he helped his brother, John, through Hampton. John had helped out so he could go; now Booker T. was helping John to get his education. Later, John became superintendent over industries at Tuskegee. Then both of them together sent the younger brother, James, to Hampton. He became the postmaster at Tuskegee.3 (78, 80, 81)

Mr. Washington seemed to have a bit of resentment for the Reconstruction period in that he felt that, with emancipation, the slave should also have received land and education so that they would be better off in exercising their newly found citizenship. He also felt that the influence of the northern whites in putting the blacks in political positions over the southern whites caused more harm to the blacks because of the already racist attitude prevalent in the South. It also drew the attention of the African-Americans from obtaining industrial knowledge and securing property. So Mr. Washington felt that political involvement right out of slavery was unwise, and should have come after education and knowledge of the trades.3 (87-88)

Booker T. taught school for two years in Malden, after which he traveled to Washington, D.C. Here, he could see the stark contrast between the school and the lifestyle of the African-American people there and those back at the Hampton Institute in Virginia. There was no industrial training program as at Hampton. The struggle for an education at Hampton, although harder, helped to build the character in the individual. While the students here in Washington had much of their education paid for them, at Hampton, the student was more responsible for helping himself. Although they wore better clothing and seemingly more intelligent, they had no real aspirations. Many had come to Washington seeking a life of ease, while others sought to work in offices and seek political positions. He also witnessed the squandering of resources by the young African-American men so as to make them appear to have money when in reality, they had very little. While there were many whose lives were substantially founded, there were too many whose lives were founded on superficiality. Even those who had steady incomes were in debt before their next sum of money came. The girls who received an education did not better themselves by learning the trades that their mothers used to provide an education for them, or to create business endeavors. Instead, they indulged in frivolous and destructive activities that kept them out of touch with what it would take to be successful in life and overcome the obstacles they would one day encounter.³ (91-94)

In his reflections as a young man, Booker T. Washington said that he used to picture himself as a white boy who, by reason of his race or color, would have no obstacles placed in his path as he climbed the ladder of success. He could be the owner of a big business or aspire to the highest political office in the land; his options were limitless. He would even have the ancestry to give him motivation because he would have a family name to live up to. In later years, he learned that success is not measured by the position one attains, but by the obstacles he had to overcome to get there. By looking at the African-American, we realize that he has to work twice as hard to be successful, but this hard work is what builds character, strength, and confidence in the individual. Mr. Washington said that "Mere connection with a so-called superior race does nothing for the individual, unless he has individual worth. And by the same token, a person who is connected with what is called a so-called inferior race cannot be held back if he possesses intrinsic, individual merit. It is a universal, human, and eternal law that merit, no matter what color skins it's found under, will be recognized and rewarded."[3] (45-46)

W.E.B. DuBois was born in the year 1868, on February 23, in Great Barrington, Massachusetts. His parents, Alfred DuBois and Mary Burghardt, owned the home in which he was born. It was a quaint, neatly trimmed five-room house with a tiny porch and a front yard full of roses. W.E.B. DuBois traces his ancestry back to a West African named Tom, who was captured and brought into slavery by Dutch slave traders to the Hudson Valley. Tom was in the service of the Burghardts, a family of Dutch descent. When the Revolutionary War broke out, Tom was registered as a private under the command of Captain John Spoors. It was his participation in the war that freed him and his family from slavery, and the Bill of Rights declared all slaves free. Tom's wife could not reconcile with her being in this country. Tom died in 1787, leaving behind many sons and a daughter named Nancy Pratt. One of his sons, Jack, took part in Shay's rebellion, and was married to Mom Bett. Later, in his second marriage to Violet, there were many children born. Harlow, Chloe, Ira, Lucinda, Maria, and Othello were their names.

The black Burghardts lived in Berkshire County, Massachusetts during the eighteenth and nineteenth centuries. They earned their living by farming, but as time passed and farming became less attractive, family members began to move away. Some moved to Connecticut, others moved west while still others moved into town and worked as laborers and servants. The children from these families usually went to school long enough to learn to read and write, but then they would drop out. W.E.B. was the first to finish high school.

As he recalls, few of his relatives went into the trades or mercantile business of the professions. They were mostly waiters, barbers, laundry workers, cooks, and the like. One of his uncles was the lifelong servant of the Kellogg family. Their daughter became the widow of a rich railroad man and helped him to enter the teaching profession.[4] (DuBois 62, 63) Othello and Sally were the grandparents of W.E.B. DuBois, and they had given birth to ten or more children. The youngest of these were his uncle, Jim, and his mother, Mary Silvina.

Mr. DuBois traces his father's ancestry back to the early seventeenth century to Cretan DuBois. Two of his sons, Louis and Jacques, settled in Ulster County, New York State. From Jacques in the fifth generation came James, who was a physician in Poughkeepsie, New York. Dr. James DuBois later moved to the Bahamas, where he took over several plantations and a salt lake. He also started a family there; his wife was neither a slave nor a free black woman.

From this union came Alexander, W.E.B.'s grandfather, and John. After their father's death, Alexander went to Haiti when he was about eighteen years old. During his time there, he got married but Mr. DuBois did not know his grandmother's name, although he did state that he may have married into the family of Elie DuBois, the great Haitian educator. At any rate, when his son Alfred grew up, he moved to Great Barrington, where he met and married Mary Burghardt. It was from this union that W.E.B. was born. Alfred was never accepted by the black Burghardts. He later moved to Milford, Connecticut. He wrote for Mary to come and join him but because of family influence, she never did.4 (65-72) Mr. Dubois attended the public school system, where most of his schoolmates were white. He knew nothing of discrimination or segregation. In his youth, he took part in excursions, hiking, church festivals, swimming, and other games with the youth in the community. As he grew, Mr. DuBois recognized the difference in his appearance from that of his classmates. He also recognized the fact that blacks lived poorer than whites. In his more immediate family, he reflected that they all would have done much better in life if they had pursued their education instead of dropping out for small jobs that led to nowhere. Instead, they joined the trend of talk with other black folks in talking about the obstacles they faced in the job market and other areas of life.

As for himself, DuBois found that he was able to outmaster his classmates in school, and his mother taught him there was no real discrimination in color; it was all a matter of hard work and ability. He himself realized the secret of life and the loosening of the color bar, then lay in excellence and accomplishment. Although his family was poor, Mr. DuBois was never hungry and never had a lack of suitable clothing. Whenever extra money was needed, there were gifts from his uncles, aunts and occasionally, white families that were somehow connected with the family.

After Grandfather Burghardt died, his family moved into town, where they lived on the Sumner estate. After the passing of his grandmother, they lived with a poor white family. It was during this time that his mother had a stroke, where she was partially paralyzed on one side. They soon moved again to a home with two rooms and a pantry downstairs, and two bedrooms upstairs. Although none of these homes had modern conveniences, they were weatherproof. The outhouse and the running water were outside and the stove heated the house.

For ten years, W.E.B. went to school ten months of the year, five days a week from the time that he was five or six years of age.4 (73-76) In 1884, Mr. DuBois had finished his high school studies and was now contemplating his future as a college student. He wanted to attend Harvard, as opposed to Amherst, Yale or Williams. Harvard was older, larger, and more widely known. His high school principal, Frank Hosmer, encouraged him to take the college preparatory test, which included algebra, geometry, Latin, and Greek. He felt that Mr. Hosmer had higher ideals for him in that his teacher didn't guide him into the field of agriculture or domestic work. Mrs. Russell, whose husband owned one of the mills, would furnish him with the books he would need. The decision was made that W.E.B. would bypass college on the first year of his graduation. Because of his youth, it was advised that he do work and study for the summer of 1884. It was also during this time that his mother died. There was a kind of gladness within him to see her at rest, for she had seen only worry most of her life. At the same time, he felt a greater urge within himself to succeed because he knew more than anything that this was what she would have wanted.

It was also during this time that Mrs. Hopkins' daughter, of the Kellogg family, moved back to Great Barrington with the millions she had inherited from her husband's interest in the railroad business. W.E.B. became a timekeeper on the construction site of her new mansion. He earned a dollar a day, with which he paid his Aunt Minerva boarding expenses. He also bought himself a new wardrobe.

His college future had fallen into the hands of three white men, his high school principal, Mr. Hosmer, Mr. Edward Van Lennep, principal of the private school, and Mr. Painter, who announced the plans for his scholarship. He had gotten together with Mr. DuBois' mother's church, as well as three others he used to pastor, and they all agreed to pay $25.00 a year each, which would be enough to support him until he completed his college studies.4 (101-105)

This resolved, it was decided that he would go to Fisk University in Nashville, Tennessee, which was an African-American college. Although he had to attend Fisk, he remained concentrated on going to Harvard.

It was at Fisk University that Mr. DuBois began to make contact with other African-Americans, and his eyes began to open up as to the conditions of the African-American community and the racist environment in which they lived. He also began to realize that the respectable jobs back in his own hometown of Barrington went to all his white classmates. The white people there, as nice as they were, still could not conceive of an African-American in local positions on that level. As Mr. DuBois studied the problem from the outside, he also learned something of the world of industry as he began to understand the importance of unions and wage compensation.4 (106)

At the age of eighteen, Mr. DuBois traveled from Fisk to the countryside of East Tennessee. He was teaching and getting as close as he could to those who suffered the pain of slavery. He was able to live with those who were the poorest of the poor, and with those who were somewhat better off. After Mr. DuBois' training at the Teacher's Institute, located at the county seat, the teachers had to search for the schools they were to teach in. For two years, Mr. DuBois taught school in a building that had no windows, no blackboard, very poor seating, and very little school supplies at all. When students did not show up for class, he went to their homes. There, he found out that school was really a second or third priority. First and foremost came the crops and helping out around the house with other chores.4 (114-118)

When Mr. DuBois returned to Fisk, his racial views had become hardened in terms of his contact with white people. He recalled an incident in Nashville where he accidentally bumped into a white woman and immediately offered his apologies, but the woman still became furious and cried out, "How dare you speak to me, you impudent nigger!" Mr. DuBois was shaken at the woman's outburst and wondered if her virulent attitude was because he continued to maintain his manhood.

Mr. DuBois was an excellent researcher, and he followed statistics on southern lynchings; each racial atrocity "was a scar upon my soul." In his "Open letter to the Southern People," DuBois wrote, "What we demand is to be recognized as men, and to be given those civil rights which pertain to our manhood."[5] (Marable 11) The fact that Mr. DuBois had never known racism during his childhood, and his mother had instilled within him ideas that merit counted over color, made him even more determined to emphasize that fact that we are human, and therefore, we should have an equal opportunity in the race for a share of the abundance of this country. To that end, he was determined to use his education and his articulating abilities to speak to these issues. In one of his writings he says of himself, "My boyhood seems, if my memory serves me rightly, to have been filled with incidents of surprisingly little importance… In early youth, a great bitterness entered my life and kindled a great ambition. I wanted to go to college because others did. I came and graduated and am now in search of a Ph. D. and bread. I believe foolishly perhaps but sincerely, that I have something to say to the world."[5] (1)

In June of 1888, Mr. DuBois graduated from Fisk University. It seems that his education at Fisk and his involvement with the African-Americans of the Deep South had given him the knowledge and insight he needed to help him to identify in a more personal way with the deeply embedded problems they suffered from as a result of slavery.

Finally, Mr. DuBois started on his most ambitious journey, which was to attend Harvard. So with the funds he had saved from his teaching experience, a traveling singing act, and a scholarship, he was at last ready to enter Harvard. By this time, however, he had already accepted the fact that he was not going to be accepted by the white students at Harvard. His social and academic life was centered around bonding with other African-Americans, therefore establishing a close-knit group that, although composed of people from different walks of life, had one thing in common, the color of their skin.4(127, 136) In 1890, Mr. DuBois received from Harvard his bachelor's degree in Philosophy, cum laude. From 1890 to1892, Mr. DuBois was a fellow at Harvard. After that, he studied at the University of Berlin in Germany.4 (146, 157)

To compare the philosophies and methods of Booker T. Washington and W.E.B. DuBois in obtaining true freedom for the African-American is to understand the background of both men. In my opinion, they were both sincere crusaders for the cause of the African-American community, and when we understand it, the greater society as well. Their methods were different, but in many ways the same. Their goals were totally the same, and they both have rightly earned the respect of all those who were interested in the same cause.

As we study the philosophy of W.E.B. DuBois, we can see that he was in favor of developing leadership for the masses as a means of leading them to freedom. Mr. DuBois spoke of an educated group that he called The Talented Tenth. It should be understood that this idea was just one of the solutions Mr. DuBois offered as a means of freedom for his people, and not the whole sum of his philosophy. He believed that through the leadership of this Talented Tenth and their knowledge of modern culture, they could guide the African-American to higher standards of civilization. Without this kind of leadership, Mr. DuBois believed that the African-American would have to accept white leadership, which might not always work in their best interest.6 (Romero 175)

As already stated earlier, this idea of The Talented Tenth is only one of the solutions offered by Mr. DuBois. This particular philosophy will only work when the goal of those who are educated is to give the masses the kind of knowledge that will enable them to lead themselves. True freedom is that kind of knowledge where a person can look into the environment and, based on what he sees, will be able to prepare himself, his family and community to meet the challenge. Therefore, this Talented Tenth would have to be universally based on knowledge, with impeccable character for the job of leading our people to true freedom on all aspects of life, morally, economically, politically, spiritually. Real knowledge in these areas of life allows a people to think for themselves and not fall victim to those who would seek to control them. We have to see all our people on an equal level with other humans, with the ability to use their G-d-given talents to propel them to the best of their potential. Aside from the idea of the Talented Tenth, W.E.B. DuBois and Booker T. Washington were very similar in their vision for the progress of the African-American community.

Mr. DuBois was a great believer in well-to-do blacks being more responsible for those who were less fortunate. He was critical of the black church because they did little to initiate community welfare projects; neighborhoods had too few libraries and readings circles. He believed that African-Americans should hold themselves to a higher criteria in cultural, social, and intellectual endeavors: "No Negro can afford to stoop to an Anglo-Saxon standard of morality."[5] (14) As we shall see in the leadership of all our ancestors, they believed in high standards and principles. These are the foundations for the kind of success that will last generation after generation. Unlike what we see today in many of our people, who have lowered their standards in order to achieve what they perceive to be success in other people's world. These low values and low standards have a way of working their way on down through our future generations and hindering their future progress. Also, unlike the high standard of excellence we see in the leadership of W.E.B. DuBois, we see the tacit approval that many of today's leaders give to the degrading activities many of our people in public life fall into.

The compatibility between Booker T. and W. E. B. was rooted in the dominant idea of the small Negro middle class of this historical era: racial self-sufficiency, education, black culture pride, "Pan-Negroism," and entrepreneurialism. In an 1898 address given by DuBois at a Fisk University graduation, he echoed words similar to those of Booker T.'s. "The German works for Germany, the Englishman serves England, and it is the duty of the Negro to serve his blood and lineage, and so working, each for each, and all for each, we realize the goal of each for all."[5] (44) Mr. DuBois is stressing the fact that when we as a people pick up the burden of our own economic and social responsibility, then we're able to take our place at the table of the society of man, not asking for anything or fearing any man, but being a contributor to the whole human society, gaining the respect of humanity as opposed to bearing the pity of humanity.

In 1897, at a meeting of the American Negro Academy, Mr. DuBois presented a paper entitled "The Conservation of Races." He asserted that each of the world's great racial groups had their distinct cultural and spiritual characteristics. "For the development of Negro genius, of Negro literature and art, of Negro spirit, only Negroes bound and welded together, Negroes inspired by one vast ideal, can work out in it s fullness the great message we have for humanity." We must see the necessity for African-Americans "to take their just place in the van of Pan-Negroism." In order to do so, African-Americans had to reject the goal of racial "absorption" and assimilation in white American society. "If in America it is to be proven for the first time in the modern world that only are Negroes capable of evolving individual men like Toussaint, the Savior, but are a nation stored with wonderful possibilities of culture, then their destiny is not a servile imitation of Anglo-Saxon culture, but a stalwart originality which shall unswervingly follow Negro ideals."

The American Negro Academy, combining its activities with black colleges, business associations, and newspapers could promote a cultural and spiritual renaissance in black America and across the black world. Within this massive effort to uplift the race, DuBois added, Negroes were "hard-pressed in the economic world by foreign immigrants and native prejudice, hated here, despised there and pitied everywhere." Blacks could not "expect to have things done for them, they MUST DO FOR THEMSELVES… A little less complaint and whining, and a little more dogged work and manly striving would do us more credit and benefit than a thousand Force or Civil Rights bills."[5] (35-36) Mr. DuBois admonishes us to maintain our cultural identity, as others have maintained theirs. Our identity is a blessing from Allah and we need to be comfortable with that. It won't be a smooth or easy journey but it has to happen, and it has to start with individuals and families. Fathers and mothers being the biggest influence in the lives of their children, teaching them the history of the ancestors. Since we have been the bottom of society, our rise to the top will be the most noticed. The victory is in getting to the top with not only our culture and our humanity intact, but also in preserving the pride and dignity handed down to us as a legacy from our ancestors. The **Black Press would be a primary vehicle in our rise, if they would promote the healthy aspirations of our people, as opposed to using sex, alcohol, tobacco, and putting entertainers before us as role models, implanting the idea in the minds of the young people that a big house and a fine car is the height of our aspirations, thus helping to keep us in a position of insignificance in terms of world progress.**

As we move on to study the philosophy of Booker T. Washington, we get a good idea of his methodology as we review his Atlanta Exposition address. In the beginning of the address, he talks about what he considers a mistake made by the black community in starting at the top right out of slavery, instead of at the bottom. This is in reference to those who attained political positions during the period of Reconstruction. He made the statement that "A seat in Congress or the state legislature was more sought after than real estate or industrial skill. Political convention or stump speaking was more attractive than starting a dairy farm or truck garden."[3] (218, 219) However, I believe that history will prove that it was because of the fact that African-Americans were in political positions that Mr. Washington was able to attend Hampton. It was because of the fact that African-Americans were in these positions that the importance of education for the masses came to the forefront in the first place. So if for no other reason, I think we should be grateful that black people not only were a part of this occurrence, but indeed led the charge for education, and other considerations for the poor and disabled. Even though it was short-lived, the rights of the common person in society were for the first time given consideration, and this laid the groundwork for future generations to build upon.

Mr. Washington goes on to describe the African-American community in the parable of a ship, lost at sea for many days and suddenly sighting a friendly vessel. "**The signal went out from the troubled ship, 'Water, water: we die of thirst!'**" The answer came back from the friendly vessel, "Cast down your buckets where you are." A second time the signal came, "Water, water, send us water!" The signal came back again from the friendly vessel, "Cast down your buckets where you are." The distress signal came a third and fourth time and the same answer was returned, "Cast down your bucket where you are." At last, the captain, heeding the injunction, cast his bucket down, and it came back up full of fresh, sparkling water from the mouth of the Amazon River." To those of my race who depend on bettering their condition in a foreign land or who underestimate the importance of cultivating friendly relations with the Southern white man, who is their next-door neighbor, I would say: "Cast down your buckets where you are"—cast it down in making friends in every manly way of the people of all races by whom we are surrounded. Cast it down in agriculture, mechanics, in commerce, in domestic service, and in the professions."[3] (219) In this parable, Mr. Washington is encouraging the black community to fish in the waters of their own human potential. He seems to be referring to the Back to Africa Movement led by Marcus Garvey in referring to those who want to better their conditions by moving to a foreign land. But at the same time, he is also saying that the same creative talents we had in Africa, we still have them here within our own human makeup. The Amazon River is symbolic of our human sentiments, and we should be about the business of realizing the valuable resources we have within ourselves. We should be developing those potentials to establish ourselves, and in time, this would put us on equal footing with others.

In the process of this development, we are to make alliances among those who are in position to aid us and stem the tide of adverse reaction to our progress. Casting down your bucket in every manly way with people of other races tells us that we are to still maintain our manhood and dignity as humans as we exhibit respect, and receive respect. To cast it down in agriculture, mechanics, in commerce, domestic service, and the professions tells us that the talents we have are too valuable to waste in foolishness and in nowhere jobs. Real respect comes when we are established. To be established means to be in a position to provide for the everyday needs of the people. As we continue to study Mr. Washington's address, he addresses the agitation method and compares it to the idea of doing for self. He says, **"The wisest among my race understand that the agitation of questions of social equality is the extremist folly, and that progress in the enjoyment of all the privileges that will come to us must be the result of severe and constant struggle rather than artificial forcing. No race that has anything to contribute to the markets of the world is long in any degree ostracized."**[3] (223)

In reviewing and understanding the background of Booker T. Washington, taking into consideration his beginning in abject poverty and the struggle he made to educate himself, I would say that particular process alone, growing from humble beginnings to a position of great recognition and respect, brought with it the kind of character and determination that makes one realize their own potential and qualities. It gives a person the wisdom and the understanding that G-d has given each individual unlimited potential in terms of the progress to be made in the society of man. Now, we understand the days of slavery, plantation life, and the physical and mental effects it had on us as a people, but equally important, we must also understand that, in terms of the goals the slavemaster was trying to accomplish, slavery was a total and complete failure. Our souls are still intact; our spirit is unbroken, as we remain human. We took the best that they could muster, and still **we rise**. Now, even though they are the ones who put us in this lowly position, it would be foolish of us to expect them to willingly recognize us as their equals in their minds.

We must realize that we cannot, and should not, try to force ourselves on anyone. This kind of acceptance would be artificial, and the people would still be resentful. If we struggle with our own talents, creating and producing for self, supporting self, then no longer would we have to beg for acceptance; others would run to us for assistance, to seek advice, to consult with us. We now have come into a position where we are the ones who are helping others, instead of protesting to make others help us. The eyes of the world will be on us to witness the excellence of the rise of the human spirit. When we began to produce for self instead of for others only, we come into establishment. We then see ourselves as having resources, just as others do. We're not asking to come into their establishments, for we have our own. So they visit us, and we visit them in terms of equal dignity and respect. We're not just on the receiving end, we now have something to contribute to the markets of the world. This kind of thinking also brings us to positions of leadership. We must refuse to allow the injustices of slavery force us to continue to look at America through eyes of hurt, because this makes it harder for us to realize our human potential and move on into the future.

The human spirit is a creation of Allah, and since its source is from G-d, man has no power over it, except what we allow. And in those circumstances with which we have no control, such as during slavery, then Allah is our protector. Allah will bring us from darkness to light. This is regardless of who we are; G-d has blessed us all with the resilience of spirit. Mr. Washington spoke of a conversation he once had with the Hon. Frederick Douglass in which he said that Mr. Douglass, on account of his color, had been forced to ride in the baggage car while traveling through Pennsylvania. Some of the white passengers tried to console him by offering their apologies that he had been degraded in this manner. Mr. Douglass responded by saying: "They cannot degrade **Frederick Douglass. The soul that is within me no man degrades. I am not the one that is being degraded on account of this treatment, but those who are inflicting it upon me.**"[3] (103,104) Even the color of one's skin is protected with this kind of positive thinking. The strength is recognized as emanating from within. Frederick Douglass recognized the fact that his skin color was not the totality of himself. His real self lies within his soul, the source of his spirit. His soul still belonged to G-d, so regardless of what kind of obstacles he faced, with this mindset, his whole human makeup was protected, even his color.

So we can see that Booker T. Washington favored not only academic training for black folk as a means of advancement in society, but most important, he believed that education in trades and industry would put us in a position to earn money through business development. This in turn would strengthen us as a community and lead to a higher sense of self-respect, and respect from others.

The differences between Mr. DuBois and Mr. Washington went further than their philosophy. Mr. DuBois saw Tuskegee as the headquarters for Mr. Washington's political influence. Booker T. Washington not only became an advisor in the Roosevelt and Taft administrations, but he also received a $600,000 gift from Andrew Carnegie for Tuskegee, which insured its future. In highlighting Mr. Washington's influence among African-Americans, Mr. DuBois didn't think that Mr. Washington spoke out loudly enough against Jim Crow laws. The laws that were being passed in the South were disenfranchising the African-American, and making legal the atrocities that were imposed on black people through Jim Crow activities. Mr. DuBois also complained that although Booker T., in his speeches, did not ignore these goings-on, he did excuse them by putting the onus on the African-American community toward their own potential to free themselves. Booker T.'s philosophy was that real respect and true freedom will come only after we're economically sound, and contributing to the society, as others are, while W. E. B. was more in favor of open agitation from an organized perspective for civil rights. However, I think its necessary that we highlight one very important thin line as it relates to the agitation of W. E. B. DuBois. His focus of agitation was geared toward the protection of African-Americans from the Jim Crow laws, as opposed to agitating for jobs and forced integration. He also favored academic achievement, as well as industrial training. There were also others who criticized the leadership of Booker T. Washington during that period of time. These voices came from among the younger educated class of African-Americans: Monroe Trotter, of Harvard 1895, and George Forbes, of Amherst 1895. Together, they started the publication of the Boston Guardian. Mr. DuBois characterized the paper as bitter, satirical, and personal, but it did print the facts.6 (175-176)

An example of how Monroe Trotter criticized Booker T. in the Guardian can be seen in the publication when Booker T. called a meeting in 1903 of men of both races from the North and South to discuss racial issues. It seemed that when the rights of African-Americans were in danger of being uprooted, Mr. Washington spoke out against the use of violence against the black community, and called for a meeting of men of both races from the North and South to come together and find solutions. Mr. Trotter, while agreeing with the idea that the violence must end, wondered what would be the use of a meeting. What good would such conferences do? He accused Booker T. of always speaking at the wrong place at the wrong time. Monroe Trotter highlighted the fact that the southern states were readmitted to the Union on the fundamental condition that universal suffrage should never be revoked or taken out of their constitution, and these conditions are still binding and obligatory.

Colored people will never consent to have their rights, which are already embedded in the national constitution, become a subject for the academic palaver and sentimental whining for a gang of busybodies, or know-nothings. He goes on to say, "Go ahead with the building of your Tuskegee, the monument to the short-lived liberty of the Negro in America, and when you have finished, let some Simonizes fitly describe it:" **Stranger, go tell the world that within this pile, the hard earned freedom of his race was laid.**[6] **(178, 179)** So this is an example of the kind of criticism that Booker T. Washington received as a result to the leadership he provided for the black community at that time. One has to take note, however, that Booker T. was a man who was acutely aware of the time period in which he lived. He knew the social and political climate that influenced the thinking of white people. He realized that, for us to survive and to live and grow in influence, we as a powerless people were no match for the Jim Crow-backers who thought nothing of shedding the blood of innocent African-Americans upon the same soil from which those same African-Americans had produced wealth for them.

Booker T. chose diplomacy over agitation because he believed that agitation would only worsen our situation. And he did put the onus on us in order to force us to look to ourselves for our own salvation. W.E.B.'s philosophy also contrasted even further in that, while he didn't mind the differing of opinions, he felt that the situation had gotten so severe in terms of the persuasiveness of Washington's influence that all opinions that differed with his were shut off. He identified what he called the Tuskegee Machine. That is to say that Tuskegee had become the information center for the black community. Here is where presidents, governors, congressmen, philanthropists, and other people of influence conferred. Appointments to certain positions were made. Mr. DuBois also argues that this machine was being financed in part by certain white groups and individuals in the North who were not interested in the black community's political ideals, or any other advancement in society for blacks. They only saw the black community as a labor force to counter demands made by northern, white labor unions. Mr. DuBois stated that the controversy between Booker T. and himself was not entirely a differing of ideas, but more in the direction of other blacks having the right to express their own ideas.

If Mr. Washington didn't agree with it, that idea was not heard. This point, more than anything, brought division to the black community. Many black newspapers found it to their advantage to agree with Mr. Washington, and the largest and oldest of these was bought up by the white friends of Tuskegee. So Mr. DuBois' differences with Mr. Washington were not all together over ideas, but in the method used to implement those ideas. Mr. DuBois favored more open agitation against the wrongs done to black people, and he resented the choking off of any kind of opposition to Mr. Washington in both the Negro press and the white.6 (176,177)

We have made reference to the Institution of Slavery and its effect on its victims, and their descendants. To try to get a feel or some type of understanding of the period of slavery, we must first understand that this was not just the physical enslavement of a people, but it was designed to capture and manipulate the total being of the person. This is why it's referred to as the Institution of Slavery. In order for one people to inflict the kind of treatment experienced by the African-American community during their slavery, they had to convince themselves that they were not dealing with humans. This was the only way they could justify within themselves the brutality and the torture they meted out to those unfortunate ones that came under their rule. So then, when we think of institution, we usually think of a physical structure or a school designed to teach and train its students and all those involved, a certain knowledge or a certain way to think. Our reference to the Institution of Slavery is to be looked at in this same manner, except that it's not a physical structure, rather, it's an open society that is closed to everyone except those who are directly involved. Its sole purpose is to teach and treat the slaves in such a way that not only will they look at white people as their gods and masters, but in the end, they will even consider themselves inferior in terms of their human development, and therefore, fit only to provide perpetual servitude to those who rule them. Hence, the Institution of Slavery, while is not a physical structure, is a mental climate that shapes and molds the minds of not only the ruled, but the ruler as well, in whatever fashion those in control chose, thus hindering the human development of both. It should be noted here that not only the slave traders, but indeed, the government as well, knew that these people came from highly civilized governments in Africa.

According to Nashid Ali Muhammad, in his book, at least 20 percent of the Africans brought to America were from Islamic empires governed by Muslims. Documented cases show that they came from the coastal and interior regions of Ghana, Mali, and Songhai. These people were enslaved because they were African, but when it was discovered they were also Muslim, their suffering was compounded. They were tortured, hung, shot, burned alive, unless they renounced their religion and their names. It was the social life and language of the direct descendants of the first Muslim community that helped form the inspiration of the African-American Muslims, known as the Gullah people, whose language helped facilitate communication between the various tribes. Some common words used in the South, such as goober (peanut), gumbo (okra), ninny (female breast), tote (carry), yam (sweet potato); names like Bobo (one who cannot talk), Geeji (a language and tribe in Liberia), Agona (a country in Ghana), Ola (that which saves), Samba (a Hausa name given to the second son), and Zola (to love), all came from the influence of these people. Muslims also contributed many Arabic words that are found in English, such admiral, algebra, amber, atlas, banana, cable, camel, checkmate, coffee, cotton, jasmine, lemon, magazine, mask, musk, rice, sofa, sugar, syrup, and zero; all these and more came from Muslim-African influence.7(Muhammad 13, 14, Introduction) Since European writers and storytellers have been primarily responsible for what most people know or knew about Africa, a very distorted view has been given as it relates to the African people. They were presented to western civilization as brutes, animals, and something less than human. This was, of course, no excuse for the brutal treatment received by one people at the hands of another.

I believe that the slave trade was so profitable to white people that they just outright excused the humanity of the African people to make it easier for them to enjoy their blood-soaked luxuries. These same white people told themselves that since the Africans had no culture and no history, slavery came as a blessing to them, which rescued them from the savage jungle and brought them to American society. This kind of rationale eased the conscience of those who profited from the activities of the slave trade. As we travel along the banks of the Nile around 3200 B.C., we see the highly evolved civilization of Egypt, with their people becoming engineers, artists, high priest, and bureaucrats, with an alphabet and a calendar. The Kushites were masters in the field of iron working, and they grew wealthy through trade and exports.

As we continue to travel through a small portion of Africa's past, we see the kingdom of Ghana which goes back to around the A.D. fifth or sixth century. By the eleventh century, Ghana had an army of two hundred thousand men, palaces of wood and stone with glass windows, and extreme wealth. As Ghana grew into a large empire, it developed sophisticated bureaucratic and governmental structures. It had become a state in every sense of the word. With the advent of Al-Islam, we see the rise of another great empire in virtually the same place that Ghana was before falling victim to a Moroccan people called the Almoravids. This empire was named Mali. The Malians had a highly centralized and stable government, and was noted especially for its peace and tranquility. Mali had become a recognized world power by 1324, when the great emperor, Mansa Musa, visited

Mecca. Soon, trade and cultural ties developed between the Arabs, Egyptians, and the African people of the sub-Saharan area. Successors after Mansa Musa could not hold the empire together. The people of the city of Gao rebelled and the empire ceased to be of any political importance.

One of the vassal states of Mali was the kingdom of Songhai. Close to the beginning of the eleventh century, the ruler converted to Islam. Shortly after the conversion, the capital was transferred to Gao, and that city began its period of great growth. During that century, Songhai revived the empire-building efforts of Mali and Ghana. Prominent among its rulers was Sunni Ali Ber, who ruled from 1464 to 1492. He was a master in the military aspect and gained control over territories around Gao, as well as being able to conquer the great cities of Jenne and Timbuktu. The Askias were the last dynastic rulers of the Songhai Empire, the most famous of whom was Askia Mohammed Ture. He was an able administrator who perfected the centralization of his government. He established a university and regulated banking, taxation, credit, and commerce. Gao and Jeanne became intellectual centers, and at the University of Sankore in Timbuktu, students studied literature, law, geography, and the sciences under black scholars. Another great city that flourished between the thirteenth and the eighteenth centuries was Great zimbabwe, which was almost exclusively a product of local Africans.[8] (Wesley 4-10)

So, here we can see that the people of Africa were not being rescued by the slave traders, but instead, it was human life being brought into a system that was designed to strip them of their humanity and reduce them to brute beasts. In order to execute this evil deed, the slave master had to instill this kind of thinking into his own offspring so they could operate without being bothered by their conscience. This is why they could look at us as mere animals with no souls, beating us, scarring us, and taking away our children as if they were taking away a calf from the mother cow, with the idea that we wouldn't feel anguish because we were only brute beasts with no idea of what it's like to have our loved one taken from us. Many claim they didn't know, but they knew of our rich history; they knew of the cities and civilizations we came from. They knew that in many cases, we were more civilized then they were.

So the purpose of the Institution of Slavery was to destroy the soul of the African-American, kill the spirit, and create a perpetual beast of burden. This is why we were fed like animals, given very little clothing, and lived in slave quarters that did not protect us from the elements. We were thought of as having no feelings that were human, therefore, we could endure whatever treatment they give regardless of how terrible it may have been. So these terrible treatments could be inflicted on us without conscience. This term, Institution of Slavery, can also be looked at from another level as well. It was also sanctioned by the highest court in the land, as in the case of Dred Scott v. Sanford, where Dred Scott sued John F. A. Sanford for his freedom. Chief Justice Roger B. Taney wrote the decision of the court.

The following is a paraphrase of some excerpts from that decision: "The question is simply this. Can a Negro, whose ancestors were imported into this country and sold as slaves, become a member of the political community formed and brought into existence by the Constitution of the United States, and as such, become entitled to all the rights to sue? The Constitution was formed only for those and their posterity who lived in the states at the time of its adoption, and histories of the times, and the language used in the Declaration of Independence, show, that neither the class of persons who had been imported as slaves, nor their descendants, were meant to be included in that memorable instrument. They had, for more than a century, been regarded as beings of an inferior order, unfit to associate with the white race in neither social nor political relations. So inferior that they had no rights which the white man was bound to respect. So inferior that the Negro might justly and lawfully be reduced to slavery for his own benefit. The slave is considered property, the owner of said property is free to traffic with it where and when he pleases, as he would any ordinary article or pieces of merchandise."[6] **(90, 91) So we can see that the Institution of Slavery was sanctioned in that we were regarded as something less than human, therefore, we had no human rights, and this kind of thinking was institutionalized**

in the fabric of American thinking. Also, in all too many of us, we ourselves became institutionalized. We came to see ourselves as inferior beings. This was done through the process of genocide.

Normally, when we think of genocide, we think of whole races of people being slaughtered to the point of extinction. However, this term only relates to genocide in the physical sense. The genocide that was performed on the African-American people was far more heinous and far-reaching.

As stated before, the Institution of Slavery was designed to create a perpetual beast of burden, so the intent was not to kill us all off in a physical sense, but to keep us under the whites control morally, mentally, and spiritually, in perpetuity. It's evident that this plan succeeded to a great degree by the way we as African-Americans treat each other today.

When we look at the word "genocide," we see two words. The word "gene" is the means of transmitting hereditary traits. These genes travel by means of the chromosomes. "Cide" is a suffix meaning killer, or killing. So when we talk about being institutionalized, we're saying that this idea of being inferior was placed in our genes, this idea of ourselves being less than others and looking up to white people as gods, and caretakers of the world.

The violence, the fear that was placed in our spirit, in our soul, through slavery, went so deep that it became a part of our human makeup and passed on down through generation after generation, and we still suffer from those effects today. Now this process didn't take place overnight; it took centuries, but we can see its effects in the black-on-black crimes, the love we have for others, and the hate we have for ourselves. So when we say the chains were taken off our ankles and placed on our brains, this is what we mean. Even though we're not in physical slavery, we're still begging others to do for us what we can do for ourselves. It is as if they knew that we would one day be physically free, and prepared us to continue to be their servants mentally. No other people in the annals of history have suffered as the African-American, and still by the mercy of Allah, we continue to rise, with our spirit still intact, our humanity still reaching out to help others, our souls still belonging to G-d.

I say to you that this is the true test of the human spirit. Again, let me point out that we are not to use this history as an excuse to continue to fail, for indeed, when the world sees our success, it gives them hope because now they know where we came from. Because of the fact that we came from so low, our light of success will be brighter, our cry for the sake of humanity will be louder, and our voices for moral uprightness will be heeded. As we have stated before, the Institution of Slavery failed miserably in its attempt to reduce us to animals, because it was G-d who made us human, G-d who created all aspects of the human makeup together; it was G-d who made humanity one, and what G-d has joined together, let no man put asunder!

There is an obligation on us today to "Rewrite The History." Rewriting the History means that it has to be revisited so that we may obtain an accurate understanding and new knowledge from it, so that we may get new inspiration. The words and deeds of our ancestors take on new meaning for us. We cease to just recognize them at a certain period in the year. We also cease to look at them as just historical figures, and their only value is what they did during their lifetime. We begin to study their words and their values, and use them as measuring rods for our own success. This is really the true purpose of history, to understand the wisdom and the knowledge, not for the purpose of a celebration or holiday; more importantly, it is for the ability to see how we learned from the mistakes they made, as well as to understand the motivation and determination of the ancestors, thus using that motivation and determination to push ourselves on to greater heights of progress. **So this history is too valuable to let it slip away and not gain any benefit from it. We see where they found their strength and recognize those same qualities within ourselves, and just as they struggled to improve themselves and the environment they lived in, we are also able to see the strength of character develop within ourselves. With every victory, there was more strength and more knowledge. This is why the ancestors did great things, because they didn't step back from the responsibility. They knew that the success would be based on their inner strength, and not on the color of their skin.**

When we allow others to control us through color consciousness, we forget the real strength that lies in our soul, our spirit, and our humanity. If we only look for respect and equality based on superficial things, then we will only get superficial respect. The deeper we reach within ourselves for the life that G-d wants us to have, the greater our contributions to the society of man. In the words of The American Society of Muslims spokesman, Imam W. Deen Mohammed, "Words make People."9 (Mohammed) We should not take this to mean the spoken word only, but that we are formed mentally by the environment we live in. Therefore, we should understand that a word is anything that leaves an impression on our minds.

So, here again, we recognize the fact that education is the foundation for individual and community progress. But this education must not be seen as a necessity to just fit in or to be accepted. Nor should this educational process attempt to replace the history or cultural ties of those receiving it, but rather it has to not only encourage students to use their minds to their fullest potential, but also make them aware that they are the ones who will be responsible for the environment they live in. This means taking responsibility for the kind of influences that come into the community in which we live. These influences shape our minds and our character, thereby determining the kinds of activities we participate in.

We must see our communities as a type of womb that is molding and shaping us morally, mentally, and spiritually. We think back to when we were in the womb of our biological mothers and how that process formed us physically, and we fed from the umbilical cord, and our bones and flesh developed. The various organs of our bodies developed and grew. So after development in the physical womb, we are born into the womb of society. So now, this means that just as we respect and protect our biological mothers, we have to look at the society we live in as our mothers as well, and this is an even bigger responsibility. We must protect the communities in which we live because they are now the womb that is shaping the way we think and will also shape the way our children think.

So while this knowledge that words make people is nothing new, it does make us more aware of what our responsibilities to society are, and that the educational process doesn't end at the school house door. Our various ethnic and historical contributions help us to respect each other more. More than anything, they help us to develop a healthy value system, for we know that without a sense of values, we lose our standards, and human society begins to degenerate. Our vision becomes blurred as to what is healthy and unhealthy. When we call on the advice of the ancestors and we find strength and vision, we should remember that the ancestors believed in and worshipped the one Creator, and we, by following their example, become successful as well. We need to remember that no matter how modern and technically advanced a society may become, what never changes is the foundation for the success of those advances. That foundation is high standard, based on strong moral principles. Moral thinking, moral vision and moral growth are what makes society progress.

Again, we hear from the great leader of this day, Imam W. Deen Mohammed: "Moral behavior graduates. It is when you just know good and bad, beautiful and ugly, hot and cold, which is on the baby level of morality. As we graduate, we come into what we call ethics and moral rules for the intellect and for the total behavior, flesh, mind, and spirit. We graduate from moral sentiments and moral feelings to the understanding of moral logic."10 (Mohammed 11) **This kind of understanding is designed to not only maintain the basic moral foundation that Allah has given to each of us, but it also evolves us into people with moral vision to give direction in terms of how society and those institutions that support society should operate. Not only do we advance as caretakers of our own society, but even outside our borders, we are seen as people who are concerned about the weak and the oppressed. Crime is reduced, and those ills that place a burden on the society are reduced as well. So there is value in every regard in recognizing the history of us all and in having that history work in tandem with our modern-day development of society.**

Those among us who are considered leaders must echo the importance of education that strengthens the ability we possess within ourselves to advance ourselves in this world. Also, our leaders should point out the weaknesses we have in our own community, which hold us back. I believe that these two areas of concern, if echoed louder than the constant cry asking others to do for us what we can do for ourselves, would do more for us as a people in terms of bringing out more of our creativity, productivity, and adding more of our contributions to the society of man. If we as African-Americans can see education as a legacy of our ancestors during the Reconstruction period, I believe we would come to value it more, and understand that it is our only way to a productive future.

Again, let me say that we live in America, and our treatment in America has been the worst that any people can receive at the hands of another. We have reasons to look back at the pain, but for the sake of our present self and future self, we have more of a reason to look forward to the success of the future. Not only do we have reason, indeed, we have an obligation, for if we continue to look back at the pain, we will continue to find excuses not to prosper.

The great abolitionist, Frederick Douglass, said; "Our destiny is largely in our own hands. If we find, we shall have to seek, if we succeed in the race of life, it must be by our own energy, and our won exertions. Others may clear the road, but we must go forward or be left behind in the race of life. If we remain poor and dependent, the riches of other men will do but little for us. If we remain ignorant, the intelligence of other men will do but little for. If we remain foolish, the wisdom of other men will not guide us. If we are wasteful our time and money, the economy of other men will only make our destitution the more disgraceful and hurtful."[2] **(28)**

It is when we hear this kind of language from our ancestors and compare it with what we hear from the leaders of today that we see a vast difference. Our ancestors spoke of independence, not because the framers of the Constitution said it, but because they listened to the voice that G-d put inside them, and declared themselves free. They also knew that with freedom comes responsibility, and by their own abilities given them by G-d, they prospered. This is what is meant when we say **"We** must rewrite history." We are not only to look at their words, we are to study the words, and put those words into practice.

Charity from others means nothing but disrespect from those giving it, when we as a people continue to squander our own valuable resources on foolishness. Our resources must produce for us, or else we will continue to say "It's the white man's fault." Because others have acted wisely with their possessions, we become envious and jealous, when our future, our destiny, are really in our own hands. If we could hear this kind of language coming from the leaders of today, we would be more motivated to move in the direction of progress. As it is with the leaders of today, they seem to want to continue the same tactics we used in the sixties, where we demanded that others accept us. They seem to be visionless, and the demands they make society, on our behalf, only make us as a people who seem silly and unproductive in the eyes of the world. It would be a major tragedy for us as a people to enter the twenty-first century with the same old gripes and the same tactics for solutions to our problems as we had in the twentieth century.

Chapter 3

Civil Rights or Human Rights?

Civil rights, when rightly understood, does not mean that we should be singled out as African-Americans for special treatment or privileges. Civil rights does not refer to integration in business, education, real estate, or any of these new definitions that have found their way into the struggle for equality in the African-American community. **In the words of the great leader, El-Hajj Malik El-Shabazz:** "Our people have made the mistake of confusing the method with the objectives. As long as we agree on the objectives, we should never fall out with each other just because we believe in different methods or tactics or strategy to reach a common objective. We have to keep in mind at all times that we are not fighting for integration, nor are we fighting for separation, we are fighting for recognition as humans in this society."[2] **(32)**

We find that according to Webster's New World Dictionary, the word "civil" means "of a community of citizens, their government, or their interrelations as in civil affairs." Furthermore, we find that the word "civilization" means "the state of being civilized, social organization of a high order," also "advancement in social organization and the arts and sciences." This kind of language refers to the society of man and his responsibility to advance that society. It also talks about human interaction with other humans, based on our ability to recognize the inborn goodness we all possess.

So we see that all the modern technology, computers, means of travel, and communication are not the measuring rods that characterize a civilized nation, but rather it's the simple civilized attitude of courtesy, refinement, and acts of kindness that we carry out toward each other as human beings. This kind of thinking, this kind of attitude, is the foundation of a truly civilized society. It is only when we recognize our human qualities, regardless of the color of our skin, that the higher principles of human development come into play. Principles such as merit, honesty, integrity, respect, etc. When we can get past the color of our skin and see each other as G-d intended, in our true human makeup, then the positive development for human society is unlimited. Then we will see that the human is not denied the right to vote, the human is not denied the bank loan or the job promotion. The human can live, work, eat, educate, start businesses, and prosper based on his own merits, heritage, and culture.

The fact is, we all have something positive to bring to the table of the society of man. We then cease to be concerned about small things like food, clothing, and shelter, for these constitute the very basic necessities of life. Even the animals of the jungle have these without any hindrances. Allah tells us in the Holy Qur'an, "He has made us of different tribes and nations so that we will know each other, and not despise each other." Since G-d is the author of all that is good, we can learn and grow from each other. Explore the depth of each other's historical contributions, traditional exchanges, and all the possibilities that will help society to advance toward a better future. This is the human excellence Bro. Malik Shabazz spoke of. If we can understand the fact that because many of us achieve more in life than others, this does not mean that we should use our positions to hinder others, nor does it mean that we're better than others. It only means that through the mercy of G-d, and through some help from men, we were able to excel. But it means more than that also. We should understand that when Allah blesses the human being to grow in material wealth or influence, these achievements are on loan to us from the Creator. We own nothing. We created nothing. We brought nothing into this world. So Allah put us in charge of these things to see how we will manage them. Will we hoard them as if they are exclusively ours to use for our own good times and pleasure, or will we see ourselves as being in a better position to advance more humanism in the world? Now this meaning of civil rights becomes clearer to us, and we cease to relegate it to the low level of social and material trinkets thrown by the rich at the poor and the less fortunate. "Civil" and "civilized" are big words and it takes a big human being to live up to them. So these definitions of civil rights goes deeper than mere rights; now, we have to understand them in terms of obligations and responsibilities more than anything else. This kind of understanding puts the onus on us to get into the race for all that is good to better the society for all mankind.

Again, we say that when we study the words and actions of the ancestors, we will see that they have always had this realization within them. There has never been a time in American history when the African-American wasn't in the forefront, pushing America on towards its greatness. As African-Americans, we have always had the idea of civic responsibility, but have been hindered from exercising it. Our history teaches us that we are descendants of great civilizations, some of which would even rival some of what we see today as civilized societies. So then, it is in these later years that we seem to have had our vision blurred as to the difference between civil and human rights. This is because we have allowed someone else to create our agenda for us. Someone else has defined and dictated our cause for us instead of ourselves.

When we look back and reflect on the achievements of the ancestors, both men and women, we see evidence of the excellence of the human potential. Not the black potential, but more so of the human potential. We see this evidence in the African-American's contributions to the greatness of this country clear across the board in every aspect of life, including social, political, and military. African-Americans have always had the care to not only improve their own lot, but to help others as well.

From the very beginning, we see African-Americans going into battle for the freedom of the human spirit. Some of the first blood to be spilled on American soil was that of Crispus Attucks, as he was one of the leaders of the charge that rallied America into the war of freedom from England. Because he had known the pains of slavery, he gave his own life, thus putting America on a journey that she will never be able to turn away from. That is the journey to true human dignity for all men.

As the Revolutionary War broke out, we find that there were African-Americans who distinguished themselves in battle above and beyond the call of duty. The Muslim Revolutionary warrior, Saleem Poor, won distinction as a soldier in the battle of Bunker Hill. He attracted such attention that a statement was sent to the Massachusetts legislature by fourteen white offers describing his conduct. The statement dated December 5, 1775 reported that "A Negro man called Saleem Poor of Col. Frye's regiment, Captain Ames' company, in the late battle at Charleston, behaved like an experienced officer, as well as an excellent soldier... in the person of this said Negro centers a brave and gallant soldier."

In another incident, Peter Saleem, also a Muslim, distinguished himself at the battle of Bunker Hill. He is reported to have fired the shot that mortally wounded Major John Pitcairn. Peter Saleem also fought in Lexington and Concord. His gun is displayed at the Bunker Hill Monument. Samuel Charlton fought in the battles of Brandywine, Germantown, and Monmouth. Oliver Cromwell served in the Continental Army for six years and nine months. During this time, he fought in the battles of Trenton, Princeton, Brandywine, Monmouth, and Yorktown. He also crossed the Delaware with General George Washington on Christmas Day of 1776. At the siege of Savannah in 1778, the famous Black Legion, composed of free Negroes from Haiti serving with the French under Admiral D'Estaing, covered the retreat of the Americans and by their fierce counterattack, saved the Americans from a crushing defeat and probable capture. The Rhode Island regiment of Negro soldiers fought with valor at the defense of Red Bank, where four hundred Negroes successfully defended their position against fifteen hundred Hessians. There were also African-Americans in the navy, and on the privateers that preceded the formation of the navy. As early as 1775, a sign was posted at Newport, recruiting "yea able-bodied sailors, men, white or black, to volunteer for naval service in yea interest of freedom." A free Negro gunner, Benoni Brown, served on a vessel commanded by Commodore Esek Hopkins. Johnnie Breenmer was a gunner on the Bonhomme Richard, commanded by Commodore John Paul Jones. This is the vessel that distinguished itself in the battle with the Serapis.

There were many African-American sailors in the navy during the Revolutionary War. It has been estimated that African-Americans fought on at lease one-third of the fifty vessels maintained by Virginia. Perhaps, the most prominent of the Negroes in the Revolutionary Navy was James Forten, who served under Steven Decatur, the commander on the Royal Louis. The British frigate, Amphyon, captured this vessel. A friendship was started between Forten and the son of the captain. Forten was offered free passage to England. He refused to renounce his American citizenship, and as a result, spent the rest of the war as a prisoner in a floating dungeon, called the Jersey. Forten later became wealthy as the inventor of an improved mechanism for sail handling, and was a leading abolitionist.[1] (90-98)

As we move on from the Revolutionary War to the War of 1812, we see African-Americans once again laying their lives on the line for the sake of the future of America. Even though they had fought for the freedom of America in the Revolutionary War, they were still put back into slavery and treated as brute beasts, good for nothing but working to increase the wealth of others.

Then as the war broke out, African-Americans stood out once again as examples of excellent soldiers of bravery.

In December 1814, General Andrew Jackson, finding himself sorely in need of a larger force to defend New Orleans against the British, appealed to the Negroes, calling them America's "adopted children." After the fighting, General Jackson said that the Negro volunteers had conducted themselves with great courage and tenacity.

When the British at Mobile, Alabama were attacking the American troops, a Negro named Jeffery placed himself at the head of the troops and successfully rallied them to a charge that repulsed the British.

Again, at New Orleans, an African-American by the name of John Julius, despite being wounded by bayonet gashes, continued to fight. Congressman Robert Winthrop, speaking at the House of Representatives, stated that "No regiment did better service at New Orleans than the black regiments." Commodore Stephen Decatur said of the Negro troops: "They are as brave men that ever fired a gun. There are no stronger hearts in the service."

African-Americans were also in the navy during this war. Two black men were on board the Governor Thompkins and were slain at their post during an early battle. One of the men, named John Johnson, was mortally wounded by a twenty-pound shot; yet he lay on deck, shouting encouragement to the others. The other black man, John Davis, also shot repeatedly, asked to be thrown overboard so as to make way for the surviving fighters.

The crews on the ships on the Great Lakes also included African-Americans. Commodore Oliver Perry was in command. When he first received his reinforcements, he explained to Commodore Chauncey that he had been sent "a motley crew of black soldiers, and boys." Chauncey replied that the men he had sent to Perry were not surpassed by any in the fleet and that he had "yet to learn that the color of skin, or the cut of the trimmings of the coat, can affect a man's qualifications and usefulness." Soon, Perry was convinced of his error, for he was to write to the Secretary of the Navy of the bravery of the black sailors. 1 (148-150)

As we continue to travel through history, we continue to see evidence of the willingness and the ability of the African-American community to answer the call to duty for the defense of their country. They saw their interest in America as the same as that of others. They asked for no special treatment, only to be regarded as human beings from the same Creator as others.

We now move from the War of 1812 to the Civil War, and still we can see the African-American standing on the path of human excellence, beckoning to others to come and follow, for this is the true path of freedom. Those who tread upon it see more than just the complexion of another person's skin; they see the human potential of that person and deal with that person out of mutual respect.

This, in my opinion, is why this history and indeed, all history, has been preserved, not just to recognize the people who made it, but to recognize the lessons taught, and the lessons learned. History takes on new meanings all the time; therefore, it is too profound, too deep, and too valuable to allow it to slide into oblivion. **"We Must Continue to Rewrite the History."** As we continue to progress into the future, not only will we learn that we all have something of value to offer, but we will explore as well this valuable creation given to us by Allah for our continued progress and development.

As the Civil War progressed, we see again that African-Americans were present in the fighting for the freedom of the whole country. In the Battle of Milliken's Bend, it was the bravery of the African-American troops that secured General Grant's position on the Yazoo, where he had established a new supply post at Haynes Bluff. Grant withdrew all his major troops from Milliken's Bend, leaving three regiments of Negro soldiers, and one company of white troops. They were the Ninth and the Eleventh Louisiana, the First Mississippi, and the Twenty-third Regiment of Iowa. When the Confederates drove the Union troops within sight of Milliken's Bend, where they took refuge, the Confederates began to cry, "No Quarter." Two gunboats, the Choctaw, and the Lexington, opened fire on the Confederates, and the Negro troops rallied. With only two weeks of training and with faulty weapons, they fought. They fought in hand-to-hand combat, and with a determination that would have failed lesser men. The Confederates withdrew and made no effort to renew their attack.

When the black troops began to enter the army, as they had throughout Grant's move into the South, they were coming in so fast that Chaplin John Eaton of the Twenty-seventh Ohio Infantry wrote as follows: "Their coming was like the arrival of cities. Often they met prejudices against their color, more bitter than they had left behind. There was no Moses to lead, or plan in their exodus. The decision in their instinct or unlettered reasoning brought them to us. They felt their interest were identical with the object of our armies."

The first black regiment into battle was the Seventh United States Colored Infantry, also known as the First Kansas Regiment.

They defeated rebel forces at the Battle of Island Mounds in Bates County, Missouri.

The First Carolina Volunteers were commanded by Colonel Thomas Wentworth Higginson, a Harvard graduate, abolitionist, an admirer of John Brown, and former Captain of the Fifty-first Massachusetts Militia. His was one of the first regiments of freed slaves enlisted in 1862. They fought near the St. John River in Florida, and the St. Mary's, and Edisto Rivers in South Carolina. Higginson, in praising his troops, stated that, "It would have been madness to attempt with the bravest of white troops what (was) successfully accomplished with the black ones." He added, "No officer in this regiment now doubts that the successful prosecution of this war lies in the unlimited employment of black troops."

On July 16, 1863, the Fifty-Fourth Massachusetts Regiment, under the control of Colonel Robert Shaw, was attacked by Confederates on James Island and compelled to withdraw from the field of battle, but not before inflicting heavy losses in the ranks of the enemy, who out numbered them. By this action, they saved three companies of the Tenth Connecticut Regiment. An attack was then ordered on Fort Wagner. The Fifty-fourth Massachusetts was the only regiment of Negro soldiers in the line of battle and was assigned the post to lead the charge. They marched toward the fort until they were about sixteen hundred yards away from it. They then got into battle formation, and marched four hundred yards closer. With the order from Colonel Shaw, the regiment advanced in quick time, then double time. They came under heavy fire when they were about two hundred yards away from the fort. Though their ranks were seared and divided by losses of fallen men, they continued to march forward across the three-foot ditch of water and mounted the parapet. Sergeant Major Lewis H. Douglass, son of Fredrick Douglass, reached the ramparts shortly after Colonel Shaw had shouted to his men, "Let's fight for G-d and Governor Andrew." The flag was planted there by Sergeant William H. Carney. Colonel Shaw fell wounded while shouting "Onward, boys!"[11] (Romero 81, 82, 85, 88)

So, as we have seen, black folk have been in the forefront of America's historical development from the very beginning, not demanding special treatment, even though we were in the least likely position to achieve success. The only thing we wanted was the opportunity, and history tells us that whenever that opportunity presented itself, we excelled.

As we continue to travel through history, we see that not only did we fight militarily to preserve this great country, but after the Civil War was over, and when the smoke had cleared and the rebuilding had begun, we find it was the African-Americans who stood up in the halls of politics, leading the charge to speak for the common people during the period of Reconstruction.

In reflecting on this era once again, we must remember that the Reconstruction was more than just the passing of legislation. This legislation and the issues debated at the constitutional conventions left an imprint on the minds and the hearts of the people of this great nation to be considerate of other men. America was now on its way to considering the human aspect of the nation. Although this human consideration would be out of reach of those who had helped to generate it for many years to come, still, the idea was put into motion. America was becoming whole again, and thus, was able to move on to greater progress, and we can see the hand of the African-American at every level of growth and development. In every war that America has been involved in, black folk have been there. The Spanish-American War, The Mexican War, World Wars I and II, the Korean War, Vietnam, Desert Storm, and on into this present day of peace.

We have seen examples of African-American participation in areas of war, and some political involvement, but it must be noted that black folks have excelled in virtually every area of endeavor. There have been examples of manufacturing and financial facilities established by African-Americans here in America. We have also seen medical and educational facilities established by African-Americans here in America. Our participation in social and community affairs is well documented. We take note of these kinds of involvement not because they are unknown, but we highlight them because we seem to have forgotten that these accomplishments were made because we saw ourselves as humans, part of G-d's creation, with the same capabilities as anyone else. We refused to see ourselves as anything less, so we looked inside ourselves for the answers to our own problems. And it is because we have forgotten the quality of our own creativity that we have gotten off the track of dignity and productivity. This, I believe, was also the downside of the Civil Rights Movement. We got so used to marching and demonstrating for the things we needed for our survival that we forgot we already had the means of accomplishing whatever goals we needed to accomplish within ourselves. And I believe that Allah has left these examples here for us to realize that it can be done. This is why we continue to emphasize that "We Must Rewrite the History." That is to say that we don't want to know our history just from an academic standpoint only, but we want to take the words of wisdom of the Ancestors and put them into action in our own lives because when we understand the success they had against all odds in their time, then we will realize the limitless potential we will have for success with the opportunities we have available to us in these modern days.

Just as we see our obligations to defend our country outside its borders in times of war, we now look within our borders, and more importantly, within ourselves for examples of success that tells us it can be done regardless of the obstacles. We see great accomplishments that were made because people looked and listened to the voice within themselves, given to them by Allah, that guided them to great heights of success in human society.

So African-Americans have always had this sense of civic responsibility. It was some members of white America that tried to close the door and shut out the advancement of society because their whole idea of what is human is based on skin color. So again, we say that polished nails, a fine suit of clothes, material gain, and technical advancements, these in and of themselves are not the hallmarks of civilized society, but rather it's the simple and basic treatment, and recognition we have of each other as human beings, created by Allah with the same potential for growth and development.

So now, we see the Civil Rights Movement was not about affirmative action, or of blacks moving into white neighborhoods and begging for jobs, etc., for as we shall see, in many cases, not only did we create our own jobs, but we were proud to live in our own communities.

The Civil Rights Movement was initiated because one people tried to deny the humanity of another people. The following examples will show the low human position occupied by some white people on the evolutionary scale of human development because of the savage treatment they inflicted upon black people, thus showing that although they were possessors of wealth and position in society, the definition of being "civic" and of "civilization" did not apply to them.

History tells us that by the year 1910, every former Confederate state had disenfranchised the African-American, and many of them had gone so far as to adopt constitutional amendments that would limit the African-American vote. Northern states that had fought so diligently for human rights suddenly became silent when it came to African-American suffrage in the South. Although state and federal courts upheld the Fifteenth Amendment, which limited states rights to control voting, still, some Southern states passed laws that would eliminate black participation in the political process.

To tighten this kind of control that the South exercised in politics, we see the advent of the "white primary." This white primary was used to keep blacks from participating in the nominating process. This was a tacit agreement to between registrars and other white officials. A writer for the Atlanta Constitution wrote in 1907, "We already had the Negro eliminated from politics by the white primary."

In other areas of concern, white lawmakers tried everything from barring African-Americans from entering the United States to placing a ban on jobs that was desirable for whites, to outright restricting African-American education. Florida and Kentucky passed laws making it a crime for a white person to even teach blacks 1(99). In Brownsville, Texas, in 1906, the military sent three companies, B, C, and D of the Twenty-fifth Infantry Regiment to relieve a battalion of the Sixteenth Infantry which was white, and had had clashes with the civilians of that area. The civilians already did not like the idea of soldiers in their town, and when they heard that these soldiers were black, tensions ran extra high. The city rioted on August 14, with one person getting killed, and two others getting wounded. The African-American soldiers were charged with shooting up the town and starting the riot. The soldiers were given dishonorable discharges en masse, without the benefit of a hearing, by President Roosevelt. Senator Joseph Foraker of Ohio found the evidence "flimsy, unreliable, insufficient, and untruthful." South Carolina's old populist, "Pitchfork Ben" Tillman, called the dismissal "an executive lynching."

After reviewing the evidence in detail, pointing out its errors and discrepancies, Senator Foraker summed up the military record of the discharged soldiers in these words: "Faithfully and uncomplainingly, with pride and devotion, they have performed all their duties and kept their obligations. They asked no favors because they are Negroes, but only asked justice because they are men." Again, let me re-emphasize that our struggle was to be recognized as humans. Brownsville was to remain a potent political issue for some time to come.

A manufacturer of pneumatic tubes, named John Millholland, a Republican, was key in working with Booker T. Washington in the fight for the soldiers' acquittal. Mary Church Terrell and Gilcrest Steward were two other African-Americans who worked for a reversal in Roosevelt's order.

Ida B. Wells Barnett, a prominent, black Chicago woman journalist who crusaded tirelessly for anti-lynching laws, dispelled a popular myth through her revealing study of police records. She found that contrary to popular belief that blacks were being hung because of some felonies that people had said they committed, she found that these people were the victims of lynch mobs and had died because of minor offenses and misdemeanors. Many Americans demanded anti-lynching laws, but the state and federal governments failed to curb it, so the atrocities continued.[12] (Robinson.105-107) In 1899, the Afro-American Council of the United States called upon Afro-Americans to observe a day of fasting and prayer to protest Jim Crow railroad cars, persecution instead of justice in the courts, arrest and jailing of the innocent on suspicion, and the torturing and hanging of Negroes.

In an open letter to President McKinley in 1899, Massachusetts Negroes stated the core of the issue: "We have suffered, sir. G-d knows how much we have suffered since your ascension to office… And you have seen our suffering. Witnessed from your high place our awful wrongs and miseries, and yet you have at no time and on no occasion opened your lips in our behalf. Why? We ask. Is it because we are black and weak and despised? Are you silent because without any fault of our own we were enslaved and held for more than two centuries in cruel bondage for your forefathers? Is it because we bear the marks of those sad generations, generations of Anglo-Saxon brutality and weaknesses that you do not speak?"

So now, we see more black awareness rising from the black community. Many black authors began to write, and thus further increased African-American pride. It was during this time period that we heard from such authors as George W. Williams, author of History of the Negro Race in America from 1619 to 1880. Edward A. Johnson's A School History of the Negro Race in America from 1619 to 1890. This book highlighted the valuable contributions made by African-Americans that had been left out by white authors. Johnson charged these white authors with the sins of omission and commission, and said that they seem to have written their books for white children only. He said that their history also to implied that the Negro was inferior. In 1902, W. H. Crogman wrote Progress of a Race.

There were many more African-American writers who came along at that time. The Colored American Magazine called upon Negroes to summon their inner gifts of creativity. It urged them to forge the bonds of racial brotherhood, which alone can enable a people to assert their racial rights as men. The first black biographer, William J. Simmons, wrote Men of Mark: Eminent, Progressive, and Rising; and Booker T. Washington's Story of the Negro in 1909} (108-109) So we see all through the twentieth century, and all over America black folk were being persecuted. In his book, The Souls of Black Folks, W. E. B. DuBois wrote, "The problem of the Twentieth Century is the problem of the color line." "This book is dangerous for the Negro to read," a Tennessee newspaper editor wrote, "For it will only incite discontent and fill his imagination with things that do not exist or things that should not bear upon his mind."

We continue to see the denial of the humanity of the African-American people, which goes much deeper than the color line that Mr. DuBois spoke of. I say here that the color line is only the beginning of white people's refusal to recognize the humanity of the African-American.

With the opening of the twentieth century, there were many organizations formed to promote black progress. There was the Negro Independent Movement, The National Association for the Advancement of Colored people, The Equal Rights League, The National Urban League, and the National Negro Business League. The National Association of Colored Women was already working on racial equality. So we see African-Americans from all walks of life getting themselves involved in bringing America to the level where it will eventually have to recognize all its citizens as equal not only in G-d's sight, but in the sight of man as well. The opposition they found themselves up against was overwhelming. In some states, the anti-Negro feeling was so strong that many black citizens just fled their homes in large numbers. The white vigilantes ran rampant through the southern countryside, committing violence wherever they were resisted.[1] (114-115) In 1905, W. E. B. DuBois called what was to be the first meeting of the Niagara Movement. This group drew up a "Declaration of Principles," which began by citing Negro progress from 18951905. The statement singled out for praise, the increase of intelligence, the buying of property, the checking of crime, the upliftment in home life, the advance in literature and art, and the demonstration of constructive and executive ability in the conduct of great religious, economical, and educational institutions. The declaration ended by spelling out the responsibilities Negroes should assume upon themselves. "The duty to vote, respect the rights of others, to work, obey the laws, be clean and orderly, to send our children to school, to respect ourselves, even as we respect others." After a few meetings, the Niagara Movement faded off the scene and was replaced by the NAACP. In 1910, in New York, the formal structure for the NAACP was set up. Most of the all black members of the Niagara Movement merged with this biracial group. DuBois was made director of Publicity and Research. At its first conference, the

NAACP had adopted five major demands: to ensure voting rights, to ban white-only policies in public accommodations, to promote free labor relations, to urge a school program that would not educate youth as servants and underlings, and to require equal justice under the law.

There was a great influx of African-Americans to the northern cities around the turn of the century, and it caught the attention of urban social workers. There were several groups already existing in New York in 1905. One group, known as the Committee for Improving Industrial Conditions for Negroes in New York City, worked with Dr. George E. Haynes. The National League for the Protection of Colored Women also worked with Dr. Haynes. Among some of the leaders were Hollingsworth Wood, William H. Baldwin, Francis Kellor, William J. Schiefflin, A. S. Frissel, Fred R. Moore, and Dr. Eugene Roberts. They all worked separately, but in 1911 they merged to form the National League for Urban Conditions among Negroes, with Dr. Haynes as Executive Secretary. Later, the name was changed to the National Urban League. The league sought to organize skilled and unskilled workers into associations to promote their welfare and efficiency. It also opened a vocational bureau of labor exchange. This bureau worked with charitable and job placements groups to find employment for Negroes, guided them into training programs to suit their abilities, and tried to develop an appreciation for Negro labor among employers.[1] (116-122)

In New York back in 1881, an immigrant Jew by the name of Samuel Gompers founded the American Federation of Labor. This group was an offshoot of an earlier group known as the Knights of Labor. Their creed was "The working people must unite and organize, irrespective of creed, color, sex, nationality, or politics."

Although the creed itself was noble in principle, its reality was virtually non-existent. In order to broaden its influence, the AFL had to let other affiliates join its ranks. Many of these affiliates did not permit African-American participation. In 1902, W. E. B. DuBois wrote a conservative estimate of the strength of organized labor as 1,200,000, with 41,000 being black. Many of these locals outright discriminated against blacks, while others claimed lack of applicants or workers in the trade. Still others barred blacks from apprenticeship programs. So while trying to retain solidarity with all the workers, Gompers had to yield to the tempers of the times in which he lived. Until this integrated solidarity could be reached, blacks were encouraged to form their own unions in those trades where they had been barred. The AFL organized them into affiliated federal unions, or separate local unions. In theory, we know the AFL's Executive Council is supposed to look out and represent the best interest of all the unions when dealing with management. In practice, however, the assistance in contract negotiations and grievance settlements were minimal.

The NAACP and the Urban League attacked the AFL for its hypocrisy, but the discrimination would continue against African-Americans for many years to come. In a letter to the AFL's 1918 convention, from a group that spoke for Negro unionist concerns, four basic demands were made: (1) The press should be given the AFL's published statement of welcome to Negroes; (2) The Federation should hire qualified Negro organizers; (3) Cooperation among Negro unions should be encouraged.; and (4) The Federation should take a more enlightened look on the issue of Negro workers. The letter was referred to committee. The AFL unanimously adopted the letter, but still nothing happened. The National Urban League met in Detroit in 1919 and adopted a resolution on organized labor, which said: "We believe that the Negro should begin to think more and more in terms of labor group movement, so as to ultimately reap the of thinking in unison. To this end, we advise Negroes to organize with white men wherever conditions are favorable. When this is not possible, they should ban together and bargain with employers and organized labor alike. With America and the whole world in labor turmoil, we urge white and black men, capital and labor, to be fair and patient with each other, while a just solution is worked out."[1] **(128-130)**

As we study closely the methods used by the African-American community in the kinds of demands they put forth in their quest to attain some sort of reconciliation to get on an equal footing with white people in terms of employment, and to have white people recognize the quality of African-American labor, we see a certain kind of thought pattern in the African-American emerging. The language shows that our focus is not on our own human potential.

We've forgotten that white people must certainly already know the quality of African-American labor. We've forgotten that it was on the backs, and on the blood, sweat, and tears of African-Americans that the country was built in the first place. But now, we see white people are making money off the labor we used to do for free. The reason we were shut out of the paid work force is that we were still considered to be less than human, not worth being paid. We were still considered to be brute beasts, and you don't pay beasts of burden to work. As stated before, we obviously had forgotten our own human potential. We were not thinking independently. It seems that our whole quest was to be accepted by others, which ultimately leads to putting our lives in the hands of others, therefore giving control of our future and our destiny to others. Instead of independence, we settled for integration, thus the seeds for perpetual begging were planted. The decision about what goals the African-American community would fight for was put in the hands of others. Instead of pooling our resources and recognizing the needs in our own community, our focus went toward being accepted by others, who did not have our well-being at heart. It seems that we, too, had begun to think of ourselves as inferior beings. We had forgotten the fact that we too, were rulers and builders of whole countries, and that whatever skills white people had, for the most part, they had learned from us.

While it's true that we would have had to start from the bottom, the fact is that we were already at the bottom; therefore, though progress would have been slow, it would have been secure in that the foundation that was laid set in motion our continued progress because we would have provided our own jobs and operating our own businesses in our own communities.

It seems that this idea of agitation became the mode for progress in the African-American community. Although I do think that the use of some agitation is highly necessary, however, I do believe that the use of agitation and protest for everything that happens to or in the African-American community puts the obligation on others for the progress of our community instead of on us. And as stated before, this leads to others making our decisions for us, as well as setting our goals for us.

Due to the fact that America had grown and many Americans had come to accept all people as human beings, and that America presented itself to the world as a nation that respected human rights and called upon other nations to do so as well, these variables came together to make agitation highly necessary and successful during the leadership of Dr. Martin Luther King and the Civil Rights Movement of the 'sixties.'

Through the media, the tactic of agitation introduced to the nation and to the world the mistreatment and the disenfranchisement America put on its own people. People at home and abroad could sit at home and see that Jim Crowism was alive and well in the South. So agitation in this sense made a positive difference. It made America take a closer look at itself and the cruel and inhuman treatment of its own citizens. Racist politicians, such as Senator James O. Eastland and Senator John Stennis, stood boldly in the path of progress for African-Americans, referring to the Civil Rights volunteers who came from other parts of the country to work on voter registration projects in the south as "outside agitators." The way that these two senators talked about those of us who were involved in the movement, one would think that the volunteers were from another country instead of being United States-born citizens. Further, to hear them talk, one would think that the political and social work being performed was unconstitutional, instead of upholding the high standards the constitution stood for.

Senator John Stennis served over four decades in the congress from 1947-1989. During that time, he served as the first Chairman of the Ethics Committee, as well as the Chairman of the Armed Services and Appropriations Committee. Senator John Stennis was a man of great power and influence, but instead of using his power to ensure equal justice under the law for all the citizens of his state, he helped to draft the Southern Manifesto. This was a document that was signed by 101 Southern Congressmen to oppose desegregation.

Senator James Eastland was first appointed to office in 1941. He then was elected to a full term in 1942 and remained in office until

1978. He served as chairman of the Judiciary Committee. Senator Eastland served six terms in Congress and was well known as one of the most formidable defenders of racial segregation.

Now, as for the public life of these two men, we know their views and their records in so far as race relations were concerned. But from this kind of public thinking we see coming from them, we can only imagine the hurt and misery and pain that they may have caused individual African-American men and women to suffer in their private lives. Senators Eastland and Stennis, instead of standing for truth and justice in service to all the citizens of their state, became two of the most powerful gatekeepers to the Institution of Slavery, and in doing so, put themselves in direct opposition to G-d.

So it was against this political backdrop that brought together the Southern Christian Leadership Conference (SCLC), the Student Non-Violent Coordinating Committee (SNCC), the Congress of Racial Equality (CORE), and the Mississippi Freedom Democratic Party (MFDP). These organizations came together and formed the umbrella group known as the Council Of Federated Organizations (COFO), and it was through COFO that much of the 1964 Voter Registration Summer Project was carried out. In virtually every community in the state of Mississippi, voter registration projects were set up. Community meetings were held at churches and in the homes of private citizens. People were being educated as to their rights and responsibilities as citizens. The total atmosphere was charged with positive thinking. Celebrities such as Harry Belafonte, Bill Cosby and other nationally known people became concerned, and offered their help in the struggle for human dignity. Even the music of the day gave the masses a feeling and a mentality of positive being, and purpose.

Curtis Mayfield and the Impressions were singing, "We're a Winner," James Brown was singing, "I'm Black and I'm Proud and Stay in School and Get an Education," Aretha Franklin was singing, "To Be Young, Gifted, and Black." Stevie Wonder was singing "Blowing in the Wind." Other musical artists such as Pete Seeger, Peter, Paul, and Mary, and Joan Baez added their contributions to the positive charge in the atmosphere and the people were inspired to "Keep on Pushing." Even the young people got involved in going

Civil Rights or Human Rights?

door to door, talking to older people about "A Change Is Going to Come." These were young people who were not even old enough themselves to vote, but still they were in the struggle for human dignity. No one came in trying to be a hero, although some paid the supreme price for the freedom of others, making it much more important for us to not only remember the history, but to remember it more heartily, for in doing so, not only do we never forget the history, we don't repeat it. And we always remember crusaders like Denise McNair, Addie Mae Collins, Cynthia Wesley, Carol Robertson, Vernon Dahmer, Medgar Evers, Schwerner, Goodman, and Chainey, and all those too numerous to list who exhibited courage in the face of oppression.

So while COFO worked and got people registered to vote, the MFDP had selected three strong black women to challenge the legitimacy of Senators Eastland and Stennis. These three were Mrs. Annie Devine, Mrs. Victoria Gray, and Mrs. Fannie Lou Hamer, very outspoken and fearless women. This effort by the MFDP culminated in a huge march on Washington where petitions signed by registered voters from the state of Mississippi were presented to show why these two senators did not represent all the citizens of the state. Even though the effort failed, the victory lies in the fact that the masses were educated, they got registered, and many have looked after their own interests since that time.

It should be recognized here that while Dr. King was the recognized spokesman for the movement, the backbone that really made the program go forward was the common, everyday people who couldn't step out front, but helped out in many other ways, like putting up their property to bail many of us out of jail, providing housing and shelter for the volunteers, giving food and clothing to those who had not the wherewithal to provide for themselves, and so many other ways.

Then there were people who went into the community to bring political education to the people. People like Sisters Jewell Williams, Annie Pearl Spears and Sarah Singleton, who worked on the Madison County Project along with the project director, Brother George Raymond. There were also James Cheeks and Sears Buckley, who stood steadfast in the face of danger in spite of the many personal threats on their lives. There was the Clarke County Project with people like Jessie Smith, Bill Kirksey, Sam Wallace, Curtis Horne, and Solomon Marshall, Ina Faye Tillman, and Ann Miller. Fred Roy Henderson was another who paid the supreme price for human dignity. Sarah Knox and her whole family were unshakable in their courage in the cause of freedom. It should be noted here that these were high school students who were very much aware of the times they lived in, and devoted their lives to making things better. Mrs. Ally Jones and Mrs. Dora McLaughlin, two of the homes we often had to take refuge in because of the danger of driving after dark. Robert and Lorraine (Sister) Hand, W. C. and W. B. Bester from Stonewall, Mississippi. These are just a few examples; not even the tip of the iceberg when it comes to who was really the nuts and bolts of the movement. Without the help of these and others like them, there would not have been a movement. Warner Buxton, who not only had courage, but was an exceptional leader. Little Mary Green, young, gifted, black, and very courageous. Brother J. T. Thomas, the Washington McKenzie family, Harmon (Ham) Hailes, Randall and Shirlene (Dena) Sumrall. Sister Elsie Cameron. George Smith, and Sam Brown, Mrs Polly Heidelberg, Mrs. Crowell, and Mrs. Smith from the Lauderdale County Project. Mr. Ben Morgan, Dave Dumas, the Miller and Itson families of Clarke County. Rev. J. C. Killingsworth, a leader among leaders, one who never backed away from his role as a leader and lay his life on the line countless times for the future of his people. Mrs. Jimanna Sumrall, whose voice could be heard from the dusty roads of Mississippi to the halls of the Justice Department, calling for justice for all G-d's people. Also, what is so very important to remember here is that a strong emphasis was put on the fact that the Civil Rights workers were to educate the local people, and in doing so, they would "work themselves out of a job." One of the purposes of the Freedom School was to educate the people as to their rights and responsibilities so they themselves could become more involved in improving their own lives.

The goal of the Civil Rights Movement was never to keep the focus of the people on the ills and problems that we had been dealing with during the 'sixties'. The idea of perpetual agitation and blaming others for our inability to make progress, I don't believe, was ever the goal that Dr. King envisioned. I believe that others have taken over these positions of leadership in the African-American community and created celebrity status and a job for themselves that keeps the masses at the rich man's table, begging for any crumb that may fall. We are in a state of perpetual dependency in every area of life here in America, while others come from all over the world with nothing, and it seems that almost overnight, they are enjoying the fruits of independent living here in a country where our ancestors have been living for over four centuries. Today's leaders of what is called Civil Rights are nothing more than the gatekeepers for the Institution of Slavery.

The emphasis should have been placed then, and now, on our own ability to develop our own potential, which would fulfill every necessity that we have. This was the philosophy of the Honorable Elijah Muhammad. Not only did he preach a program of independent economics, but he also started an educational system that is alive and well today, and in many of the major cities across the country. The basis of the teachings of the Honorable Elijah Muhammad was that the so-called American Negro living here in the hells of North America has to begin to straighten up his own life, stop falling victim to drugs, alcohol, nicotine, and other harmful lifestyles that not only are harmful to the physical body, but also kill us off psychologically as well. For the first time, as African-Americans, we were told that we were better than white people, therefore we were well able to do for self, the same thing we had done for white people, which made them successful. The teacher of Elijah Muhammad was Fard Muhammad, an immigrant Muslim from the East who gave him a distorted teaching of the religion of Islam. He taught the Honorable Elijah Muhammad that the black man was G-d, and that the white man was the devil, which in reality was nothing more than the reverse of what white people had been teaching themselves and us for centuries. But the Honorable Elijah took this teaching and called it Islam, following the instructions of his own teacher. We know that it was not true Islam, but this kind of teaching served a particular purpose for a particular time.

The economical program given to us by the Honorable Elijah Muhammad was a three to five-year savings plan. Although this plan was nothing new because others were already doing it, it was the fact that coming in the context of all the other new teachings we were getting, it was just one more thing that inspired us to move on ahead. Suddenly, African-Americans began to realize that we could have money just like other people, all we had to do was manage it right. The Honorable Elijah Muhammad also had mega-tons of fish being imported all over America, thus providing jobs for men to work and earn a living. Then there were the sewing factories where our women made their own clothing. The bakeries, restaurants, and snack shops across America. The buying-up of thousands of acres of farmland was also another aspect of the do-for-self mentality. So although most of the material accomplishments from the Nation of Islam are gone, the do-for-self mentality which was the real jewel of the NOI's is still alive and well. And those of us who came under this kind of teachings practice it even today.

Also, along with this teaching of cleaning up our own lives, we began to look at our women in a different way. We were taught that the black man was G-d of the universe, and the black woman was Mother of Civilization. So as African-American men, we developed a new respect for our women and began to hold them in the highest regard.

Along with this personal development, we lost all fear of the white man. As Muslims, we saw ourselves standing toe to toe with any white man, not feeling any sense of inferiority.

I remember one incident where one of the fish crews from San Francisco was out selling fish, going from door to door in Newark and Freemont, California. We were well dressed, not disturbing the peace, being well-mannered, and making some business. Suddenly, both the day and night shifts of one of the city's police departments ran down on us, and we found ourselves in hand-to-hand combat. Of course we went to jail, and thanks to a very courageous white lawyer, we were eventually acquitted.

The Universities of Islam was the name given to the schools under the leadership of the Honorable Elijah Muhammad. So not only were we self-sufficient, but we had our own educational system, which stands today under the name of the Sister Clara Muhammad school system. Sister Clara Muhammad was the wife of the Honorable Elijah Muhammad and the mother of Imam W. Deen Mohammed, who is responsible for the name change.

Because the Honorable Elijah Muhammad taught self-sufficiency and love for self and kind first, the media put out distorted information that he was teaching hate. I must say that I, as a person, never heard any hate teachings. The central message of the Honorable Elijah Mohammed was, if we want to be equal with the white man, then we must produce like the white man. I believe the media used the hate-teaching part as a tactic to turn African-Americans away from the NOI because even though they knew it wasn't true Islam that he was teaching, they knew the idea of economic independence was powerful, and would build self confidence in all those who came under its influence.

So by giving Dr. King and the Civil Rights Movement all the positive reports, and giving the public a distorted view of the teachings of the Honorable Elijah Muhammad, the media was able to keep the masses of African-Americans away from the kind of thinking that would eventually give us true freedom.

A study of the Nation of Islam will show that there was also corruption going on inside that movement as well, with many of the ministers living off the backs of the membership, riding in fine cars, living in expensive homes and wearing the finest of clothing. Those of us who were known as foot soldiers sold the products for the Nation, donating much of our money back and leaving us with inadequate income to care for our families. So after the passing away of the Honorable Elijah Muhammad, some of the ministers continued to teach that same old distorted teachings of the Nation Of Islam, and just like those leaders in the Civil Rights Movement, they continued to blame others for the inability of the African-American community to make progress. Any people who are on the bottom of society will always like the idea that they can blame others for their downfall. This way, when they make half of an effort at success and fail, they can always blame it on somebody else. "It's the white man's fault." "If it wasn't for the white man, I'd do this or I'd do that." Those ministers who came along after the passing of the Honorable Elijah Muhammad are either ignorant or criminal to continue to teach that which holds our people in bondage, and like the visionless leaders of today's Civil Rights Movement, they have become the gatekeepers for the Institution of Slavery.

So we have between Dr. Martin Luther King and the Honorable Elijah Muhammad, virtually the same divergence in philosophies, as did W.E.B. DuBois and Booker T. Washington. The philosophy of agitation and protest that was used for equality by Dr. King not only dealt with our right to practice our civil and civic responsibilities, it also carried on over into education, employment, housing, and other areas of life. But we must remember that agitation was only a tactic that was used by Dr. King, it was never meant to become a way of life for the African-American community. In my opinion, these issues are our own responsibility. I don't believe Dr. King would use these same methods of social protest today.

The Honorable Elijah Muhammad's tactic was to teach black people that they were superior to white people and therefore, we should work to build up our own communities and develop our own economic foundation. He taught us that we were originally a dignified people by nature, and that we were to come away from gambling, drugs, alcohol, and foolishly throwing away our money when we could use it to develop our own community development. He initiated a three to five-year savings plan for black people to have their own resources to start their own businesses. He started a private school, with locations across America, that was known as the University of Islam, now known as the Sister Clara Muhammad Schools. The emphasis was also on African-American family life and respect for the African-American woman, to see her as the mate that stood by us during the brutal and inhuman days of slavery. Never flinching, always supporting. To see her as the first teacher of our children and therefore, the preserver of our future generations. To always hold our women in the very highest esteem, because a community is judged based on the way they treat their women. Strong family life makes for strong community life.

It is reported that the Honorable Elijah Muhammad told Dr. King that black people already have the resources in their own community to do what he was asking others to do for us. So we see that just like W. E. B. and Booker T., even though their philosophies may have differed, there is no question about the sincerity of either of these men concerning the advancement of us as a people.

As we look further down through the annals of history, we see other shining examples of human success that Allah has allowed to remain so as to let it be known that He hasn't given anyone something that He didn't give us all.

Madam C. J. Walker was born Sarah Breedlove Walker in 1869 to parents who were ex-slaves. She was born a pauper in Louisiana, and her parents died when she was six years old. She married C. J. Walker at the age of fourteen, and became a widow at the age of twenty. She did laundry to make a living and experimented with hair oils so as to remove the Negro curl from her hair. The oil did make it softer but did not remove the curl. In 1905, she developed the straightening comb, which took out the curls. Madam Walker went on to open up a school of cosmetology to train her operators. She employed agents to sell her products and built a factory to produce them.

We see here in this example of achievement a woman who looked within herself and found her G-d-given potential. Even the brutality of slavery and its intent to harm the human spirit failed in its purpose to reduce her below the level of her G-d-given human form. Slavery had failed in its effort to pass on the gene of inferiority, and Allah has allowed her to remain so that others will prosper from her shining example.

Before her death, Mrs. Walker had more than 2,000 agents selling and demonstrating the "Walker System" of hair styling and cosmetics. Not only was she able to supply jobs and employment for people in her own community, but she gave $100,000 for the establishment of an academy for girls in West Africa. She also donated large sums of money to Negro institutions and charities here in America. Evidence of her success can be seen in the door-to-door method many of the cosmetic companies use today.

Again, we say, "We Must Rewrite the History."

As we continue on our journey through history, we see another example of the rise of the human spirit in the person of Maggie Lena Walker, born in 1867 in Richmond, Virginia to a poverty-stricken family. Her family lived in an alley where her widowed mother made a living doing laundry. Maggie was a gifted child and finished high school at the age of sixteen. She took a course in business, then left the teaching profession and went to work as the executive secretary of the Independent Order of St. Luke. The purpose of St. Luke was to provide assistance to its members in their sickness, old age, and in meeting funeral expenses. Mrs. Walker's duties were to collect the dues, verify the claims, and keep the books. She conceived the idea of members saving and investing their money. When she assumed the job of secretary-treasurer, the order had only 3, 408 members, no reserve fund, and no property. By 1924, she had increased the membership to 100,000, had acquired a home office building valued at $100,000, organized an emergency fund of $70,000, and had established the St. Luke's Herald newspaper. In 1902, she proposed the plan for the founding of the St. Luke Penney Savings Bank, of which she became president. The bank was later known as the St. Luke's Bank and Trust Company. Mrs. Walker helped those who helped themselves. For instance, she once encouraged a one-legged shoeshine man to save his pennies. When he had saved $50.00, she helped him first rent, then buy his own place. Children were encouraged to also save, with the definite purpose of using their money wisely.[12] (138-139)

So here, we see yet another example of the human being calling on her own G-d-given qualities, and at the same time, urging others to also look within themselves and find the inner strength to do for self. We see people who not only see themselves as being as intelligent and dignified as others, but also able to establish themselves to a level of independence so that they can be of service to others.

This is exactly what we mean by true leadership. Reaching out to give a person a helping hand so that person can go on to being in a position to provide for his or her own needs. Clearly we can see that these were people who did not have the same idea about leadership, as we see in the examples of what we call leaders today. The so-called leaders we have today seem to want to keep the focus of the people on them. So instead of giving the people the motivation and the information they need to become self-sufficient, they continue to issue out programs of dependency. As stated before, there is not even the slightest bit of similarities between any of the language used by today's leaders and that of our ancestors.

This philosophy of dependency we hear coming from the leadership today is not the average idea of dependency, for it is more serious than that. That is to say that this agitation for dependency today has to be seen in the context of degenerating morals and values. Therefore, when we continue to be dependent on others to include us in on their successes instead of maintaining the high standards of dignity and respect handed down to us through our ancestors, we not only take on the values of others, we hand these values down to our future generations, and so we create a vicious cycle of perpetual dependency, and we're seen as a people with very little honor and self-respect. We must shed this idea of wanting to force others into doing for us what we can rightfully do for ourselves. The standard for quality leadership should not be lowered or compromised. Instead, it should be raised. If in days gone by, our ancestors were able to achieve the seemingly impossible goals that they did with less to work with, then why is the African-American community still in a state of dependency in these modern times of enlightenment, with not only unlimited resources to work with, but with the laws and the language of the Constitution being enforced? There is no excuse for failure, and we need to be about the business of establishing ourselves with an economic foundation so as to be equal in today's society, and a moral foundation that will enable us to set the example for our own future generations, and for the broader society as well. The best resource that we have is our own human potential, and when we use that, then all else that we need will come to us. "We Must Rewrite the History!"

In Tulsa, Oklahoma, in 1921, in a 36-square block of the city, there were over six hundred black businesses that prospered. These were doctors, lawyers, educators, business owners, and entrepreneurs who controlled their own destinies by doing for themselves. There were bus lines, cab service, restaurants, movie theaters, schools, hospitals, movie theaters, banks, schools, hospitals, and the like. Whatever was needed to only operate a community was there, but black folks who lived there established, indeed, an entire city in Tulsa at that time. The black dollar remained in the black community for over three years because there was no need to go outside for anything. Everything that was needed was already there.[13] (Wilson. Forward)

In Philadelphia, in 1800, African-Americans accumulated $250,000 worth of assets and owned two insurance companies. What was so amazing about this was because this was during the period of slavery. Black economics and self-help are not new ideas in the black community. As early as 1853, an economic convention was held in Rochester, New York, where slogans such as "Buy Black and Double Duty Dollars" were heard. It has been reported that in 1865, the African-American community had accumulated up to $50,000,000 in assets. Again, this was during the period of slavery. In 1889, we conceived our first privately owned bank in the state of Virginia. We had a reported number of 31,000 businesses in 1890. Booker T. Washington and Fred Moore led the business convention that started the National Negro Business League in 1898. Again, the slogan was "Buy Black and Double Duty Dollars." Also at this time, one of the largest black insurance companies was founded in Durham, North Carolina. The North Carolina Mutual Insurance was started by a barber named John Merrick, who had no formal education, and Dr. Aaron McDuffy Moore. These same two men went on to develop the Mechanics and Farmers Bank in 1908. They also invested money in North Carolina Central College. The Haiti Business District, so named after the Republic of Haiti, was established in the business section of the black community. The Haiti Business District housed up to 150 black businesses. The black banks in Durham actively recruited black folks for business development and brought economic development into the area by providing business and property loans that could not be had at the white-owned banks. What really stood out is the fact that none of these businesses failed during the Great Depression. This was mainly due to the fact that much of what the black community needed was provided by these businesses, and the community supported these businesses.[14] (Kunjufu, 15-17) These are just very, very few examples of what a people can do when they recognize the fact that they have within themselves the power to lift themselves up by their own bootstrap. This statement by Booker T. Washington is telling us that we have the mind, the spirit, the potential, and all else that is needed to create our own success. The bootstrap is symbolic of all these assets, working together to accomplish what is needed for individual and community prosperity, but we have to want it to achieve it.

Our aspirations must go far beyond just wanting enough money to pay the bills and go out and party on. Our definition of freedom has to move to a higher level of interpretation. Our ancestors didn't establish themselves because they had permission from the United States Constitution. They established themselves because of the constitution that Allah established within them. This inner constitution proclaimed them to be free. They understood that Allah had made every human being with a desire for the real life in this creation, and that this creation was put here by Allah to be of service to man. This kind of simple knowledge is inherent. It is a part of the natural makeup of the human being. Another simple but great realization that we see in the thinking of the ancestors is that no civilized or intelligent people want to have their daily needs taken care of by others. We must understand that along with freedom comes responsibility. So the word "civil" is automatically a part of the natural human makeup.

The establishment of the United States Constitution is to be understood as that document derived from the G-d-given nature of man that protects the right inherent in all men's nature to grow and reach their fullest potential. It should not be interpreted to mean that people have the right to force themselves on others. It is the verbal interpretation of the human spirit that protects individuals as they grow and earn the respect of other men, thereby putting themselves in a position of influence so that they may become part of establishing a truly civilized society.

This is the real spirit of that great and wonderful document we call our Constitution. There are those who would attempt to prevent others from growing and reaching their fullest potential. Their desire is to control the masses mentally, so as to maintain political and material dominance over them. Some men want to be masters over others, and there is no other example that is more blatant than the treatment of the African-American under the whip of the slave master. The United States Constitution recognizes the human being, and the unlimited possibilities for growth and development in the individual. In stark contrast, we find that the Institution of Slavery's primary objective was to reduce the African-American to the level of a beast of burden so as to perpetuate the slave mentality in us as a people.

The fact that a person cannot be held in physical bondage says that that particular person can, and should, use their minds to establish themselves through the ownership of property, business development, and control of their own community against those negative forces that will tear it down. This is called "civil establishment." This civil establishment brings about awareness and responsibilities in civic affairs, affairs that we, as citizens, should be involved in. So we say that the African-American community has shown more allegiance to this great country than any other people. We say this because not only were we the first to shed blood for this country, but we did it even though we owned no land. We enjoyed no pleasures or privileges at that time, and the fact that we were thought of as less than human meant we didn't need anything to do with civil responsibilities.

Today, however, because of the psychological residue from the Institution of Slavery, most of the problems we experience today are self-inflicted. Therefore, we must not only demand that others treat us as human, but we must treat ourselves as human as well. The cruel and inhuman treatment we inflict on each other is based on the fact that we have let others develop our agenda for us, therefore, we become victims of whatever negative influence they inject into the atmosphere. One of the main reasons for this is because we fail to educate ourselves and to establish ourselves economically. Therefore, we continue to look to others for everything, including our lifestyles. In the words of that great emancipator, Booker T. Washington, who said, "At the bottom of education, at the bottom of politics, even at the bottom of religion itself... there must be for our race... economic foundation, economic prosperity, economic independence."² (30) Again, I say, **"We** Must Rewrite the History." We must live the language of the ancestors. In this time of opportunity and in this land of plenty, we as a people must find independent establishment. That is to say that we must put ourselves in a strong economic position.

Mr. Washington is telling us in this statement that with an economic foundation, we, like others, can set the standard for our own educational system. The students of our future generation will see our people as the role model to follow. We have to control the knowledge that goes into our children's minds. To do that, we must be the primary contributing force behind the educational system. This same principle applies in politics. If we want our political representatives to see us as more than just another vote at election time, they have to know that they are the dependents, not the people who put them there. We should ensure that they are able to legislate the kind of laws that would not only be of a political benefit, but of a moral benefit as well. This can only be done with a strong economic foundation. Religion must also be seen as more than just a spiritual force, or some place to show off our new fashion or to release the stress of the previous week through emotional outbursts. Religion has to be seen as touching all aspects of our lives, moral, economic, political, intellectual and spiritual. Allah is the G-d of all the worlds of knowledge and science. And he is the motivation behind our involvement in these areas. Our obedience to G-d shows us how to use our success in his creation to help advance the positive development of mankind. We no longer see ourselves as recipients of charity and opportunity from others, but rather, we have become the producers and contributors, and we can take our own rightful place as world leaders of human society.

This is the kind of language we need to hear from our leaders today. There is an obvious difference between the philosophy of the ancestors and the language we hear coming from the leaders today. The very idea that a privately owned business should create a position so as to hire us is utterly ridiculous. The tactic of arm twisting through the boycotting of businesses so they will hire us is shameful to us as a people. This is especially true in these modern times, when we as a people are as rich collectively as some countries. When we listen to the advice given to us from our ancestors, we find strength, stability, courage, and progress.

The economic success we experienced during the 1800s and early 1900s came despite the fact that we didn't have equal protection under the law. And although they couldn't pass legislation to deny our rights, the unwritten law of Jim Crowism was in full effect. Still, we rose despite the persecutions and the injustices; still, we maintained our dignity and continued to progress. So, when we hear in the news about success based on merit, just a very slight glance at African-American history will reveal the epitome of that success.

As a people, we can ill afford to continue to look back and allow the hurt of the past to hinder us from the success of the future. To do that would mean that not only would we have failed the ancestors, for their greater success lies in our doing far and away better than they did. It would also mean that there would be no future for the next generation, and so the vicious cycle of failed communities would start all over again. And lastly, we would have succumbed to the sub-human standards intended for us by the Institution of Slavery. At all costs, we must be successful, striving legitimately, respectfully, and with integrity.

This success should not be looked at as just ordinary success, but indeed, it must be predicated on the higher meanings of life. We must think of the ancestors as if they are actually looking at us and urging us on. This periodic and shallow academic lip service we give to the ancestors need to stop. The best tribute we can possibly pay them is to lift ourselves up to the moral, economic and spiritual levels that Allah intends for all His servants. Therefore, they will find their fulfillment in our success.

Some of the telling marks that identify the shallow thinking of the leaders of today's movement can be seen in the fact that whereas in the early part of the twentieth century, we could see where our vision was beginning to become blurred, now, its as if we are totally blind. The tactics that were used to show the nation and the world the mistreatment of the African-American community has suddenly become the goal. Our struggle has gone from our demand to be recognized as members of the human race to the "give me a job" mentality; the "I want to sit and eat next to you" mentality, or the "I want to go to school with you" mentality.

A civilized society means that a person should be able to eat, get educated, and come and go as they please, but the way to attain these goals is not to force ourselves on others, but rather we need to develop these needs for ourselves, and the respect will grow so fast that others will fly to us because we know how to do it better, anyway. When we understand it, all that we protested and demonstrated for, we already had the ability to create for ourselves, but somehow, we began to focus on the very basic elements of life and this impeded our progress. We must realize that as long as we view these basics as the goals of life, and as long as others control these things we're struggling for, our fight will never end. The issue of civil rights will never die. It is only when we realize that we are human and that our humanity is as creative as others are that racism as we know it today will come to an end.

When we are operating from a position of strength, we position ourselves to make sure the laws are being enforced, and justice is flowing equally for all people. No longer do we have to worry about civil rights because through our human efforts, we've gained the respect of others. We can now sit down anywhere at the table with anyone and sip a cup of coffee on equal footing.

We take notice of Sister Rosa Parks as she boarded the bus in Montgomery, Alabama, tired and weary from a hard day's work. Her thoughts, in my opinion, were probably on just getting to the nearest seat and resting herself. When this white man came and tried to force her to move, her spirit cried out to him, saying, "I'm as good as you are! I have a mind and a soul, and I'm as much human as you are! I'm made by the same G-d as you and I ain't moving!" Even though Mrs. Parks stood her ground based on her humanity, she was arrested based on her color.

Black folks stopped riding buses and found alternative ways of travel to take care of their business and getting to work. Think of the progress that could have been made by now by black people if someone had started their own transportation system. Think of how much advanced we would be if the slogans of the day had been "Buy Black, and Double Duty Dollars!" Think of where we would be if that was the battle cry today, instead of continuing to demand handouts from others. Once again, we say the issue for us as African-Americans is human rights, as opposed to civil rights. And even more importantly, this fact has to be recognized by the African-American community, more so than anybody else.

When we look across America, and indeed, the whole world, we see other groups and organizations marching and demonstrating for rights. We see every kind of group from those who advocate rights for animals, to save the environment, pro and anti-abortion groups, and even people over in China. Although various groups have always used marching and demonstrating as tactics in the past, it was African-Americans during the Civil Rights Movement which really made it a popular form of protest. Most of these and other legitimate groups have been very successful and have gotten much accomplished in terms of highlighting their cause to the public.

We also see other groups that are not legitimate but who want recognition for their cause. They align themselves and their cause with the Civil Rights Movement, so as to garner sympathy from the unsuspecting public. One such group is the gay and lesbian community. When the homosexual community began asserting themselves on the public, they already knew that the gay lifestyle would be hard for the public to accept as legitimate. We used the term "legitimate" in this case, in the same sense as we mean "ethnicity." The gay community's strategy is to present their lifestyle to the public as a minority in the same sense as that of African-Americans and Latinos, and other racial groups are considered. Their way of getting the public to accept their lifestyle as legitimate is to compare their cause with that of the African-American experience during slavery, on up through the Jim Crow period and the Civil Rights era. This is a tragedy, and a heinous crime. What's more of a tragedy is that not only have our leaders not spoken out against this slanderous and ridiculous comparison, but some have actually come out in support of them. We see politicians who want to get the gay vote come out using slogans like "witch hunt," which is to imply that the citizens would march through the streets to drive the gays out of town. Of course we know that there is nothing farther from the truth, but they use this kind of language to gather public sympathy for the gay cause, which increases their chances of getting elected.

When we think about the Institution of Slavery and what it is designed for, we realize that this is more than just physical slavery; this is the kind of slavery that is designed to rob those who are enslaved of their very humanity. We have already explained genocide, and how the fear and intimidation, the complex of inferiority, feeling less than human, and of self-hate was bred into the genes of the African-American, and thus, through the process of heredity, was passed down from generation to generation. In order to make our case a little more clear, it is necessary for us to briefly revisit just a few of the atrocities we've already mentioned.

The fact that we were considered less than human was evident in the scanty clothing we received, the drafty and leaky quarters we were given to sleep in that were only adequate for livestock. We were tortured and burned in an effort to break our human spirit, branded like cattle so as to be identified as the property of another human being. Our manhood was destroyed when our women were taken and disrespected right in front of us and our children, and we men were so powerless that we could not even come to the aid of our families. This is a profoundly deep, hollow, and hurting feeling that one can only know through the experience.

Unspeakable acts of violence and torture were committed against our people. The type of treatment experienced by us as their slaves not only scarred us from the outside, but also left an everlasting psychological scar of inferiority and self-destruction on the black community. There was the hurt and the misery felt by the black mother as her baby was snatched from her arms and sold without conscience to another plantation, because since we were on the level of animals, we weren't supposed to have those human feelings of love and affection for our children anyway.

Then to endure the period of Jim Crowism, where a black man or woman was hung just to instill more fear into the heart and soul of the rest so as to keep them submissive. We've just witnessed Rosewood in Florida and Tulsa in Oklahoma. The mass destruction and obliteration of a people because their color wouldn't allow their humanity to be seen.

On up through these modern times, a black man could lose his livelihood or his life for just exercising his rights of citizenship. Many times, the fear would not allow him to speak in his own defense as any person should be able to do.

The effects of this kind of treatment can still be felt today as we move on into the twenty-first century. We witness the self-hate manifested in black-on-black crime in the African-American neighborhoods and the practice of taking our resources outside our community to spend them with other than self, thus keeping us as a people at the very bottom of the economic ladder.

So then, this is just a very brief history of the treatment and the psychological effects of that treatment African-Americans have had to suffer here in the hells of North America. This is just enough to give us an idea so we don't forget.

How can we stand by silently, and allow this immoral and slanderous comparisons against us as a community to be made without even so much as a whisper of protest? We hear many in the gay community say "This is who I am." Meaning living the gay lifestyle, and basing their identity on the way they perform sex is how they identify themselves. I say, that's fine; we have no problem with a person being gay and making that lifestyle their identity. But as African-Americans and with any other ethnic group, our identity is not based on a sexual style. Our "total" human makeup is who we are. Black people weren't persecuted because of their lifestyle; we were persecuted to prevent us from ever living life on the human level. Homosexuals call their lifestyle their sexual orientation, or the way they were influenced to go. As African-Americans, we were not influenced into being black; we were born black, and this is something that does not change.

When we talk about ethnicity and what identifies us as a people, we're talking about traits that people who are of the same geographical and cultural backgrounds have in common. Ethnicity has to do with language, food, music, religion, culture, etc. It has nothing whatsoever to do with how someone indulges in sex.

One has only to reflect on our African heritage and the rich and beautiful languages spoken by the various tribes, or on some on the history of Timbuktu, Mali, Ghana. Later, we will witness the conquest of European Spain, which led to the enlightenment of the world and took the Europeans out of the "Dark Ages." The beautiful garments and tasty African dishes, the differences in the shades of the skin— some the darkest of dark, while others, the lightest of light— and all beautiful. When we reflect on the beautiful music, that is part of our African heritage and how that rhythmic sound has influenced the whole world. It instills within us a feeling of pride. The African dance that has flavored the dance styles of many other ethnic groups. The industrial and agricultural contributions exported from Africa to the rest of the world, especially America, which has been the primary recipient of great African contributions. The various inventions and discoveries given to America by her African citizens that has helped to make America the great world power that she is.

This is just a very, very small tidbit of what's behind the door of African and African-American culture, heritage, contributions, and suffering here in America. So we see, in terms of legitimacy, homosexuality is not even on the same planet. We are African! We are American! And we are proud! We reject the gay lifestyle, and we insist that you cease and desist in comparing homosexuality with the black experience.

Sex is what we, as humans and animals, all have in common, and it is the method by which life is perpetuated. Sex between two people of the same gender is an aberration all over the world, and although it is allowed, it is not considered to be normal, although Hollywood tries to make it seem normal. Nor is it elevated to the level of ethnicity. Homosexuality is just a perverted lifestyle, nothing more, nothing less. There is no such thing as "gay culture." (Let me stop here and say that no one has the right here in America to visit violence upon anyone because they want to be gay. Anyone who does violence to others should be punished to the fullest extent of the law.) Also, I am not talking about rejecting people, but I am talking about rejecting anything that's immoral, be it drugs, white-collar crime, political corruption, and homosexuality; all of these are immoral diseases and should be rejected outright by civilized society because they go against the grain of positive human development. Again, I say emphatically, gay rights are not the same as the black experience here in America.

African-Americans in movies and television should really consider the impact they have on the minds of children when they go in front of a camera. No amount of money and fame should be worth your leading our future generation down the wrong path.

We see the media present the sitcom where they make it seem as if the society is mistreating the homosexuals. It should be understood that sitcoms, and sometimes even the news, are products of the people who write them. So the general public should not allow themselves to get caught up in a fictional storyline written by some writer on a sitcom or any television program, and perceive it as reality. Hollywood, in their movies and television programs, try to win the sympathy of the unsuspecting public by making it seem as though the person is being rejected because of their humanity, and we know that's just not the case at all. The tactic used in misleading the public is to raise homosexuality to the level of ethnicity and then make it seem as if that person is discriminated against because of some imagined ethnic makeup. They present the gay community in the same light as the black community as it relates to civil rights, using the same language such as discrimination, prejudice, etc. They play upon the emotions of the public, then the society's, especially black people, since we came from that kind of experience with racism. We all jump on the bandwagon, supporting gay rights, when it's not about that at all. In reality, it's about standing for human decency, and the whole of the African-American community should be up in arms that this shameful hoax has been played on our community, and those among our leaders who supported it should be publicly condemned.

We see gay and lesbian activists on talk shows, talking about being treated as second-class citizens and being discriminated against. Nothing could be further from the truth. Those who push this misinformation know full well that homosexuals have not been discriminated against as a people. The gay community enjoy America in all its fullness, as do other citizens, and this kind of language used by them to promote their cause only highlights the dishonesty employed by them to push their movement. I don't believe that we should allow society to degenerate to the point where our sons and daughters will feel that it's normal to marry a member of the same sex, as it is normal to marry the opposite sex. When we look at our society today, we realize that we've progressed tremendously in terms of technology, but our morals have gone by the wayside, and we will find that this is the root cause of many of the symptoms that are plaguing America today.

Many of our leading African-American magazine publishers have begun to help promote the gay lifestyle in the black community. They start off by printing traditional African-American news, culture, and other related interests, then all of a sudden, they come with this gay lifestyle information, which, by its mere presence in the magazine, helps to sanction the lifestyle. As African-Americans who realize the rich heritage and culture we came from, we should let those who represent us in the media know without a doubt that we're not with that, and that we request that they cease that practice. As the concerned public who supports these black publications, we should be very concerned about the kind of information they put into the black community, and we should let them know that we are holding them responsible. We should not accept information just because it comes from someone black; we should accept it based on its soundness, as well as its being designed to promote positive thinking for our people.

When we look back over the history and study the value system handed down from generation to generation, we find the black family, for the most part, closely knitted together despite the treatment they received under slavery. Even though it has been in the community, black folks have never sanctioned this lifestyle and have even condemned it in the community. It is only today's leaders that have been bought off financially or politically that have stood in favor of gay rights. So here again we witness the tragedy of the failure of our so-called leaders.

Society must draw the line somewhere to maintain human decency. When we look at society, we see the sexually transmitted diseases, as well as the ones that were already here, getting worse and harder to cure. I believe because of this focus on sex, society has produced all kinds of perversions, and although they try to say that AIDS is not a gay disease, I say we did not begin to experience this tragedy until the gay community came out of the closet. I am not a doctor or medical scientist, but I have sense enough to know that after millions of years of man-and-woman relationships, for us to try to make AIDS everybody's disease is a crime as well, and it is my opinion that it is the gay political clout that fuels this misinformation.

Lastly, when we look into the universal order of things, we see nothing that supports gay lifestyle. Everything operates on opposites. Progress for the society of man is based on man's observation of G-d's creation. In the Holy Qu'ran, we find that G-d gives the human being a clear picture of His intent for the progress of society, and to follow these signs in the creation is to have unlimited progress. Allah says to us, "So glory to Allah, when you reach eventide and when you rise in the morning. Yea, to Him be praise, in heaven and earth. It is He who brings out the living from the dead, and the dead from the living. And among His signs is this, that He created you from dust; and then, behold, you are men scattered far and wide! And among His signs is that He created for you mates from among yourselves, that you may dwell in tranquility with them, and He has put love and mercy between your hearts: verily in that are signs for those who reflect. And among His signs the creation of the heavens and the earth, and the variations in your language and colors: verily in that are signs for those who know. And among his signs is the sleep you take by night and day, and the quest you make for your livelihood out of His bounty. And among His signs, He shows you the lightening, by way both of fear and hope, He sends down rain from the sky to give life to the earth after it is dead: verily in that are signs for those who are wise. And among His signs is this, that heaven and earth stands by His command: then He calls you, by a single call, from the earth, and behold, yea straightway come forth. It is He who begins the creation; then repeats it; and for Him it is most easy to Him belongs the loftiest similitude we can think of in the heavens and the earth: for He is exalted in might, full wisdom." **Holy Qur'an 30:17-27. So we can plainly see the plan or the intent of G-d in the Qur'anic verses above.**

Everything we see, from the farthest reaches of outer space to the precious life that we see in the creation all around us, the plant life, animals, and the human race, the progressive life of us all, is based on opposites, or the male-female principle. Life comes from the dead, and light comes from the darkness. To preserve our physical life, we take sleep to rejuvenate the body after work. As human beings, we have the power to live any kind of life we choose, but to live a productive life the way Allah intends, we only have to observe His creation. There are those who say to those who are trying to be upright, "Who are you to tell me how to live?" Or they will say, "This is my lifestyle given to me by G-d." I say to you, G-d did give you the life, but you chose the style, and although you are free to practice it, we will not stand by and see you try to legitimize it off the trials and tribulations of the African-American community. Homosexuality works against the creation. I also say that there are people who study the creation, and as we shall see later in this discussion, man's life has benefited from his study of the creation.

The point is this, while we cannot tell anybody how to live, you cannot stop me from speaking out against what I know to be wrong. We know the difference between what's right and what's wrong. G-d did not leave the human being without guidance for his life. The life examples and the words of the prophets as well as other dignified people we see down through the annals of history, and this magnificent creation He has given us to advance our lives as He intended. So then, if a person wants to be gay, he has the right to do so now, and had always had that right. We become concerned when they try to legitimize it so as to make it normal, or be accepted as part of the norm by society. I say to you all, we are not without guidance for our lives! "Glory to Allah who created in pairs all things that the earth produces, as well as their own human kind and other things of which they have no knowledge." (Holy Qur'an 36:36)

There are other verses that refer to the word pairs, which, when understood rightly, also means mates. The word pair or mate is from the root word ***zauj***, which means to join in pairs, or couples. To germinate, to marry, join in wedlock. Even the earth itself, where all life is produced, when studied in relationship to that life, we still see the principle of opposites, working in Allah's plan for human productivity. In our own human makeup, we see that two left shoes or two right gloves don't make a pair. This is the same as two men or two women in same-sex relationships. Although they may be nice shoes or pretty gloves, they are not a pair. As we go further from the universal order of things to the natural environment, to the signs we see in our own human makeup, we come to the modern inventions of man himself, which are based upon G-d's natural pattern of creation.

From the very basic use of the modern appliances and equipment we use everyday to make life livable and enjoyable, their operation is based on opposites, or the male-female principle. The very sacred act of bringing life into the world, we see progress for the human being, is based on diversity, and the greatest diversity is that of male and female. All are based on the signs man see in G-d's creation. There is absolutely nothing in G-d's creation that supports homosexuality. From the outer reaches of space to the new soul born into the world that helps to perpetuate the natural development of the human being, in these are signs for men who are wise. Allah also tells us in His Holy Book: "O mankind! Fear your Guardian Lord, who created you from a single person, created, out of it, his mate, and from them twain scattered like seeds countless men and women; fear Allah, through whom you demand you mutual rights, and be heedful of the wombs that bore you: for Allah ever watches over you." Sura 4:1 G-d is telling us here that He created the person, or the soul, and from that creation He created his mate, and we see the human race perpetuated over the world. So again, we see this word "mate" connected with the continuing life of the human being. The physical differences between men and women constitutes their being opposite each other and this is what makes them a pair. But there is also a physiological difference as well. It is that physiology that sends the male into the world. His ability to protect, maintain, and provide for his family puts him in the right frame of mind to protect and maintain the community life to make it a safe environment for not only his family, but for others as well.

The woman's physiology, for the most part, keeps her at home, with her attention focused on the family, giving them a value system to live by. After all, she is their first teacher, making sure that the home is in order, and all those kinds of things that helps to make the home a safe and happy environment to live in. In today's society, there are as many women who work as men, but still it is primarily the man whose responsibility it is to provide for the family. We are to understand that both these functions in the male and female, while different, are equally important, for one cannot survive without the other. Also, this does not mean that women cannot be active in community affairs and positions of leadership as well, but they both must bear in mind that the family and its proper development must come first. So we have this physiological difference that makes us mates to each other. We see more support for this kind of thinking as we read further in G-d's Holy Book, "That it is He Who granted Laughter and Tears; That it is He Who granted Death and Life; That He did create the pairs,—male and female, From a sperm drop when lodged (in **it's** place); That He hath promised a Second Creation (raising of the Dead)." Sura 53:43-47

There are two words here that again give us G-d's intent. The first is ***dhkir***, used for the male, which means to think or reflect, to take counsel, negotiate, confer the remembrance of G-d. This is masculine grammar, and some have mistakenly used it to refer it to a duty of men only, but as G-d tells us, this duty belongs to the female as well. The second word is ***unsay***, which is feminine grammar, and refers to the female, is also being called upon by G-d to think, to reflect, negotiate, remember G-d, etc. So we see here where the minds of the male and female have come together on a higher level of mating. Now we see intellectual development, ideas being formed that will help to keep society moving forward. Plans are being made for not only the children of one family, but for the family of mankind. Government, laws, rules and regulations, home planning, city planning, the total life of society is moving forward. So we see that the word "mate" doesn't mean just physical, it also takes in the total development of the human being. Ideas from both genders being brought together from a balanced perspective, which makes for a balanced society. Even the language bears witness to this truth. The Qur'anic language, which is the revelation of Allah to man, is still in its original form and is based on masculine and feminine genders. In terms of its originality, it has never been changed. So we see then that it is the words of G-d that should form the thinking of the human being, and not the political aspirations of man.

Again, I say, if people want to be gay, that is their choice, but we as African-Americans demand that you cease and desist in trying to legitimize your lifestyle off the blood, the injustice, and dehumanization that we as a people have suffered in this country. Sexual techniques cannot be compared to a people's humanity. They are not the same, and we will never accept them as such! Sex between two men or two women is not mating in terms of the way G-d intended it to be. It's only sex for the sake of sex. It produces no life, therefore, their claims for the concerns of the society cannot be the same as that of those men and women who produce families. The very premise on which they base their lives is against human life and development.

Life is sacred, so sex should be looked upon as something given to us by G-d as sacred as well, for it is the process that we use to continue the life. Sex is not for procreation only, but to be enjoyed lawfully between husband and wife for the good of the community. So as Brother Malcolm said, "The struggle for the black man is to be recognized as humans in this society," and the first step in that process is to "Rewrite the History." That is to say, take the words of the ancestors and materialize them. Recognize our own great human potential so that we can achieve some dignity and honor in our own community. This is how we honor the ancestors. This is how we encourage the future generations to do better than us. This is true freedom.

We should not, we cannot, we will not allow ourselves to fall into this immoral trend and give up what we know to be right in terms of a value system that has brought our ancestors over the rough waters of society. The struggle has been too hard, the cost has been too great, and the goal is too near for us to give up the struggle now for a few trends and fads that will make our glorious past meaningless. We must be the ones to decide what's right and what's legitimate for us. We have to be the ones to record our own past, present, and future so that the generations that are to come after us will be able to see what it is we have done. "We Must Rewrite the History!"

Chapter 4

Why we Regressed an Imposed Culture

At the beginning of the nineties, and throughout most of that decade, there was a statement being circulated around the country that said "The black man will be extinct by the year 2000."

Now I don't know the source of that statement, but when I heard it, that's the way it was phrased, and it made a very powerful impact on the African-American community. I've talked with many of my friends and colleagues, Muslims, and non-Muslims, and with some who were members of the Afro-centric culture. We discussed this statement extensively, trying to determine just how something like this would take place. The extermination of a race of people was no small matter. And we knew through just plain common sense that whoever put that statement in the atmosphere had to be dealing on a much higher plane than the Ku Klux Klan, or some other hate group.

"The black man will be extinct by the year 2000," a statement that was being discussed across the country, and as stated before, it made a big impact on the black community.

As I was driving cross-country from California to Mississippi, I thought back on a statement made in a speech by Imam W. Deen

Mohammed. The imam said "Man means mind." (9) So when we're talking about man, we're not referring to gender as much as we're referring to ideas that are generated by the mind. Ideas are not necessarily masculine or feminine, but when they enter into the mind of another person, they begin to shape, mold, and form that person in a certain way.

Then I thought about the statement the imam had made earlier, when he said, "Words make people." (9) So then, what all this is telling us is that although we are walking around in masculine and feminine bodies, the real person is the mind. So that tells us further that the statement that the "black man will be extinct by the year 2000" is not talking about the male gender, but it has reference to the African-American community as a whole in terms of leadership, on an individual, family, community level, as well as the values and principles that determine the quality of that leadership.

When we can understand the relationship between the human being and the influences that pervade society, we can see that that statement is not talking about physical extermination or physical incarceration. This statement has much more ominous ramifications than that. This statement is telling us that the process that began with our physical enslavement back on the plantations will still be in motion even in the year 2000. That is to say that even though we are walking around, going where we please, doing what we want, wearing nice clothes, living in nice homes, driving nice cars, and we're able to associate with white people without being lynched, even though we have all these things, we're still under a heavier form of slavery than ever before. There is a saying that goes, "If you forget your history, you're destined to repeat it."

During the days of physical slavery, we were running, always trying to escape the brutal treatment of the slave master. What is even more significant is that, not only were we trying to escape the brutal physical treatment, we would not submit to the mental enslavement. Here is another man, demanding that we look up to him as G-d, telling us that he is our master. Telling us that he is the one that decides our future, and the future of our children.

So the slave wasn't running away from work, for he was used to work, building great cities, and civilizations. The slave was running away from the capture of his real self, and that is his mind.

The African knew that the same G-d that created the white man created him, and that he had freedom of mind to grow to his fullest potential, just like the white man. He looked at himself as a man, just like the white man, and he refused to see himself as other than that. So he ran, trying to cling to his pride, his dignity which is part of his true self. Our motto was, "Our physical bodies may be enslaved, but our real selves are still free, and we won't stop until our whole self,—our mind, body, and spirit—is free!"

So then, when we look at the African-American community today. Even though we have all these material accomplishments, in reality, we still have nothing, because not only is everything that we have produced by someone else, we have even given up our pride and dignity. It seems as if we're living out the intent of the genocide process inflicted upon us during the days of physical slavery. The self-hatred, the sense of ill-responsibility and dependency, the idea of being less of a human than others, the love of pleasure more than establishment, is being manifested in our character today more than ever, and it seems that not only are we not able to get ahead, we can't even get equal. The very few that make it are of no consequence, because most of them are so far out of contact with who they really are in terms of their historical and ethnic background that they just melt in with those they're around with; they just go with the flow. They're just glad to be there. They don't see the importance of maintaining their own identity. They forget that it was Allah who gave them their identity, their colors, their distinctive features, etc., and these are to be cherished and protected.

Now this is not to say that we are to flaunt and put ourselves on people, and that every other word that we utter has to be about something referring to blacks. No, this is not what it means at all. We only mean that we should be as secure in who and what we are, as others are secure in who and what they are, because the same G-d that gave them theirs gave us ours. Our relationship should be one of mutual respect, and this should be the case, even if we are the only one of our kind in the entire city. We must have a positive sense of selfhood. But the only way to have this is to know who we are, and what we are about. We must not only stay in touch with the history, "We Must Rewrite the History!"

The most deadly aspect of this form of genocide is that it allows us to walk around in this society disconnected from our true self, not even knowing that we have a problem. We are, in fact, morally, mentality, and spiritually dead.

As we can see, the slavery process is still in motion in this day and time because, as already stated, during the plantation days, we were forever trying to escape. This was because only our bodies were enslaved, our minds were still free and trying to run so that we could find the freedom to exercise our own potential.

We came from a background that wouldn't allow us to accept another man as a master over us. It is recorded that up to 30 percent of the slaves brought to North America between 1731 and 1867 were Muslims. Many African Muslims were brought to America from the south of the Sahara Desert, between Senegal and Lake Chad. They were Fula, Fulbe, Fulani, Hausa, Manding, Mandinga, Kanuri, Kassonke, Serahule, Tenne, Mende, Moor, and Arab. They were of the Islamic empires of Songhai, Ghana, and Mali, and came from places like Timbo, Futa Jallon (now Guinea), Conakry, Ghana, Congo, Angola, Senegambia, Sierra Leone, Nigeria, and Bundu.

During the 1730s, there were among the Muslims who were taken away into slavery, at least three who became well known. They were Job ibn Solomon, Yarrow Mamout, and Lamaine Jay. Later in the century, there was Ibrahim Abdul Rahman, who was known as a prince among slaves, and Mohammed, a well-known runaway slave from Georgia. Later, in the 1700s and 1800s, came Kunta Kinte, Lamen Kebe, Omar ibn Said, Salih Bilali, Samba, Bilai (Ben Ali, and Abu Ali), Charno, Osman, Abu Bakr, Mohammed Kaba, Mohammed, and Abu Muhammad ibn Abdullah ibn zaid Ali-Qairawani. Some came from powerful and prominent families. They were teachers, cavalry leaders, religious leaders, and students of law.[7] (10) So what we are saying here is that since many of the slaves were

Muslims, they came from an orientation that said they should bow to no man. They looked at no man as being superior to themselves. Muslims see G-d as the only force greater than themselves. We see evidence of this when we reflect back on the first episode of Alex Haley's mini-series, Roots, when the baby, Kunta Kinte, was held up in a symbolic gesture to the universe to "Behold the only thing greater than yourself."

So in many cases, rather than bow or submit to another man as master, many of the slaves would run, or find some other way to maintain their Islamic practice. Some, such as Job ibn Jallo, who as a slave, was given a place to pray and some other conveniences to make his slavery easier. Some slave masters were well aware of the contributions of Islam to the enlightenment of the Western world, and they recognized Muslims as learned men who were monotheistic in their worship.

Job was a hafiz, or one who memorizes Qur'anic scripture. He wrote out three copies of the Holy Qur'an by hand from memory. After two years of slavery, he was taken to England and set free to return to his homeland. Lamine Jay was from Futa-Toro, Senegal. He was captured with Job in 1730 by Mandingos while trading in Gambia. He was known as a linguist, or translator. He was returned to Africa in less than five years because of his friend Job's intelligence, personal dignity, and religious piety.

Kunta Kinte was born in 1750 in the village of Juffure, in Gambia. He was captured at the age of sixteen, shipped to Annapolis, Maryland, and sold to a planter in Virginia. Kunta fought hard to hold on to his Islamic heritage. As alluded to earlier, he was the great, great, and great-great-great-grandfather of the renowned writer of Roots, Brother Alex Haley.

Paul Cuffe was a noted shipbuilder, captain, and philanthropist. He was a descendent of a Muslim family from Ghana. His father's name was Saiz Kofi. Paul became very wealthy, and was responsible for the repatriation of many slaves back to Africa. He was the first black to petition the government to free every slave, and allow those who wanted to go back to Africa the freedom to do so.

There were many Muslim runaways as well. Muhomet (Muhammad), with documents dating back as far as 1774, was one of the earliest recorded Muslims in Georgia. He escaped from John Graham's plantation on Augustin's Creek, near Savannah, Georgia. He had been free over three years and was last seen at a settlement near the Indian line on Ogechee. On May 24, 1775, two ads appeared in the Savannah, Georgia Gazette reporting runaway slaves. The first ad named three Muslims: Quamie, Sambo, who was also a Moor, and another Sambo. The second ad named another Sambo, who was born in the county. In 1787, the Baltimore Advertiser and the Baltimore Maryland Journal advertised two Muslim runaways, one named Mingo, and another named Anthony. The ad read, "They both had the appearance of Indian or Moor." Osman was another runaway, and was known as the leader of the Dismal Swamp Maroon Community from 1852 to 1862. Osman's leadership proved useful when he made a military alliance with the United States Government against the Confederate States of America during the 1860s.7 (11, 14, 21) In 1753, Abdel Conder and Muhamut, who were Moors from Sali, on the Barbary Coast of Africa, were taken into slavery after losing a battle to the Portuguese. They were taken to South Carolina, to the Daniel LaRoche plantation, and enslaved for fifteen years until they petitioned the authorities for their freedom.7 (7)

So we can see that many of the Africans that were brought to America for the purpose of servitude to others besides Allah refused to submit willingly, and for the most part, these were the ones who had to be tortured most brutally in an effort to break their spirit.

In the Islamic culture, the words, "Allah is Greater," is whispered into the ear of the newborn baby. This serves the same purpose as when Kunta Kinte was held up to the universe to behold the only thing greater than himself.

In my own opinion, I believe that those who stood out most for freedom during the slavery period were of Muslim descent. They were those who led wars and insurrections; those who spoke out so eloquently about the attributes of G-d being in each and every man. I believe that they were speaking from their Islamic heritage. It was their devotion to Allah that made them refuse to bow to another man, and I believe that same spirit existed in those leaders who came along in later years to set the example for true leadership. It is only in these latter times that we hear the voices of dependency and willing submission.

We understand more clearly now why we were not allowed to keep our family names, and why the babies were snatched away from their mothers as soon as they were born, so not only would the child not have any family life or tradition, they would also never know G-d as their real source of life. The goal was to put in the mind and the very nature of that slave child that everything he needed to sustain his life would come from the slave master. Therefore, the slave master would be his god.

This same situation could very well apply to us today if we do not step up to the plate of responsibility. We must realize that slavery did not end with the Emancipation Proclamation. In fact, it was just the beginning of true slavery. When we say true slavery, we mean willing servitude, living a life of self-destruction willingly, willingly depending on others to do for us what we can, and should do for ourselves.

Let us ask ourselves a very serious question. How did we come to this condition we find ourselves in today? If we were to look back at some of the leaders of the society and the country during that period of physical slavery, I'm sure that we would come to the conclusion that these were very smart and intelligent people. These were leaders who made decisions not only for the people they represented, but they helped to decide the future of the nation. So we can conclude then that these were men of vision. These were people who knew that one day, physical slavery would come to an end. The Emancipation Proclamation did not take them by surprise. They already had another plan in motion to keep the slave a slave by the time physical slavery ended.

During physical slavery, the mind of the slave had already been put under fear. So after physical slavery, the quest really began in earnest to capture the total mind of the slave, for until you have the total mind, you don't really have a slave. So knowing the slave's true allegiance to their religious beliefs and their deeply rooted spirituality, the scientists of human nature came into the mind of the slave and weakened them with the very instrument that had been a source of strength for them in the past. That instrument was religion. History tells us that for the slave to attempt to read or learn to read anything was punishable by death for black people, and imprisonment and for any whites who would try to teach them to read.

So armed with the knowledge that physical slavery was coming to an end, the powerful forces that really ran the country found a way to continue the slavery process without the physical ball and chain holding the slave down. Again, we say these were the people of vision, those whose job was to be able to look into the future and determine what is going to be needed to keep the nation going, and the method that will be used to accomplish that goal.

We should never believe that a country is ran on a haphazard, day-to-day basis. The operation of society is very orchestrated and there are always minds at work to come up with the plans that are needed to keep the masses under control.

In this situation, America was still growing and not yet strong enough to sustain herself in terms of paying for the kind of labor that was needed to build the physical, economic and political infrastructure needed to become a world power. Nor did America have the knowledge that was needed to make it a truly civilized and creative society. As we shall see later, America knew the creative abilities of the slave because America knew the history of the slave. So the slave had to be made a "willing servant" in order for America to tap into our creative abilities. Knowing our devotion to G-d and religion, we were given their interpretation of the Scriptures, an interpretation by the slave master that would bind us to them until these modern days and times. Until the time that someone, blessed by Allah with a sincere heart and the genuine well-being of the masses as his primary concern, was born into the world to bring the clear understanding of G-d's word to all the people, representing True Salvation for the world.

So their interpretation of religion and the manipulation of the senses are the main tools used to keep the masses in check. Let me be very clear here. I am not saying that the Bible is not the word of G-d, or that it's a bad book. As a Muslim, I believe in the Bible and all the revealed books of Allah. In fact, a person cannot call himself a true Muslim unless they proclaim belief in all the revelations of G-d, including Biblical scripture, and the prophets of those scripture as well.

What I am saying is that the language the slave master gave Biblical Scripture to us in was what has held us in check for them. Scripture as we have it today was given to us by white people, and in order to keep us in a position of looking up to them as being our providers to reward us when we do good, and to punish us when we do bad, they gave us both the language and a picture of themselves as G-d. We have always heard the saying that "A picture is worth a thousand words," so we were given this picture of a white man hanging on the cross, and we were told that this is G-d, or the son of G-d, and then we were taught to bow down to this image and worship the image as G-d. And in time, when we looked at that picture and then looked at the slave master after the savage brutality that had been inflicted upon our minds, we began to really see white people as being superior, and being in the family of G-d.

This image has had the effect on our minds so much that when we close our eyes to pray, we see G-d in the image of a white man. So to us, everything white is better, and everything black is offensive. This image, along with their interpretation of Biblical scripture, tells us to obey our masters, no matter what the primary reason for us being in an inferior position in society today.

This kind of language has also had a harmful effect on white people because it has made them think of themselves as something bigger than human, and this will lead to a total disrespect for Allah, and the creation of Allah, thereby leading to their destruction.

Once again, let me say that I am not talking about the true Christian faith, nor am I talking against the Prophet Jesus, I am only making it clear to us the detriment that has been caused by this image, which is a creation of man that has been presented to us and to the world. Not only this; it also goes against the teachings of the Biblical scripture. Just to give one example of those teachings, for there are many in Biblical scripture, in Exodus 20:4-5, we are told,

"Thou shall have no other gods before Me, and not to make images." This is the first law of the Ten Commandments. Jesus said, "I came not to destroy the Law, but to fulfill the Law." That is to say, Jesus was the living, perfect example of that law. In other scriptures, Jesus said, "Worship G-d in spirit and in truth," and that his teachings, and that of all those prophets that came before him were the same, to wit: "Love the Lord thy G-d with all thy heart, soul, and mind, and thy neighbor as thy self." Jesus is telling us here that the focus of our attention should not be on him, but rather on the One that his focus is on, and that One is G-d. He is telling us that when we love G-d first, our relationship with him, with the rest of the prophets, and with our neighbors fall into the right perspective. G-d is not to be seen as a physical entity, but rather, we are to understand G-d with our hearts and our intelligence. As we have seen, and history bears witness, any other teachings besides these, will eventually lead society off the straight path of serving G-d, and before we know it, we have been reduced to the position of serving another man.

As we study the changes in the attitudes of the planters as it related to the slaves, we find that in the mid-1840s through 1860, the planters of the Deep South demonstrated a growing interest in religious instruction to the slaves. The shift in the planters' attitudes was linked closely to the political, social, and religious developments in the final antebellum years. In 1844, in New York City, at the General Conference of the Methodist Episcopal Church, the issue of slavery erupted, as it did in all other American denominations. Nearly three-fourths of the southern clergymen were, or shortly would be, slave owners. Other American churchmen were soon forced to take sides on the slavery issue. In 1845, the Southern Baptist split away from their northern brethren in support of slavery. Meanwhile, the Old School—New School Presbyterians divided over the issue after the formation of the Confederacy. The Episcopal and Catholic allied themselves with the slaveholders. Thus, during the 1840s, virtually all the southern clergymen allied themselves with the slaveholders. They purged their ranks of any lingering antislavery influences, attacked abolitionist heresies, and endorsed human bondage with Biblical arguments.15 (Touchstone 100) The southerners stressed the message of social control within the context of the harmonious Christian community. Bishop William Green observed that instruction and worship, especially when begun with young slaves, brought about a "blessed change in their spiritual condition which will make them orderly and obedient upon principle and not from fear alone." "The days of fogyism in the management of Negroes have gone," wrote an Alabama planter who sponsored religion for slaves, "the time for brute force is past, and men must admit that there is another way to make Negroes contented and profitable, a way in which, while it improves the moral status of the Negro, will strengthen the hold of the master upon him."

One crucial argument for religious instruction appeared again and again. Christianity would make the slave contented, happy, and faithful. It thereby promoted control and prevented rebellion. Planters echoed it in their private papers and their leading agricultural journals. John C. Jenkins, one of the largest cotton growers in Mississippi, claimed that many Christian slaveholders, himself included, adhered to Biblical arguments supporting slavery and remained true to their conviction by caring for the souls of their servants. He maintained that the divinely ordained Institution of Slavery saved southern blacks from heathenism. To delineate and popularize the idea of the benevolent Christian masters and the contented Christian slaves, agriculture and religious organizations offered prizes for the best essays on the duties of masters and slaves. Articles and sermons deluged the south. Planters were told they resembled the old patriarchs of the Old Testament.15 (104-108)

So, as we can plainly see, that with this kind of religious instruction coming directly from the slave owners or their designates, we can see more clearly now why we as African-Americans have such low opinions of ourselves. We were taught that we were ordained by G-d to be slaves. That slavery was our permanent station in life, and that we were supposed to love our masters more than we loved ourselves. This kind of message supported by that image of what they say is G-d in the flesh is the worse hoax that can ever be played on anyone, and again we say, that it is the primary reason why we as a people are on the bottom of society around the world.

So by beating us down and treating us like brute beasts, the slave master was able to convince himself that the slave was nothing but a heathen. Then they came with their religious teachings and bound the slave to them in such a way that they willingly stay and suffer.

No matter how free we may be physically, our minds are still tied to that peculiar institution, "The Institution of Slavery." One would be hard-pressed to imagine the turmoil and confusion going on inside the mind of the slave. The pain, and the hurt of knowing that deep within, as a human being, we're supposed to be as free as everybody else, yet, we still feel this strange allegiance to the slave master.

Through some strange mixture of greed, guilt, and sick rationale, white people came up with the idea that they were saving the wretched heathens from themselves. They fed the slaves, gave them shelter, clothed them, and all that the slaves had to do was give them a lifetime of service and devotion.

Through the physical, brutal, and animalistic type of treatment, coupled with the psychological doctrine of Caucasian interpretation of Christianity, African-Americans were almost completely taken out of their human form that was given to them by Allah and turned into a despised, rejected, and hated people. And when we use this kind of language, we're referring to the attitude we have toward ourselves as a community. So now, when we look back through history, we can understand more clearly why the Institution of Slavery is referred to as the "peculiar institution."

When talking about slavery, this word, "peculiar" is used only when referring to the African-Americans. It means "special," "like nothing else," "in a class by itself." We emphasize this point because in an environment such as we live in today, full of fads, fashions, and trends, we want people to get the full impact of its significance as much as possible. The knowledge of what was done, and why we still suffer from its effects today.

I believe it was back in the sixties when Brother Marvin Gaye sang a song called, "Ain't that Peculiar." Some of the lyrics of the song said, "You do me wrong but still I'm crazy about you. Stay away too long but I can't live without you. Every chance you get you seem to just hurt me more and more. But each hurt makes my love for you a little stronger than before. I know flowers grow from rain, but why do my love grow from pain. Ain't that peculiar, peculiar attitude, ain't that peculiar, peculiar as can be."

Now the person who listens to this song would naturally think that he is singing about a love-hate relationship with a woman, and this is true on one level of understanding. But on a higher level of understanding, when we see the position and the attitude of the black community toward the white community and how the society has been operating from generation to generation, this song also fits that situation as well. No matter how bad they treat us, we still come running back to them like a love-sick lover to a hurtful relationship. "We love them because they give us nothing… but pain." So we can see that the Institution of Slavery is a peculiar institution that produces a peculiar kind of thinking.

Also, let me put special emphasis on a very, very important point, and that is this, although these terrible things did happen and they are facts of history, still, we cannot use that terrible time in our history as an excuse for failure. We have too many shining stars in our past as examples of success, and the triumph of the human spirit. Moreover, we must remember that it was Allah who gave us our souls and the spirit that emanates from it, and it is only Allah who can take that soul from us.

Now let us go back to that bold statement that said the black man will be extinct by the year 2000. I believe that this statement told us that the seed of psychological slavery that was planted so many years ago in our subconscious has only come of age in these modern times. After the destruction of our history, the emptying out of our humanity, and filling us with their influences, we have become more destructive to self and kind then ever before. The psychological chains of slavery are stronger than ever now because its strength lies in its ability not to be recognized.

The proof is the fact that many of us are in positions of power and influence, yet we control nothing, and subconsciously, we still have the picture of that image in our minds of G-d being a white man, and so we continue to look at Europeans as all powerful. Some of us get upset and mad and start cursing and fighting physically, but all this end up being just a temporary venting of frustrations and anger at realizing our lowly position in the world. So when the smoke clears and all the anger and anxiety have died down, we see that the same people still have the power.

This statement is saying that due to that psychological control and the emptying out of all that is valuable to us, and our adapting the values of this society means that what we had is no longer with us, and that we're operating on what we've gotten from someone else. This has been detrimental to us because in our seeing others as superior to us, we forgot the fact that we are people too, and it has been a constant struggle on our part to be like everyone but ourselves.

When we go back to that physical abuse and the inferiority complex that was passed down through our genes from generation to generation, and then add the religious element, for a great many of us, our mindset had already been put in motion. All we had to do from that point was act it out.

This savior, given to us as the image of a European and pounded into our subconscious over a period of centuries, proved to be the death nail in the coffin of freedom and independent thinking for African-Americans as a people. Now, if we were to just stop and think about our position in the world and where we came from in terms of slavery, we would see that we had no control over our present or future selves. We were completely subdued, both physically and mentally. We had this all-powerful European over us, exercising total control. This man thought he had the power to destroy us both inside and out, and this he set out to do. We are the vessels whose own cultural identity had been stolen, and whose motivation for self-sufficiency had been subdued. So it stands to reason that when we're thinking with a mind that has been given to us by others, then they are always in control, no matter what position we may hold in society. No matter how equal we may be made to look, we are not equal when we don't control anything. The first thing we need to do is get control of our own minds, and the first thing we need to do in that area is get the right concept of G-d.

Imam W. Deen Mohammed, who is primarily responsible for highlighting the harm caused by this image, has said we are not to see G-d in any image at all, for G-d is above all creation. We have to understand that Allah is Creator, not creation. The very first commandment is to worship the one G-d, and to not make any graven images from the creation depicting G-d.

This idea about not making any images is given to man for the purpose of keeping the worship of Allah pure. When we begin to use innovations and letting small things creep into our faith, pretty soon, these small things become big things, and over a period of time, we find that we have strayed away from the pure worship of the one G-d. The one who created everything and everybody, including the Prophet Jesus. Jesus said, "Worship G-d in spirit and truth." This statement alone eliminates him and the image from the position of being worshipped.

To worship G-d in spirit means that we are to bring our whole self to live an upright life according to what is revealed to the prophets by G-d. To be one with G-d as Jesus was means that in striving to obey G-d, we have given ourselves over to Him, and now we are thinking with the mind that He has given to us, so our purpose is His purpose, and His purpose is our purpose, and that purpose is to work to make the world a better place for all mankind to live.

To worship G-d in spirit means that we can't see G-d, but because our faith tells us that He is the one who created us, we know that we are in His presence at all times, and even though we don't see Him, we know that He sees us, and we should act accordingly. This kind of regard for the Creator brings us to a greater understanding of truth.

So the mission of Jesus and the mission of Moses was to bring freedom to the people. Moses' people were under bondage of the pharaoh in Egypt, and Jesus' people, under the Romans. Now if we study the scriptures very closely, we will see that both of their messages to their people was for the people to realize that they had the power within themselves to free themselves. The prophets didn't give them that power, G-d gave them that power. The prophets, through their life's examples and their teachings, brought this realization to the people. We must remember, the only power pharaoh has over us is the power WE give him. So this imagery and making another human being into G-d goes totally against the teachings of scripture.

Even some African-Americans who own their businesses become just as detrimental to our people as others, because we're thinking with the mind that was given to us by others. Examples are some of the black-owned businesses, such as liquor stores and night clubs. Those who open these kinds of businesses only see them as quick profit makers. Unfortunately, they don't see themselves as continuing the detrimental lifestyle that has plagued our people for so long. Then there are the record labels and music companies that produce the sexually explicit music lyrics, the promotion of violence, gang lifestyle, and other negative influences that help to destroy the future of our youth, and add to the destruction of family and community life. These kinds of business activities show that we have been well indoctrinated with self-hate and destruction, and just like the slave master who disregarded the human being for the sake of the profits of physical slavery, that same principle applies to those of us who conduct our businesses in a negative way, regardless of the human loss. The profits are all that matters.

We see entertainers from the African-American community on worldwide television accepting awards given to them by the entertainment industry, and the first thing they say is "Thank you, Jesus." The first thing we should realize is that what they really mean is "Thank you, white man," because that's the picture that comes to mind when they think of G-d. Secondly, with all the profanity, the violence, and the sex that many of them have in their music, how can they even think that G-d or Jesus would be involved in whatever success that they think they have? G-d is the author of all that's good, and He promotes only that which is good. All the rest of that stuff is just a new wing that's been added to the Institution of Slavery.

We can now further see the detriment of worshipping G-d through images, and having idols in our homes and places of business. The danger is that we give others the credit for that which G-d alone is responsible for, and we fear them with the fear that belongs to G-d alone.

To ascribe partners to Allah is the worse sin that could be committed, and as stated before, this is not our original mode of worship, for our original faith brought us face to face with our own personal relationship with G-d directly. What we have now is mostly what has been given to us through an alien understanding of religion with the language that we preach.

Now when we stop to think about the effect this indoctrination has had on the black community, generation after generation, century after century, then we can get an idea as to the reason we are still at the bottom of society, always looking up to others to supply our daily needs. We continue to see ourselves subconsciously as inferior beings. Many may argue this point, but when we look around and see who owns most of the factories and the jobs those factories provide, the skyscrapers, the fast-track trains, buses and airlines, huge trucking companies, the computer and the telephone companies, etc., and the dependency of other nations on them for their survival, we can see why we see them and why they see themselves as being members of the family of G-d. The language of white superiority has given white people the self-esteem and the motivation to go out and subdue the world. Now the correct understanding that we are supposed to have concerning Jesus is that he is the type of man that G-d would have us all to be. In other words, Jesus, the human being, is the expression of Divine Mind. The word "Christ" means "to be anointed." That is to say that G-d anointed or gave Jesus a Divine Mind. We've already talked about the mind being the real person, and how words form the character of the person when the words enter the mind of that person. So the mind of Jesus was formed by the word of G-d. Divine revelation, higher knowledge, this was given to all the prophets of G-d, from Adam, Noah, Abraham, Moses, Jonah, John, Jesus, Muhammed, and other prophets of Allah. All were men that lived among other men and had to eat their daily bread. Some even had families they had to care for while still toiling for their Lord. Their lives were a demonstration of the fact that all men have the potential given to them by Allah to walk upright, and teach other men that it is their duty as well to demonstrate in their own lives the life that Allah would have them to live. So Jesus was the type of person that represented the ability of the human being to live above corruption in his individual life. We see this same representation in the community life of Muhammad, as he was involved in politics, economics, military, etc.

When we read the story of the temptation of Jesus, we're really reading about the trials and tribulations each of us are faced with on a day-to-day basis. Jesus exercises self-mastery over the temptations of Satan as an example to let us know that we have that same power when we live by every word that proceeds out of the mouth of G-d. These same words from Allah that established the Christ mind in Jesus is still here, and are available to anyone who is willing to stand for truth.

The bread in the story represents materialism, and while we need it to improve our lives, it should not become the motivating factor in our lives. Truth is what we should base our lives on, not materialism. Even when we grow intellectually and spiritually, we are to understand that all we have come from G-d and that it must be used for His glorification, and not ours.

Something that I think is worthy of note here is that when we hear the story of Jesus being tempted by Satan, all the emphasis is placed on Jesus and what he did when more emphasis should be placed on the fact that Jesus was setting the example for us and what we should do. Also, we must remember that Jesus gave all the praise to G-d, and those who follow his example must do the same.

We should also remember that when we fast for moral and spiritual strength, our total concentration is on getting closer to Allah. Therefore, all our senses or appetites are drawn above the desires of the world. The reason that we were created in the first place, which is for the service of Allah, comes back to us and reorganizes and strengthens our disciplines so that when the fasting is over, even though we may thirst for the world as it said of Jesus in the scripture, still, our morals and our discipline stay in check, and our lives continue to be devoted to the service of Allah, as Jesus' was.

As human beings, we were born with the five basic senses of hearing, smell, taste, feeling, and seeing. We should also realize that our senses could also be used to control us. That is to say that whatever it is that we have an appetite for, this environment can give it to us. What's even deadlier is the fact that if we don't have control over ourselves, this environment can create the appetite for us, and feed it to us. If it feels good, do it. If it taste good or smells good, looks, or sounds good, don't think, just do it. If we're not careful, this society will turn us into a mass of nonthinking, impulsive thrill-seekers whose appetites are confined to this physical environment. So the Satan in this story not only represents the negative influences in the environment, but in our own ego as well, which will influence us to seek praise for ourselves.

So the whole story of the temptation of Jesus represents the fact that we have the ability within ourselves to overcome the negative influences in this society that lead to destructive lifestyles.

This is not just a fast from food and drink, but it means to refrain from all the foolish activities we involve ourselves in. So now, we see that we can bring our senses back under our own control, thus getting our lives back into our own hands, no longer allowing this society to manipulate us into a life of self and community destruction.

Now with this enlightened understanding of the scripture, we're no longer looking at an image, but rather our own personal relationship with the Creator. We're not looking at any image of color or kind. Our focus is wholly on our service to G-d and mankind. We now feel the same responsibility to self and mankind as others do, and we also feel the same closeness to G-d as others do. Not through imagery, but through the characteristics emanating from us as a result of the clean and productive life we're living through the correct worship of Allah. When we read the book of Genesis as it tells us about this vast creation Allah has given to us, we cannot find anywhere in the scriptures where it said that G-d gave white people alone dominion over the earth. G-d told all men to share in this dominion. We look at the earth itself, the vegetation, the air we breath, the birds, the land animals, fish in the waters, all G-d's vast creation is meant for us to prosper from.

When we study the creation, we find that everything we see has more than one purpose. When man first started, he saw only a limited use of the creation. However, as we continued to grow, we began to find more uses for this great creation given to us by the Creator. An honest study of history will reveal to the seeker that the so-called poor, heathen slave, whose soul the slave master was trying so desperately to save, was in fact the very one primarily responsible for increasing the development and use of G-d's creation. It was some of these same heathens, as we were called by the slave master, that was responsible for what is known as the European Renaissance, or the age of Enlightenment for Europe. This was the period of the rebirth of the sciences, art, philosophy, and all that goes to make up civilized society for mankind.

It was during this time that Europe lived in the Dark Ages, and the church held sway over all intellectual and scientific thought. If it didn't agree with church doctrine, it wasn't allowed to be heard, and those that propagated it were silenced with exile or imprisonment.

As we review again just very briefly the practice of degrading the humanity of the African slave, we should realize that this was not done wholly out of ignorance of the great contributions of the Africans, because many Europeans, especially those who held powerful positions of influence, were acutely aware of the fact that the Muslim African influence was primarily responsible for European progress. So by this degradation of the Africans' humanity, in my opinion, it was the only way the European could see his own superiority in his own mind.

African contributions to the progress of human society were almost completely eliminated by European writers and historians. The results of the process of elimination of facts on African history can be seen in the ignorance of the American public in general, and the African-American community in particular. Again we emphasize the fact that a people that has no history has no life, and is therefore non-existent as a people. When one set of people allows another set of people to write their history, then that people become whatever or whoever the writer wants them to be.

There must be a rekindling of the interest of the black community in our culture and our heritage so that we will always be able to look back with pride, and go forward with dignity and direction. We as a community should be primarily responsible for writing our own history, and when others do write it, we should be ready to make public any distortions or misinformation.

When people see themselves as descendants of scientist, explorers, conquerors, great soldiers of war, leaders of nations, then they see the great possibilities of their own human potential. They see themselves as rulers, and in some cases, they see themselves as gods. So then, when these people encounter a people whose history has been distorted, omitted, ignored, misinterpreted, or just wiped out, they think to themselves, "These are a people that are uncivilized and have no accomplishments. They have never lived in a governed society, therefore, they never had a sense of culture or heritage that ever amounted to anything. These are people that are savage and deserve no respect, therefore, slavery will not only be profitable for us, but it will be a salvation for them." It is really worth noting that in this time of enlightenment, this kind of ignorance pervaded the thinking of the masses of the society. This is the reason for the attitudes of many of the average white Americans, and unfortunately, many African-Americans see themselves in the same light.

We find that many of our young people today know absolutely nothing about their history and the great contributions of the ancestors, and in too many cases, many of our older people share in this ignorance as well. So there are many people who don't like us because we don't like ourselves.

To be aware of one's own history and ancestral contributions is to instill within that person a higher sense of purpose and responsibility. We say these contributions are the foundation of the society in which we live, so now, we see its incumbent upon us to become more responsible for the things we do, so that through our actions, an appreciation for these contributions will live on. Also, it raises the aspirations of the individual to not settle for the handouts of society, or just a good job, but because we find ourselves connected to such a rich past, we call on the best within ourselves to emulate it to the best of our ability. This also raises our value system as well because now we want to establish standards of life to live by. We become more G-d conscious, as we are now in control of the things we do. In effect, we have become masters of ourselves.

So this idea of preserving the history of the ancestors means more than just shallow celebrations, quite the contrary. It means that we are able to keep alive the contributions of the ancestors through our actions, and this lays the foundation for future generations. It means that instead of passing on the genes of self-destruction that were imposed upon us during slavery, we are now able to recreate our own past, thus allowing us to decide our own destiny. It means that the moral and material contributions made by the ancestors can now be recreated on an even broader scale, thus contributing to the greater advancement of mankind.

To highlight the words of Dr. Carter G. Woodson as he spoke on the African-American contributions and on the urgency of the African-American community being educated on these contributions, he said: "The achievements of the Negro properly put forth will crown him as a factor in early human progress, and a maker of civilization. He has supplied the demands for labor of a large part of our country... he has given the nation a poetic stimulus, and he has developed the most popular music of the modern era, and he has preserved in its purity the brotherhood taught by Jesus of Nazareth.

In his native country, moreover, he produced in the ancient world a civilization contemporaneous with that of the early Mediterranean, he influenced the culture then cast it in the crucible of time, and he taught the modern world the use of iron by which science and initiative have remade the universe. Must we let this generation continue to be ignorant of these eloquent facts?"[2] (28)

Just a very brief review of history will give us some insight on Dr. Woodson's words and meanings. We've already talked about African culture and civilization, and of the great Nubian Kush that lay south of Egypt on the Nile River. The Kushites were some of the oldest known masters of iron working techniques. In fact, Meroe, the second Kush capital, attests to the presence of one of the largest iron-working centers in antiquity. We've mentioned the great kingdom of Ghana, which was responsible for transporting most of the gold that was used in Western Europe during the Middle Ages.[1] (4-7) We've also talked about Mali, Songhai, and the great educational center, Sankore, at Timbuktu, whose greatness was enhanced even more so with the advent of Al-Islam. As we travel to the interior parts of Africa, we discover the great kingdoms of Kanem-Bornu, and the Hausa states which lie between Kanem-Bornu, and Songhai. These were centers of exchange and trade, as well as of agricultural development. These kingdoms were frequently visited by Arab scholars and developed a written language based on the adaptation of their language to the Arabic script.

By the eighteenth century, the Hausa confederation was a center of handicraft industries and had begun to manufacture cotton textiles. In modern Tanzania and Kenya lived a people called by the Arabs the "Zanj," who were skilled metal workers and traders. They were heavily involved with the Arabs in the Indian Ocean trade. It has been suggested that the famous Persian swords used by the Europeans during the Crusades were made of African iron.1 (10) So we can see that with the advent of Al-Islam, Africa, which was already known for its great civilization and highly developed culture, became even greater. It is only because of the slave trade and European oppression that we see Africa in the scattered condition it is in today. But all praises are due to Allah; we can see signs of that great homeland of ours coming back to life.

Al-Islam entered Africa through Egypt, which is the northern part of the continent, and moved on through Morocco. So besides moving on into the interior parts of Africa, Islam moved on through Africa and into Europe by way of Spain. The Muslims subdued the Moroccan people in the conquest of North Africa, and except for Cueta, all Morocco was converted to Islam. Musa-bin-Nusair gave an African chief by the name of Tariq the rank of general in the Muslim army. Tariq later became governor of Mauritania. He entered into friendly relations with Count Julian, Governor of Cueta who urged him to invade Spain. Tariq, after much deliberation delegated the task to Tarif, an officer in his army. An army of four hundred men and one hundred horses was shipped out to Spain in boats supplied by Count Julian Musa. Their place of landing was named Tarifa in honor of Tarif. It was here that the Moors levied a tax known as "tariff," also in honor of Tarif. After this successful expedition,

Tariq invaded Spain in full force. He built a fort at the foot of Mons Calpes, where he landed. It was renamed Gebel Tariq by the Moors who were African Muslims in honor of Tariq. The Spanish called it Gilbraltar, which is a corruption of the Moorish name. As the Muslim African Moors moved into Spain and established themselves, we saw education begin to flourish.

We saw learned men in the schools of Cordoba in Spain corresponding with learned men in Kairowan, Cairo, Badgered, Bokhara, and Samarkand. Nothing genuine was discarded. The Greek classics, such as the works of Plato, Aristotle, Hippocrates, Galen, Discorides, and Alexander of Aphrodisiacs, Ptolemy, were rediscovered by the Muslims and translated into Arabic. The Muslims materialized the useful theories that came from these great thinkers. The old Roman numbers were discarded and replaced by Arabic numbers, which we use today. The zero was given numeric value. Arabic words like "Algebra" and "chemistry" were in common use. It was through Africa that the new knowledge of China, India, and Arabia reached Europe. It was the Muslim military protection that allowed education to take root and grow. It was the Moors who established the silk industries, as well as the introduction of rice, cotton, sugar cane, dates, lemons, and strawberries into Spain. They built underground silos to store grain.[16] (Jackson, Introduction) So we can understand better now why Dr. Woodson was so concerned about teaching our people, both old and young, about the fact that we are descendants of a people with such a glorious past. People who had a history of military might, of building cities and educational centers, of improving science and technology, which laid the foundation for man to advance to where we are today in medicine, agriculture, space exploration, and many other areas of progress that man has advanced in.

Dr. Woodson was saying that people who know their history can use their glorious past as a springboard to encourage them to do even better. It is important that our people know that we were more than just slaves in forced servitude to someone else, we must also know that we are a people of pride and dignity, not just in words alone, but in the fact that our ancestors took the creation that was given to them by almighty G-d and produced feats that helped to bring mankind the world over to a level of growth and development that has made this great nation the superpower it is today.

So we asked ourselves, "What made these people so great? Why were they so fond of education and the preservation of the history and philosophies of other people?" One point to consider in answering that question is the fact that, unlike the Europeans, the Muslims had no desire to rob others of their past or their history. They were aware that all knowledge comes from Allah alone, therefore, they could take credit for nothing. Their desire was to bring the knowledge forward so that it could be used for the progress of mankind. Their motivation for this kind of thinking was their study of the Qur'anic scriptures. When the sincere seeker of truth and knowledge reads the Holy Qur'an, he will not find any pictures or images depicting G-d, or the angles, or the prophets, or any pictures of any sort for that matter. The Holy Qur'an is in its pure text, as Allah revealed it to Prophet Muhammad. The revelation has never been changed, and although the reader will find several people mentioned in it as in the Bible, the only words that are in the Book are the words of G-d. None of the prophets spoke. It is only G-d's words we read in the Qur'an. It is the revelation from G-d to the Prophet Muhammad. So the Holy Qur'an is the word of G-d in its purity.

I believe that this is what makes Al-Islam so great, and its influence so far reaching. The reader is being motivated by Allah, and they see themselves being told by Allah that they have the same potential for growth and development as anyone else.

Allah also lets us know that all the prophets were mortal men, including Jesus, Moses, and Muhammed. And as stated before, they were men that lived among other men, and had to eat their daily bread, as other men did. This is so people will have an example they can follow, as well as identify with.

The first revelation to Prophet Muhammed from G-d was a stimulation to his mind, or his intellect. Since all creation was put here so that man can use his mind to develop it for his use, the first revelation of the Qur'an to Prophet Muhammed was "Read." This revelation came in the form of a command. Since the Holy Qur'an was revealed in the Arabic language, the Arabic word for read is iqra, which comes from the root word, qira'a. This word carries with it very significant meanings. Not only does it mean to read, but it also means to proclaim, recite, to teach, examine, study thoroughly, search, explore, investigate. When we expound on these words, we will also get establishment, institution, consolidation, etc.

Now we've already established the fact that a word is not just relegated to the spoken or the printed word, but a word is whatever leaves an impression on the mind of the individual. Not only did the revelation of the Holy Qur'an to the Prophet leave an impression on his mind, but indeed, since it was revealed on his heart as well, it made him even more of the sincere and sensitive person Allah wanted him to be. The Arabic word for heart is qalb, which means the middle, the essence, the best, or the choicest part. The heart is also known as the seat of the intellect. So now, we see the heart and the mind of the Prophet Muhammed being stimulated by the same force and out of that revelation, we see unbridled progress for the whole of mankind.

"Proclaim! (or Read) in the name of thy Lord and Cherisher, Who created—Created man, out of a leech like clot: Proclaim ! and thy Lord is most bountiful, He who taught the use of the pen. Taught man that which he knew not." HQ 96:1-5. So we see that even with all the philosophers out of Greece and elsewhere the marginal progress that man had made in other parts of the world up until that time, we see that what we thought man knew was nothing compared to the progress made by man after the advent of Muhammed the Prophet, and the revelation of G-d's word. Not only did Prophet Muhammed learn to read the word, as he was unlettered, or had no academic training at the time, he also taught the word, and he went even further and established the word.

So Allah, in appealing to the mind of Prophet Muhammed in this first revelation, is opening up a whole new world of enlightenment to mankind which up until now, lay in utter ignorance. Man had gone as far as he could go as far as civilization was concerned. Jesus had said that as long as he was in the world, he was the light of the world, but after him, the world would come under mental darkness.

The Dark Ages came as a result of man trying to destroy the divine inspiration that comes to us from G-d through His prophets. The truth that Jesus Christ brought was from G-d, and it was designed to free the minds of the people. Jesus' message was the worship of the One G-d, and that all knowledge, all power, and all progress emanate from that One Source... G-d. So this direct worship of G-d is man's passage to progress. It puts every human being on the same level to use their G-d-given potential to be the best that they can. Not looking at an image purporting to be G-d, and subconsciously placing one race of people above another, but rather each human being is motivated by the word of G-d to reach inside themselves and pull out the best of themselves to the utmost.

So the message of Jesus had been corrupted and the world came under mental darkness or ignorance, and it was only after the revelation of the Holy Qur'an to Prophet Muhammed that the light of intelligence began to dawn upon the minds of men. Again, we should keep in mind that the people carrying the torch of enlightenment for the world progress at that time were Africans who had converted to Al-Islam, and in later times, were among the people who were captured, brought to America, and enslaved.

So in reading G-d's word from the Holy Qur'an, man's mind is stimulated to activity. Christian Europe rejected reason and considered those of intellectual and scientific abilities to be against the church. Even as late as the great scientist, Galileo, the church was condemning rational and scientific thought. Also, during the Dark Ages, the Catholic Church was asserting its claim to dominate the conscience of the western world ... All that was independent, all that was progressive, all that was persecuted for conscience's sake, took refuge in the courts of Africa. Art, science, poetry, wit, found congenial homes in the orange-shaded arcades of Hez, in the palaces or Morocco, and in the exquisite gardens of Tripoli and Tunis. (16)

As we look further into G-d's Holy Book, it says to us, "It is He Who sends down rain from the skies: With it we produce vegetation of all kinds: From some we produce green crops out of which we produce grains heaped up at harvest; out of the date palm with it's sheathe or spathes comes clusters of dates hanging low and near: And then there are gardens of grapes and olives and pomegranates, each similar in kind, yet different in variety: When they begin to bear fruit, feast your eyes with the ripeness there of. Behold! In these things there are signs for people who believe." HQ 6:99. **In another verse, we read;** "And it is He Who spread out the earth, and set thereon mountains standing firm, and flowing rivers: And fruits of every kind He made in pairs, two and two: He draweth the night as a veil O'er the day. Behold, verily in these things there are signs for those who consider! And in the earth are tracts diverse though neighboring, and gardens of vines and fields sown with corn, and palm trees-growing out of a single root or otherwise: Watered with the same water, yet some of them we make more excellent than others to eat. Behold! Verily in these things are signs for those who understand!" HQ 13:3-4. **So we can see further stimulation of the minds of men as they gain more insight on the revelation of the Qur'an. We as humans are encouraged to subdue the creation and bring it into service for our own productive life. Again, we say, this is what Allah is telling us in Biblical scripture in the book of Genesis, when man is given dominion over creation. Not that we as humans are to abuse the creation out of greed, for surely, by natural law, creation will turn back on man, and man will be the loser. This is why we stated earlier that the revelation not only came to the mind of the Prophet, but to the heart as well, for while the mind forms and creates and puts things to use, the heart, which is the seat of the mind, governs the mind, and keeps it compassionate, and in the state that Allah would have it to be. So we see further stimulation of the minds of the Muslim scientist by Allah. They introduced new irrigation methods, as well as developed new ways of grafting to produce new types of flowers and fruits. Fertilization and soil conservation were greatly improved. (15) So we see that the human being was able to go into the creation given to him by Allah and not only improve their own personal lives, but when we look at the way the fruits and vegetables have been improved upon today, the giant farms that are able to supply food for the world. The beautiful flowers and landscape that not only beautify our homes, but our** highways and other public facilities as well, these things that are so common to us because we see them everyday without a thought as to their origin, but we would be hard-pressed to live without them. In times gone by, as well as in today's society, we know that we get many cures for various diseases from herbs, fruits, and vegetables. This passage also refers to human society and its various ethnic backgrounds, all from the same origin, but with different contributions, all coming together for the benefit of humankind. Man has gone into the waters, the land, and the sky and harnessed the elements for the purpose of useful community development. This history tell us that it was the Muslim African Moors who, by the grace of G-d, laid the foundation that brought about this advancement in agriculture, irrigation, medicine, and other areas of scientific development. These were our ancestors, some of the same ones the slave master referred to as heathens. Abu Zaceria and Ibn Alamam wrote authoritative remarks on Moorish animal husbandry, and on agriculture. Ibn Khaldun wrote a treatise on farming, and worked out a theory of prices and the nature of capital. He has been called the Carl Marx of the Middle Ages. Cooper, gold, silver, lead, quicksilver, etc., all were mined by the Moors. (16) **Again we go into G-d's Holy Book, in sura 16:12-18, Allah says to us:** "He has made subject to you the night and the day; the sun, and the moon, and the stars are in subjection by His command: Verily in this are signs for men who are wise, and the things on the earth which He has multiplied in various colors and quantities. Verily in this is a sign for men who celebrate the praises of Allah in gratitude. It is He Who has made the sea subject, that you may eat thereof flesh that is fresh and tender, and that you may extract there from ornaments to ware. And thou seest the ships therein that plough the waves, that you may seek thus of the bounty of Allah and that you may be grateful. And He has set up on the earth mountains standing firm, least it should shake with you: And rivers and roads, that you may guide yourselves. And marks and sign posts, and by the stars men guide themselves. Never would we be able to number the favors of Allah, for He is oft forgiving most merciful." **In this** ayat, **or verse, we see the lofty position that Allah**

has given to the human being. Even the mighty sun, moon, and stars, which are a larger creation than the human being, are made subservient to the human being.

So with this kind of inspiration and motivation that comes from the stimulation of the minds of man, higher institutions of learning were developed in the cities of Cordoba, Seville, Toledo, Granada, Murcia, Almeria, Valencia, Cadiz. The telescope was invented and astronomy grew to real scientific advancement from the theory of the Greeks. Observatories were built for the study of the heavenly bodies, and today, man is able to build transportation for space travel.17 (Encyclopedia Britannica 1617) This progress came from the Moors. That same African that the slave master brought into slavery and tried to reduce to subhuman standards, and justified that dreaded Institution of Slavery by saying that it saved the African heathen from himself. But for the greed and the savagery of one people to rule over another, one can only imagine the progress human society would have made today. So today, man is able to go out into space because back in history, he was motivated by the word of G-d to lay the foundation for such progress. Caliph Al-Mamun of Baghdad signed a treaty with Michael III of the Byzantine Empire in which he demanded the entire library of the city of Constantinople.

As we have seen in much of Christian Europe, valuable manuscripts lay collecting dust and withering away because there was no interest in developing and advancing the knowledge contained in them. In this particular library, the caliph found a rare literary treasure. It was the treatise of Claudius Ptolemy on the mathematical structure of the heavens. The caliph, who was also an astronomer, had the works translated into Arabic, under the title The Almagest.

Long before Magellan circled the globe in 1519, the Moorish geographer, El-Idris, asserted during the twelfth century that what resulted from the opinions of learned men, and those skilled in observation of the heavenly bodies was that the world is round as a sphere, of which the waters are adherent and maintained upon its surface by natural equilibrium. It is surrounded by air; all created bodies are stable on its surface. The earth draws to it all that is heavy, the same way as a magnet attracts iron. Muslim scholars were already teaching geography from globes before the time of Ferdinand Magellan. (16) The Moors were master navigators of the waters.

Also in the above Qur'anic ayat, or verse, we see the introduction of scientific exploration of the waters, where man can not only find food and precious stones, but we see that Allah has opened up a whole new world of scientific exploration and research for the benefit of the whole of mankind. All this progress came about because G-d appealed to the minds of men through His Prophet Muhammad, in the revelation of the Holy Qur'an, and set man's mind in motion to ponder upon His glorious creation, and hence, bring the creation under his command to benefit the society of man.

This is where the words "establishment," "consolidation" and "institution" come into their true form because in proclaiming, teaching, and reciting the word, at some point, these teachings have to be materialized. This is truly establishing G-d's word not only in the hearts of men, but in such a way that man will benefit from Allah's creation, both from within and without.

When we understand the word "establishment" and its use in the context of bringing into being the word of G-d in more than just a spiritual sense, we can get some idea of the meaning of the Qur'anic words that refer to Prophet Muhammed as a mercy to all the worlds.

In Webster's Dictionary, we find that the word means "an established order of society"; "social, economic, and political establishment"; "a code of laws." We also see the word "stable" as well.

The word "consolidate" means to join together into one whole, to unite, to make firm or secure. Now in this word "consolidate," we see the word "con," which means "to know, to learn, to study or examine closely, to commit to memory." We also see the word "solid," which means "having no break or interruption, made firmly and well, serious in purpose or character." We also see the word "date," which means "duration."

The word "institution" means a significant practice, relationship, or organization in a society or culture. An act of instituting; establishment.

When the words of G-d become the stuff we base our lives on as individuals, then we become strong and resistant to the negative influences of the environment. When individuals of like minds come together for the good of the whole and develop standards, laws, rules and regulations to govern themselves by, they are now even stronger because now they stand as a community, having no breaks or interruptions, being serious in character and purpose, institutionalizing this kind of thinking within themselves, thus making whatever establishment they create an extension of themselves. Whereas the individual will last for a limited period of time, the community will last through the duration of time. In other words, there is no date, there is no limit on how long that community will last as long as that society follow the standards set forth by Allah.

We see this kind of thinking related to the first revelation received by Muhammed the Prophet, and we see that where man has based his life on these teachings following the example of the Prophet, progress has been the order of the day.

All over Spain, education was the order of the day. City streets were well paved, with raised sidewalks for pedestrians. At night, ten miles of street lamps illuminated the streets. This was hundreds of years before there was a paved street in Paris, or a street lamp in London. Public baths numbered into the hundreds, while in Europe, cleanliness was treated as a sin. Muslim Africans lived in palaces while the kings of England, France, and Germany lived in barns lacking windows and chimneys, with only a hole in the roof for the emission of smoke. Christian Europe condemned education and had no public libraries, while the Moors in Spain had more than seventy. There were only two universities in Christian Europe, while the Moors of Spain had seventeen, including those named earlier in this writing. While progress was being made in the areas of astronomy, chemistry, physics, mathematics, geography, and philosophy by the Moors, the illiteracy rate in Europe was 99 percent. (16). Books were burned, and people were burned for reading books, because books made them think.

We continue to read from the pure words of Allah as He speaks again to the human being in sura **16:66-69.** "And verily in cattle too will you find an instructive sign from what is within their bodies, between excretions of blood we produce for your drink, milk pure and agreeable for those who drink it. And from the fruit of the date palm and vine, you get out wholesome drink and food: behold in this is a sign for those who are wise. And thy Lord taught the bee to build it's cells in hills and on trees, and in men's habitations. Then to eat of all the produce on the earth, and find with skill the spacious paths of it's Lord: there issues from within their bodies a drink of varying colors wherein is healing for men: verily in this is a sign for those who give thought."

Here again, we see how Allah has blessed the human being to use His creation to better his own life. From deep within the stomach or belly of the cow, we see how Allah has arranged the innermost parts of the animal so that that which is impure is separated from that which is pure, and all man has to do is enjoy the good and pure drink that is good for his health, and physical development. We don't have to worry about impurities getting in the milk from the cow, because Allah has already provided the means for the pure to cross between the impure for our good life, and our good pleasure.

A close study of history will show how the Muslim African Moors were able to greatly improve upon the breeding of horses and cattle, as well as developing other uses for the milk from the cow. The dairy industry has grown into many different facets as a result of the contributions of our ancestors. We will find that they laid the foundation for much of what we enjoy today in what is derived from the use of many animals.

The word for cow here in this Qur'anic scripture is an'am, which means "grazing livestock, sheep, camels, cattle, etc." It is from the root word, na'am, which means, "to live the good life, to live in comfort, or luxury." The cow here is symbolic of human society, where we have various levels of existence for human existence.

We live in an environment where sometimes, it's hard to discern the difference between that which is harmful and that which is not harmful. The Qur'anic revelation sets the example for that which is clear from that which is unclear or ambiguous. This is an instructive sign we see here in just a very simple part of Allah's creation that tells us how to avoid the negative and the deadly influences of human society. This is instruction for not only the individual life, but even more so, for the community life. When we learn to love that which G-d loves, we then begin to see immediate improvement in our lives as individuals, and as communities.

The reason that we, as a society, are experiencing so much violence and child abuse, and all the other societal illnesses, is because our moral vision has become blurred. We talk about our belief in G-d, but our activities are light years away from what we say we believe in, and as a result, while we remain strong militarily, technically and otherwise as a nation, we have become morally weak from within, and this will ultimately lead to our demise if we allow it to continue.

We have already said that the cow or na'am represents a society that has grown materially fat, and while many are living the life of luxury, the greatest concern for others who live among us is just to see another day. As a society of thinking people, we must not allow the world of commercialism dictate our values to us. We cannot allow them to interpret for us what the good life is. Many of us are led to believe that great material accomplishments, such as expensive cars and SUVs, or the big house on the hill, and staying in touch with the trends of society, are the things that determine our worth in the eyes of men. Allah tells us in His Holy Book that the best among us is the one most aware of his duty to society. In another place in the Qur'an, we read that we should live for the hereafter, or the afterlife, but we should not forget our share of this material world that we live in.

Our concern is this, if we allow the commercial world to determine our values for us, then we lose sight on what the real goal in life should be. These material accomplishments become our gods, and we grow selfish and hardhearted. We begin to think more of these material things than we do of people, and we develop into a class system of the haves and the have-nots. Apathy becomes the rule to live by, and life as we know it degenerates into the survival of the strongest, or jungle law.

There is nothing wrong with having material accomplishments, and we should strive to make life as comfortable for ourselves and our families as possible. Our point is that these things are not to be what defines us in life, but rather to be used for the service of mankind. The trends of society cannot serve as a foundation of life.

Establishments cannot be based on trends. Institutions cannot be built with trends as the basis.

The object of life should be to serve G-d. This tells us then that our material gain is to be used for our comfort and enjoyment, but also to make us able to contribute our time and efforts to the advancement of mankind. This kind of thinking helps us to develop integrity, respect, a healthy and sound value system, and we're not left to the whims of the changing environment that we live in. We are in control of ourselves and of our thinking, and we cease to be just an extension of whatever we may have accomplished materially.

If we say that G-d is the creator of everything, then we are saying that everything is created to serve G-d. G-d did not create this world for just sport and play. When man is able to go into the creation and bring out the best of the creation for the service for mankind, then not only does the human being serve Allah, but all this material creation is put into the service of Allah. Nothing or no one comes to G-d, except in the position of a servant.

The Qur'anic word for "pure" in the ayat or verse is kalasa, from the root word, kulus, which means "pure, unmixed, unadulterated, to be free, to secure one's rights, to act with integrity. Pure, faithful, loyal, sincere, etc." The word for "agreeable" is saga, which means "to be easy to swallow, pleasant to taste, enjoy, relish, etc."

If we can see the physical milk delivered to us from deep within the belly of the cow, from among the filth and excretions of the bowels, etc., and it comes out pure and free from disease and impurities, and we then take it into our bodies as infants, and as a result, we grow into strong and healthy individuals, able to manage and provide for ourselves. So it is with the pure word of G-d that is able to reach deep down in the belly of society among the interpolations and the confused ideologies, philosophies, as well as other filthy ideas of mankind. Allah has allowed it to remain pure and unadulterated for the minds of those who want to grow morally, mentally, and spiritually strong as individuals and communities. This is regardless of whatever level of society the individual is on. His nature is still intact, and all he needs to do is open himself up to revelation.

We've already talked about how the Muslim African Moors became experts in the field of botany and agriculture, developing new ways of grafting to produce new flowers and fruits, developing new irrigation methods and laying the foundation for what we see in the thousands of varieties of fruits, vegetables, flowers, and other plants. Books were written by the scientist and scholars that were responsible for these advancements, and as a result, we are the beneficiaries of this great knowledge. Just as this knowledge in agriculture was preserved and passed on down to the future scientists of today, so then society has to be cultivated, and refined so that it will be fit for human habitation. This is why we read in the scripture, for those who believe, or for those who reflect, or for those who are wise. Allah is making us aware that if we as humans really want to know Him, and what He requires of us as His servants, we need only to study His creation, for even in the lower forms of life, there are lessons to be learned.

The word fruit in this ayat comes from the root word, thamara, which means, "fruit, profit, benefit, gain, effect." The root word for vine here is a'nab, which means "grapes," from whence comes the strong drink. But this strong drink is related to spiritual instructions, not intoxication, as strong drink is sometimes called spirits. So now we have the fruit, or the profits, which is our material gain, and we also have spiritual instructions, and together they make for a balanced diet for our moral, mental, and spiritual development. The word "food" is from the root word razaqa, which means to provide with the means of subsistence, to bestow upon someone material or spiritual possessions (said of G-d). The word for wholesome is hasan, which means "handsome, beautiful, excellent, good manners, good conduct, proper, etc." This is the kind of community life that we as intelligent human beings are supposed to work to establish. We would be wise to follow the signs that Allah has put in the creation for us to live by and improve our lives with.

As we continue to study the pure words of G-d and how we as humans are to advance as a healthy society, we read where Allah inspired the bee to build its cells in hills, on trees, and in men's habitations.

When we study the ways of the bee, we find that there are some parallels in their structured community life and that of human society. Just to give a few examples, we find that a bee colony can contain from 20,000 up to 30,000 bees. The worker bees have to exploit the patch of nectar and work it in a way that saves time in that this benefits the community. This also allows the bee to gather information on the nectar supply so that the bees can adjust their visits to that particular patch.

The queen bee is decided on by the worker bees, which are all females and make up the bulk of the bee community. They have three stages of life developments, where they perform different tasks, which includes keeping the hive clean, gathering the nectar for the making of the honey, and other duties.

The purpose of the drone or the male bee is to mate with the queen; they do no work, so when the food supply gets low, they get kicked out the community. The bees have a very sophisticated form of communication, which is done by the worker bees. When one of them has found a rich patch of nectar, she comes back to the community and does a dance that indicates the direction and the richness of the patch. This dance can be very long depending on the richness of the patch, but the bees don't stay around for the complete dance, for once they have the information, they leave so that they can get the job done. Again, this is done with the well-being of the community in mind, as opposed to their own individual comfort.

Guard bees protect the colony both from within and without. Not only do they use their stingers, but also they coat the hive with certain odors that will allow them to be able to distinguish intruders from themselves. Bees are also able to control the climate of the hive in both summer and winter. This allows them to protect the young as they develop. There are many other aspects of the bee community that we can mention, but this gives us an idea of what their community life is like.

In our own human community, we find that we give the authority or the position of leadership to members of our community.

These representatives are usually chosen by the people, who for the most part, are the working class. The word for "hills" in this ayat or verse is jabala or jabal which means "to shape or mold, to have a natural disposition or propensity for something." It also means hills or mountain range. Examples are Mt. Sinai, or Gibraltar, etc. These represent for us symbols of authority and stability. This is what we have in human society when we have organizations and government set up to keep order on all levels of the society. Human society starts out with individuals, which become families, and grow into communities and nations. So from the very beginning, we see that the concerns of the individual have grown from selfish concerns to community, national, international, and universal concerns. Many of us humans are naturally born with the ability to be leaders, and the duty of the masses is to try to choose the ones better qualified. As a community of rational and intelligent people, we are able to mold, to shape and form our community life in a manner that will be conducive to positive growth and development, not only for the present, but for future generations to come as well.

As a family and as a nation, our homes and communities have to be protected from intruders, who may look like us but their aim is to control and destroy that which has been built up for the good of the whole. Just as the bee can sense the intruder by way of odors, Allah has also blessed us humans with certain intuitive abilities to know who among us is not true, and that person is eventually removed from the community.

Again, we have the word thamara, which means "fruits, profits, produce, etc.," which are the results of work. So Allah has instructed us to eat of all the produce of the earth. To subdue this creation He has given to the human being, and make it produce the good life for all mankind. We are to take advantage of all the good this creation has to offer. The word ways is from the Arabic root word subul, which not only means "ways, path, or road" but also means "for the cause G-d, or in behalf or G-d and His religion." As human beings, we should understand that we created nothing, but are ourselves created, so all glory belongs to Allah. Everything that we do should be done because we love Allah. In taking this approach, we are able to do better for our families, as well as for our nation and ourselves. This is a beautiful attitude.

The word varying is from the root word khalifah, which is also the name or title given to the human being that Allah created to be a ruler in the creation. So this tells us that the khalifah, or the mind that G-d has chosen, knows how to use the creation in all its goodness to bring about the best situation for the different aspects of human society to advance itself. The word for color is laun, which means "hue, complexion, species, to bring out the different aspects of something."

So we see here how Allah has created in every human being the potential to be the very best they can be. To add to the advancement of the society of mankind. People from all ethnic backgrounds and cultures, brought together for the sole purpose of serving Allah through their service to mankind. We all have something positive to contribute, and this is healing to the human society because now, we're not judged by our colors, but by our human worth. The word for healing is from safa, which means "to heal, to cure a disease. To restore to health."

So Allah, in His infinite wisdom, has shown us through these examples in His creation how the human being grows in a healthy state of mind after being nourished from the pure moral teachings of Qur'anic knowledge, which enables us to build a strong moral base for productive growth and development.

Then as we grow and develop, our responsibilities grow; therefore, we need stronger nourishment to sustain ourselves. This stronger nourishment from the same source not only feeds us materially, but it also supplies our spiritual food. Just like the trees, which are also symbolic of human society. They feed from both earth and sky. They grow stronger materially from the earth, and they also feed from the radiant light of the sun through their leaves, giving off oxygen for us to breathe. This material and spiritual growth helps us to be dually proportioned. Not too far to the right, and not too far to the left.

And as a result of this growth process, we have now grown into adulthood. We have become aware of our purpose in life. We see the need to exercise our economic and political strength in the development of the kind of society that will be conducive to the healthy growth of families, and community life. A society that's agreeable, palatable, easy to swallow, pleasant, and enjoyable, and something to be relished.

The word for "made smooth" is dalla, which means "humble." This has reference to our attitude in terms of how we execute the responsibility on loan to us from Allah. As long as we acknowledge G-d and refrain from developing the kind of attitude where we think we are self-sufficient, there is no limit to our growth and development. We should never allow pride and self-glorification be the motivating force in anything we do. It is then that we grow into the ruler, or khalifah that is intended for us by Allah.

This kind of inspiration that motivates man to take advantage of G-d's creation is good for the soul. The Qur'anic word for soul is nafs, which means "soul, psyche, spirit, life, mind, essence, nature, personal identity." It also means "self, to breath, aspirations, inclinations, appetite, desire, nature." So we see the soul is really the person, the complete self of mankind in all its aspects. From the soul emanates all our aspirations, our dreams, our desires, our goals, etc. The soul is bottomless. That is to say that Allah in His mercy has made progress for the human being unending. The potential for positive growth and development is limitless. But now, at the same time, we should realize that the potential for human degradation also has no limits as well. Man has the potential to continue to develop in the direction intended for him by Allah, but he can also revert back to his animalistic ways, to a life based on instinct rather than intelligence.

Traditionally, we have been taught that the soul was something separate from the person, but now we see that the soul is the person. The Institution of Slavery sought to destroy the soul or the humanity of the human being in an attempt to reduce the African to sub-human standards. It is Allah who is the creator of the soul, and only Allah has the power to discontinue it. This is the primary reason why slavery had to be so brutal, and so inhuman. Since a large percentage of the Africans were Muslims, they saw themselves as equal with any other man, created by the same G-d, having the same potential as any other man. So in slavery, in order to bring the slave under submission, the slave master had to be brutal both physically and mentally. Physically in the obvious ways that the slaves were tortured, beaten, hung, and many times, burned to instill fear in the hearts of the other slaves, and mentally, in an even more heinous and crippling way, in that religion was given to the slave in such a way that it presented one man to another as a god, thus tying the slave to the slave master in perpetual servitude, even after the physical chains had been lifted.

This idea gives new meaning to the Biblical verse that ask the question, "Will a man rob G-d?" Many preachers feed the idea to the congregation that this is talking about giving money to the church, and they play on the conscience of the people to entice them into not only paying their tithes, but giving other financial support over and above their means, and too many times, only very few benefit from it, while the life of the congregational member never improves. This is not a blanket condemnation of all Christian ministers, because I know of many who, through their own personal efforts, have not only helped to improve the lives of their own membership, but have been instrumental in improving the lives of the people in their communities.

It is shameful, and a tragic sin that instead of using the word of G-d to free the people and bring them out of this mental bondage that too many of us find ourselves in, some of our leaders continue to keep the people enslaved for their own personal gain, and in doing so, have made themselves members of those who are gatekeepers to the Institution of Slavery.

G-d is not interested in our money, for all the money already belongs to Him, whether we give it up willingly or not. What this verse is really talking about is the fact that man has tried to steal the devotion of the human being, which belongs to G-d only, and have that human devotion focused on him instead, thus taking the slaves out of contact with his Creator and leaving them at the mercy of the Institution of Slavery, and those who operate it.

So yes, man will try to rob G-d, but in the end, everything has to return to its origin, and that is the Creator of everything. Through unheard-of brutality, and the introduction of divine racism through that image of presenting G-d to the world as being white, still they have failed.

So we see that it was the soul of the Muslim African Moors that was influenced by the inspiration of the Holy Qur'an to bring into existence progress for world development. Since the soul or the person was created by Allah, then it stands to reason that only Allah can put the human being on the path to world progress. All creation is placed before the human being in such a way that the human being can see all the possible potential in it. We can see the development of some of the various branches of scientific thought, while in Christian theology, the masses are content to just sing, pray, and preach, and go home without realizing that Allah is speaking to them through His creation for the purpose of empowering themselves. Most of the people's attention is focused on the physical birth, death, and resurrection of Jesus. There is no real motivation to do what Allah really wants us to do.

These three topics of scripture form the basis of Christian doctrine, and it is because of their misinterpretation by church leadership that we find the African-American community on the bottom of society today. We say this because of the fact that the African-American community spends a large percentage of their time either in church or working on church projects, and it would seem that with that kind of dedication to G-d, our community would be the leaders of the world, but instead, we find ourselves on the bottom all around the world. Again, let me emphasize the fact that I am not talking against the church. However, I am highlighting the fact that church doctrine of today is all together different from the truth that was brought by Jesus Christ.

As we continue to study the great technical advances made by our ancestors before our being brought into slavery, we will understand that G-d's intention is for us to know him through His creation. This fact is key to our growth and development. There are really no words to give for the great contributions made by these Islamic institutions for the advancement of human society.

It was our Muslim ancestors who calculated the angle of the ecliptic, measured the size of the earth, and calculated the procession of the equinoxes. Centuries before Sir Isaac Newton came on the scene, our Muslim ancestors had already explained the field of optics and physics, and such phenomena as refraction of light, gravity, capillary of attraction, and twilight. They made advancements in the field of drugs, herbs, and foods for medication, established hospitals with a system of interns and externs, discovered the causes of diseases, and developed correct diagnoses for them.

They had proposed new concepts of hygiene, made use of anesthetics surgery with newly innovative surgical tools, and introduced the science of dissection in anatomy. And as stated earlier, they furthered the scientific breeding of horses and cattle, found new ways of grafting to produce new flowers and fruits, produced new concepts of irrigation, fertilization and soil conservation, and improved the science of navigation. In the area of chemistry, Muslim scholarship led to such discoveries as potash, alcohol, nitrate of silver, nitric acid, sulfuric acid, and mercury chloride. They also developed, to a high degree, the art of textiles, ceramics, and metallurgy.[16] (16-17)

The Muslims adopted the decimal system of numbers from the mathematicians of India, and the place notation was perfected by Bin Musal-Khwarizimal in the ninth century. He adopted the zero as a mathematical quantity, and wrote the first textbook on algebra. He was also the author on a treatise on spherical trigonometry. The Muslims made trigonometry into a science by substituting sines and tangents for the cords of the Greeks. The tanneries of Cordoba and Morocco were the best in the world. Almeria specialized in making sashes famed for their fine texture and bright colors. Carpets were made in Teulala, and bright-hued woolens in Granada and Baza. The Moors also produced high quality glass, pottery, vases, mosaics, and jewelry. They also introduced the manufacture of gunpowder into Europe. (16) It was the advent of Al-Islam that moved into Northern and Western Africa and took a people that was already highly civilized, and brought them into an even higher order of civilization to the point where they made a never-ending impact on human society for the advancement of all mankind.

It was the advent of the slave trade, along with subjugation through colonization, that stifled Africa's growth up until these modern times. But as stated before, G-d is bringing that blessed motherland back to life, never again to suffer from the yoke of physical and mental slavery. Now many may argue that the Muslims participated in the slave trade, but a close study of history will show that in most of all the areas where this dreaded activity took place, it was a practice among many of the Africans tribes to sell their captives of war to the slave traders for gold and other trinkets. The Africans were told by the slave traders that their countrymen would have a better life, and that they would receive money for their labor. I don't believe that any of the Muslim or non-Muslim Africans realized the horrible plight their fellow countrymen would face. So we can see that while the European were bringing Africa grief and slavery, Africa was bringing them progress and enlightenment.

We find that during the twelfth and thirteenth centuries, most of the classical thought and their adaptation to Islamic theology and philosophy, the sciences that had been introduced and assimilated into Islamic culture, as well as classical learning and its refinement and its adaptation into Islamic culture, was translated from Arabic into Hebrew and Latin. So during this period of time, with the translation of Arabic into Hebrew and Latin, we begin to see the awakening of Europe after centuries of darkness. As Europe absorbed the fruits of Islam's centuries of productivity, signs of Latin, Christian awakening was evident throughout the European continent.

The twelfth century was one of intensified traffic of Muslim learning into the western world through many hundreds of translations of Muslim works. By 1300, when all that was worthwhile in Muslim scientific, philosophical, and social learning had been transmitted to European-schooled men through Latin translations, European scholars stood once again on the solid ground of progress, enriched by the education they received from Africa.[17] (17) So now, when we read about the great scientists and philosophers like Sir Isaac Newton, Roger Bacon, Galileo, Rene Descartes, etc., we are now able to determine the source of their knowledge.

So then, in studying the history of Africa, Europe, and the period of Enlightenment, as African-Americans, we need to know that we, as much as anyone else, are a universal people. When we think about

Muslims, Islam, Africa, and the contribution of knowledge made to the world because of the stimulation to the minds of men by G-d's revelation of the Qur'an to Prophet Muhammed, as African-Americans, we must see ourselves as part of that great heritage. We must see ourselves as descendants of many of those great people, but even greater than that, we must see ourselves as part of the universal order of mankind, because others came along after us and continued the advancement of the knowledge. Therefore, we are no longer confined to a particular point of geography, for we can see our influence touching the whole world and beyond, as man, through the technology from that glorious era, is taking human society from the deepest points of the waters to the outer reaches of the universe through space travel.

Let us take just a very brief look at our modern-day history, beginning with the Industrial Revolution. There was the work done by Lewis Latimer in perfecting the light bulb. His patented design (recorded in January 1882 under the title "Process for Manufacturing Carbons") of the black, dense, carbon skeleton that constitutes the electric light filament gave the world a cost-efficient, longer-lasting lighting system. Black scientific minds produced much of what America and the world's livelihood depends on, for with them, what we call the great superpowers would properly be decades behind in terms of progress as we know it today. Also the railway switches of W. H. Jackson, rotary engines by A. J. Beard, refrigerators by J. Standard, electric railways by W. B. Purvis, the Graphite Lubricator by Elijah McCoy. These men and others are responsible for many great inventions that have served as an integral part of world development. In the area of communication, there is Granville T. Woods, who invented a machine that could transmit by electricity using voice signals rather than the Morse Code. Another great invention by Granville T. Woods was the induction telegraph, a system used to facilitate communication between two moving trains. It is easy to see why Westinghouse, General Electric, American Engineering, and Bell Telephone owe their success to the scientific mind of an African-American.

As we move on up to more modern times, we find great minds like that of Dr. George R. Carruthers, who developed infrared imaging, which enables telescopic vision through the dust and glare of neighboring stars. In recent years, we have come to learn that there were also African-American scientists who worked on the atomic bomb, also known as the Manhattan Project. Dr. Lloyd Quarterman of Columbia University was specifically cited by the U. S. Secretary of War. Besides Dr. Quarterman, there were twelve other African-Americans involved in the Manhattan Project. Dr. Shirley A. Jackson received her doctorate from MIT in theoretical physics. From 1976 until 1991, she conducted research in solid state and quantum physics, theoretical physics and optical physics at AT&T Bell Laboratories. Since July 1, 1995, she has held the chairmanship of the U. S. Nuclear Regulatory Commission. Bartholomew O. Nnaji, Ph. D., is a professor of industrial and mechanical engineering at the University of Massachusetts at Amherst. He is the director of the Automation and Robotics Laboratory at UMASS; founder and director of NEMESIS, the National Center for Computer-Aided Medical Imaging and Devices for Diagnosis and Surgical Invention Systems; founder and chairman of Geometric Machines Corporation; and editor-in-chief of the International Journal of Design and Manufacturing. Originally from Nigeria, Dr. Nnaji is an internationally recognized expert and consultant on robotics. Dr. Patricia Cowings is a NASA scientist and researcher, specializing in Aerospace Medicine, Human Vestibular Physiology, Bioastronautics, and Psychophysiological Biological problems of long durations in space travel. In her work at Ames Research Center at Moffett Fields, California, Dr. Cowings developed the Autogenic Feedback Training Exercise (AFTE) that includes the Autogenic Clinical Lab and biomedical monitoring system. She has been recognized as one of the top minds in science and technology in America.[18] (Om-Ra-Seti 8285, 89-91, 93, 96) These are just a very, very few by way of example to show the presence of African America. Not only in the progress of America itself, but the hand of the African-American can be felt worldwide and universally in terms of the progress of mankind. As African-Americans, we can trace the roots of our creativity back over the annals of history through European Spain, and the great empires of Ghana, Mali, Songhai, and other great cities of Africa, including the great pyramids of Egypt and beyond. The words of the great historian, Dr. Carter G. Woodson, ring truer to us today more than ever. We cannot allow this generation to be ignorant of these facts. Those who are in these positions, those who have the ear of the public, be it media, political, educational, religious or otherwise, we have to make our youth see that these areas of concern is where the future lie. Not just in sports, entertainment, fads, and trends that bring along with them undisciplined lifestyles that take away from society, as opposed to adding to the positive development of society.

While man tried to take the humanity of a people and reducethem to animal standards, G-d in His mercy has seen fit to preserve not only the humanity of this great people, but their creativity is stronger than ever. This, more than any statement that can be made, explains what we mean when we say that since man didn't create the human spirit, man cannot destroy the human spirit. There is no G-d but G-d!

As stated earlier, up to 30 percent of the slaves brought to America were Muslims, and while many here in America, especially African-Americans, see Islam as an Arab religion, it should be understood that Prophet Muhammed is a direct descendant of Prophet Abraham and his wife Hagar. It was Prophet Abraham and his son Ishmael who built the Kabah in the Holy City of Mecca, where all Muslims make their pilgrimage. Jews, Christians, and Muslims all look to Prophet Abraham as their Prophet, and all three are known as the Abrahamic religions. The message of Qur'an is a universal message for all people. This is why Prophet Muhammed is known as the universal prophet. Although the Holy Qur'an was revealed in Arabic, the Arabs are a very small part of the worldwide majority of its adherents, and as can be seen by the above historical accounts, the message is universal in scope, and is the primary reason why we see the world at this stage of growth and development today. So when we talk about Africa, we are not talking about some king sitting on a throne as just a ruler over a tribe of people. Instead, we are to see our people in a state of progress, ever moving forward and contributing to the advancement of mankind. Such were our ancestors out of Africa.

So then, with this glorious past, how is it that we come up with this bold statement, "The black man will be extinct by the year 2000?"

Again let us refer to the words by Imam W. Deen Mohammed, "Man means mind." These words are referring to the creativity, the imagination, the deep insight man has gained in studying G-d's word and using it to bring enlightenment to the world.

During the sixties, when the cry for revolution was in the air, we used to talk about the white man building concentration camps to put black folks in. Now we see that the concentration camps were not to be physical places of confinement, but instead, it meant to have control over the mental makeup of not only the black man, but also the minds of the masses in general. That is to say that when other than self determines what you concentrate on, your own mind becomes your prison or concentration camp. The negative influences and destructive activities that we participate in are what hold us in these concentration camps. There are many who are confined physically in newly built jails and penitentiaries because their destructive mentalities cause harm on the society, but for the most part, as stated before, too many of us become insignificant because we have gotten caught up in this mental concentration camp. Whether we live in the streets or in the projects, or belong to the middle class. Whether we live in the more affluent areas, or are in show business, sports, or other parts of the world of entertainment, many are still caught up in the mental concentration camps. There's nothing wrong with being in these professions, or being in ownership of these kinds of possessions. It's just that in most cases, by the time we get in possession of these kinds of businesses, we have become so indoctrinated so much that our values have become much like the creators of the concentration camps, and so the beat goes on.

In too many cases, the people on the ground become the prison guards for these concentration camps because they devalue the need for education and end up selling or using drugs, becoming gang members, babies having babies, and this lifestyle eventually becomes acceptable in the community. Black-on-black crime is the major source of homicides in the African-American community and it goes virtually unchallenged by the leaders of the African-American community, as well as the community itself. So, wittingly or unwittingly, we all become affiliated in some way with this concentration camp, which has now evolved into the Institution of Slavery. And so the vicious cycle continues.

Again we ask the question, How did this all happen? A people with such a glorious past, a people that has been one of the primary sources of advancement for human kind, how did they end up in a position of nothingness?

To answer this question in as complete a manner as possible, we must first revisit the statement that we made before in regard to the fact that we were taken out of direct contact with Allah, and given the idea from the language in religious scripture that everything white was close to G-d, and everything black was considered evil and farthest away from G-d. To reinforce this kind of religious instruction, we were then given the picture of G-d in the image of a white man, and were then told to bow down to that image and worship it as G-d. This process over a period of centuries of indoctrination has worked better than the physical chains of slavery to keep the African-American community in a position of servitude. This is the major source of the inferiority complex in the black community, and the superiority complex in the white community. Imam W. Deen Mohammed quoted a black woman as he was giving a public address. The woman said to her slave master that he looked liked G-d in the face, but he acted like the devil in his actions.

So no matter how mad or upset we may get at the white man, or how much we better him in sports and other ways we may outdo him, the idea that has been planted in our subconscious will always come to the surface, that they are better because they are closer to G-d. And that goes against all scriptural teachings in Christianity, Islam, and Judaism.

So now that we consider them to be better than us, naturally, it follows then that we should like what they like, and our values should be assimilated with theirs. Our history and our culture became less and less important to us, which in and of itself, leaves a people to become no people at all. This is what the Biblical term refers to when it speaks of the empty vessels being filled with strange wine. So now, although we were free from the physical chains of slavery, we find ourselves in the worse form of slavery in the history of mankind. At least back in the days of physical bondage, we did try to get away, but today, not only do we look at others as being better than ourselves, but we also look at them as being able to do things better than us. Instead of us baking our own pie, we continue to beg others for a piece of their pie. It seems that it's so hard for us to understand that when we bake our own pie, we decide on the kind of pie it's going to be, the ingredients that go into it, and most importantly, how big a slice we're going to get from that pie. And just as important, the only thing better than one pie is another pie. This means that just as others are able to control their own destiny, we can also control our own destiny.

After slavery, some of the ex-slaves were able to become successful in business, and while many grew rich, the majority of our people remained in abject poverty. As we slowly began to emerge and do somewhat better in our livelihood, we had started to move into the period of protest against Jim Crowism, political disenfranchisement, and other forms of oppression meted out to black people by whites. As we saw in the organization of the unions earlier, we began to demand that they allow us on their jobs, and as stated before, one of the goals was that an appreciation for Negro labor among employers be established.

The problem for achieving genuine equality for African-Americans in America is one of many complexities, and I'm sure not a single answer would have been enough. However, I do think that more emphasis should have been placed on developing our own strengths from within our own communities.

Again, the words of the great historian and philosopher, Carter G. Woodson: "At this moment, then, the Negroes must begin to do the very thing they have been taught they cannot do. They still have money, and they have needs to supply. They must begin to immediately to pool their earnings and organize industries to participate in supplying social and economic demands. If the Negroes are to remain forever removed from the producing atmosphere, and the present discrimination continues, there will be nothing left for them to do."[2] **(30)**

Dr. Woodson is saying to us here that if we look within our own communities, and do as others have done in terms of servicing the needs of the people that reside there, we soon will see our own economic independence come to establishment. We know that the black community do not have the financial resources as do the white community, but in pooling our resources, we are able to establish businesses, financial institutions, hospitals, and all the needs that a community would need to grow. As we grow materially, we develop a sense of self-respect, and in turn, respect would come to us. The needs of the African-American community are the same as those we see in other communities, and we see those needs in other communities being serviced by the people who live there, or by someone else like them. In any case, there are not enough services being produced by us for us. In order for our children to grow up with a positive attitude, they must see us as producers, rather than all of us being consumers. We can ill afford to wait for others to produce employment for us.

Echoing the words of Dr. Woodson, Imam W. Deen Mohammed said, "We should feel ashamed to have to depend on others to feed our families. We should be ashamed to depend on others to supply our medical needs, provide us with an education, patrol our neighborhoods, and generally look after every aspect of our well being." (9) Dr. Woodson is telling us that if we are to survive, we are going to have to get into the race for all that is good. We must stop looking for others to find work for us to do. Our own creativity must come into play, for above all else, this kind of thinking is what brings true freedom to the black community. The dependency on others to supply our daily needs, and the total loss of our value system together seal our demise as a people of productivity and creativity.

We begin to see ourselves on television and in the movies in very degrading positions. I believe that this fact has had the most devastating effect on us in terms of influencing the degeneration of our value system. We see ourselves as dope dealers and gangsters, dressed in clown clothes, driving shiny cars purchased with dope money, and these become our role models in real life.

In contrast, in past decades, we played butlers, maids, head-scratching buffoons, and the like. That was mostly because we could do no better at the time, so we accepted what came to us. But what is worthy of note is that even though we were forced to play those roles for the public, in our private lives, for the most part, our people maintained a certain degree of dignity. In these later days, however, when we see ourselves as gangsters and slicksters in the movies, we also find too many of us trying to act out those roles in real life. Where once we were concerned with establishing financial institutions and industrial parks for the establishment of business complexes, now all we want to do is sing, dance, tell dirty jokes, and play ball.

On the so-called black entertainment network, and the stations that produce many of the black sitcoms, I see very little, if anything, that would be considered black or African-American in terms of positive contributions to African-American society. On the BET station, blatant sex and profanity is paraded on this station without shame to such a degree that, in my opinion, this station has become one of the primary sources of some of the most detrimental influences in the black community. I tell you, this is not entertainment; this is the epitome of filth without regard to decency or responsible programming. Our African-American women sit up and laugh at dirty jokes about themselves and then wonder why they don't get any respect from African-American men. For the most part, it is because they have dropped their own standards of decency and respect for what we as men are supposed to be about, and how we are supposed to conduct ourselves around them. It is because we have lost the ability as men to provide correct examples of leadership in the home and community life, thus, our women have lost respect for themselves.

Fully 99 percent of the music from African-American entertainers is about sex, or about a friend stealing another friend's girlfriend or boyfriend. At the risk of my reading too much into some of these modern-day lyrics, I must say that it is these kinds of lyrics that influence much of the negative thinking in the society. After hearing so much of it, we then begin to try to act out the lyrics, and thus, we begin to chip away at that valuable institution we call friendship, and at other social pillars that support positive community life. As if there wasn't already enough mistrust, and distrust in the world.

I think the African-American community, in realizing the rich heritage and culture of our past, should consider it an insult to our intelligence that even in comedy, an entertainer would think that he or she would have to appeal to our baser human makeup in order to entertain us. To me, that's like saying that I'm not intelligent enough to understand humor on a higher level, or that the entertainers themselves are on such a low level that base humor is all that they know. In either case, there is nothing positive to be gained, and everything to be lost. Our black leaders are silent on these issues when clearly, these are the kinds of negative influences that are killing us off as a people. If we as a people cannot overcome the vices in our own communities, as well as the sources of these vices, we have only ourselves to blame, and no one else. Even our babies are singing lyrics about perverted sexual experiences, and we, as parents, look at them and laugh, as if it's funny not realizing that these lyrics are shaping and molding the character of our youth.

We must not forget that words make people, and with the kind of influences that we're under as a people, it's understandable why our prison population are majority black and Latino. Many of our African-American musical groups and individuals adopt names for themselves that show lack of intelligence, crime involvement, and other negative connotations. And included in all this glitter and excitement, we also find the violence and death. For the most part, all are part and parcel of each other. The entertainment industry tries to say that they imitate real life, but I beg to differ. It is the world of entertainment that sets the pace, in most cases, for what would be the need to have commercials if the public couldn't be influenced to purchase the product? By the same token, the public also buys the examples they see on the music videos, the TV sitcoms, the movies, etc.

Again, let me say that those African-Americans who have gone into the entertainment business, be it in music, sports, drama, or whatever field must get back to a sound value system, because willingly or unwillingly, they are playing a major role in the destruction of the African-American community.

We can see and understand more clearly now the bold statement, "The black man will be extinct by the year 2000." Whereas we used to create instruments for the progressive development of the society of man, we now have become a destructive force for self and others. We should understand that it was our ancestors that laid the foundation for America's space program. These days, we seem to not be able to get our minds above our sexual drives.

It is time that people whose imagination is stuck on sex, flashy jewelry, fancy cars, and a party every night be put by the wayside. We are losing too many of our precious resources in terms of our children being shot down in the streets, and serving lifetime prison sentences because they want to follow those who are in that lifestyle.

Further, what makes this cycle even more vicious is that when you have babies having babies, these young mothers are ill equipped to train, guide, and give good advice to their offspring because they haven't had a chance to develop morally, intellectually, and spiritually themselves, so the young children grow up in an environment that saps their humanity, and as Dr. Woodson said, "There will be nothing for them to do." So then, this environment of negativity is created and many of our youth end up in prisons and graveyards as areas of containment because the society has nothing for them to do. And the beat goes on.

Many of our African-American entertainers, and also the white and Latino ones parade themselves on TV and in the print media, having children out of wedlock like it's the thing to do.

They sing songs about how much they love their baby, which it is good for them to do so, but it sends the wrong message to too many of our young teenage girls and boys, and that's the kind of mentality that contributes to the negative thinking we see in so many of our young people today. These people who make the music have the finances to live the good life, and can afford the necessities needed for providing for their children, but for those whom they influence, in too many cases, find themselves in a position with no way out because too many of the fans of these entertainers are from poor to fairly well-to-do families, and the situations they find themselves in as a result of following the examples of these entertainers, more times than not, leave their lives devastated.

We must understand that this is still that genocide at work, and it is reaching its deadly hand all the way from those dreaded days of the plantation life into modern-day society, still trying to snatch the life from the human being. These are the kinds of situations that our African-American leaders need to educate our youth about so that they will be prepared to pick up the banner of responsibility and run with it.

As the situation presents itself presently, too many of our youth, both Latino and African-American, because of the environment they are brought up in, develop the gang mentality, tolerate drug-infested communities, teen pregnancy, and the like. So we see that those who sing the songs and tell the jokes seem to not have enough intelligence to entertain their audiences with class, wit, and talent, so they stoop to insult and vulgarity. In my own opinion, I say that all they're really concerned about is the profit they're able to make off the masses. Essentially, their mindset is the same as that of the slave master, profit by any means necessary. Regardless of the carnage and the young minds they are affecting, it really doesn't matter, as long as they are making money. Those African-American leaders who remain silent about this situation have become reminiscent of those white officials who, at the turn of the century, gave tacit approval to the illegal activities of those in the Democratic Primaries. They, and those entertainers who stand up in front of the public and make this garbage acceptable, have become the gatekeepers to the Institution of Slavery.

The attitude of dependency displayed by the African-American community, and the present-day leadership, has left us a third-world people, in not only a first-class society, but in the most progressive society on earth. We are fast becoming members of the servant class. Although many of us will rise above this status, too many of us will fit in it or fall below it. It seems that our primary concern is to be part of the entertainment world. We want to become modern-day gladiators for the entertainment of the movers and shakers of world affairs, for when they want to take a break from making decisions that affect the way the world is ran.

Those sources of media that have worked to break down the moral foundation of the society have influenced the masses to the point that, in these days, anything, regardless of how vulgar or insulting to the intelligence, can be made to be socially acceptable, first through subliminal seduction, then by bombarding the minds of the masses to the point that they become numb to what's really happening to them.

It must be understood that this destructive attitude we see in our young people is not confined to the black community only, for all across the nation, we see young white children committing mass murder and suicide. They have also become victims. We are all on the same bus that takes us to the extremity of the extremes. According to many news reports, the majority of drug use takes place in the white suburbs. There have been some media coverage of this fact, but for some reason, for the most part, we are led to believe that it's mostly Latinos and African-Americans that's caught up in drug abuse. This misrepresentation of the facts has left some white people thinking like an ostrich with its head in the ground, that if they don't see the problem, then it's not there. Sometimes, I don't know if those in the media just outright hate Latinos and African-Americans, because they make it seem like we're the only ones involved in crime, or they just don't want to face up to the fact that this is a problem that has grown to epidemic proportions, and it's time the responsibility be placed in the right place so that it can be dealt with effectively. Some studies show that a young, white, middle-class girl is more apt to steal than the young African-American girl that we see portrayed in that role in the media. We don't know how much credibility can be placed in studies such as these, but we are all aware of the violence we see in our communities, the abduction and abuse of innocent children, which is almost a daily occurrence. Our business people, both in small and large companies, defraud their customers, and while the average student has no conscience about cheating on exams, the state government, instead of appealing to the human excellence of the student as a means of building character in them, turn instead to playing the lottery and other forms of gambling to support education. If G-d has condemned gambling, how then are we going to use it to support education, something G-d has condoned? There can be no success there.

In recent years, we've seen numerous incidents where young white boys have gone into the school campus and committed mass murder and suicide, and when the doctors of mind and medicine make it on the scene and the sensitivity sessions are done, we come back to the news reporter on the scene, whose only statement is, "This terrible incident has left the people here in a state of shock and asking the question 'Why?'"

These are just some examples to show that all of America is affected by the negative influences in this society, and it's all our responsibility to call America back to G-d. I do not believe that it's an accident that all these negative influences are coming into the black community. It seems to me that we are a target in a concocted scheme of destruction. But the scheme has gone wrong, and now, everybody is suffering, hence, again we say, we're all on the same bus.

In terms of raising our children, I don't know who wrote the first law that made discipline in the home a violation of the law, but I believe that person was a devil. I don't believe corporal punishment is child abuse. I believe that children should know that they have consequences to face when they do wrong, and I believe the parent has the judgment to handle these things properly. When the responsibility is taken away from the parent to keep the child from dangerous behavior, then the media steps in and begin to bombard the society with all these dangerous and negative influences, so what can we expect but a society steeped in violence. A parent that cannot discipline his children because of fear of reprisals from the law is therefore forced to see their children go bad, and in many cases, even attack the parents. Some eventually end up either dead or behind bars for long periods of time. To me, that is the epitome of child abuse. I am not saying that corporal punishment is the answer in all cases, because it may not apply with some families. Each family knows it's own situation. Now there are some parents who have been just as negatively influenced by the media as the children, so they are mentally ill-equipped in many ways, in my opinion, to raise their children properly. These should seek the help of relatives, ministers, and well-trusted friends, but the goal is to raise responsible thinking children.

We are still dealing with the bold statement of the 'nineties that said, "The black man will be extinct by the year 2000." We see then that in the above passages in this writing that we're not talking about physical extinction, but the ability of our people to govern themselves in a responsible and progressive manner. We're talking about the fact that the minds of the people in the African-American community have been put on such a low level that our men have lost their manhood. We don't see the African-American man teaching family responsibility to his children and other children in the community around him. We don't see that attitude of high respect and high esteem for our women being taught to the future generation. We don't see the emphasis being put on the need for education the way it should be. We don't see the history of our ancestors being taught to our youth so as to give them a sense of pride so they can use that history as a motivation to do even better. Because of the lack of leadership on the part of the man in the family, we don't see prayer in the home like in days gone by, and therefore, the respect for Allah is virtually non-existent.

In regards to our women, we see that they have dropped their standards to such a low level that their being the first teacher of our children in terms of positive growth and development is virtually a thing of the past. It is the mother in the family who teaches the child dignity, pride, and compassion. It is the mother in the family who teaches manners, and respect for adults and others. It is the mother who gives a sense of refinement and culture to the children as they are growing up. The combination of the mother and father working together virtually assures the development of a positive-thinking generation of future leaders that truly will pick up the banner of responsibility and run with it.

These two negative factors, combined in the black man and the black woman in terms of not shouldering their responsibility in this sense, make it very difficult to see a bright future for the next generation of black youth.

So we are realizing the reality of that statement, "The black man will be extinct by the year 2000." Our respect for the real life has been substituted for the superficial trinkets given to us by the environment we live in. The fact that we have traded in our high value system means that we have lost control of not only our own families, but indeed, our total community. So then, if the statement that "Man means mind" is true, and it is, then what we're saying here is that because of our love for this artificial life we have been given, we have been reduced to that level of animalistic life, that life of the brute beast that the Institution of Slavery was designed to impose upon us. We don't think with intelligence anymore, which is the sign of the Homo sapiens, but we move more on instinct, which is the sign of the jungle life.

Again, we say that much of the bad attitudes we see in our youth today comes as a result of what they see in the media, especially those that encourage them to reject authority. And as I stated before, the media and the entertainment world are not the only ones to blame, but they are a good place to start in terms of bringing life back to the community. Let me just say right here that I am not just condemning the media as if it's not a good thing. I believe the media is a valuable asset when people and the humanity of the people are seen as being as important as the profits.

The question begs to be asked: "What ever happened to the music that was a part of our heritage and history?" The kind of entertainment that made talent a requirement. The kind of entertainment, whether it was comedy, drama, music, or whatever, which required not only intelligence to perform it, but intelligence to appreciate it. What has happened is that the comedy and music of today, instead of appealing to the intelligence of the public, appeals to our sexual drives, and generally, to the lower desires of the human makeup. And since the sex drive is one of the strongest forces in the human being and the vulgarity allows us to let it all hang out, we get caught up in the crosswinds of some of the filthiest stuff in the environment, and it becomes the primary cause of our downfall.

As we look around today and we see others taking over and monopolizing the jazz, blues, and the real R&B that the great African-American musicians brought into existence, it has to be a shame and a tragedy, not so much that others are realizing the beauty and the value of our music, but that we're not realizing it. Some may argue that the music we're hearing today is an advancement of those great musicians. I beg to differ. Not only did the instrumental music illustrate a great and profound depth of talent and spirit that the listener could move and dance to, but the music could also act as a massage that relaxed the body, mind, and soul, and allowed the listeners to stay in touch with themselves as they enjoyed the piano of The Count, or the horns of Miles, Coltrain, or Dizzy, and felt the soothing strings of Brother Wes. The vocal talent had no limits to them as well, whether it was the scatting voice of Ella, the soft, smooth, but firm voice of Carmen, the deep baritone of Joe, and the velvet sounds of Diana. There are many, many others such as Nina, Alice, Lady Day, Max, McCoy, Satchmo, Freddie, Milt, etc. Then there was Muddy, whose waters ran deep, Jackie, who had not only a great voice, but talented feet. There was also the comedy of Moms and Pigmeat, who added to the never-ending list of talent produced by our community for the world, and now we trade it for the garbage that not only is void of any musical nutrients that would be good for the soul, mind, and spirit of the listener, but what is even more tragic, reaches into the next generation and put the chains of moral and mental slavery on our future generation as well. As a people, we need to rediscover the beauty of the jazz, blues, and real R&B of the great musicians that have had a positive impact on the whole world of music and entertainment.

The dance that we see today borders on pornography, and the reason we don't see the emphasis placed on poetry like in days gone by is that poetry takes talent, and because it was one of the primary influences that motivated us forward during the movement of the sixties, with the likes of Nikki Giovanni, Amiri Baraka, Maya Angelou, and later, The Last Poets, Gill Scott Heron, Sonia Sanchez, etc.

Even the lyrics in some of the gospel music of today really have no redeeming quality to them. There is really no message that can be garnered from what we call religious music that would profit the listener to any real degree of growth and development. Even in some of our African-American writers, too many of them write books depicting African-American men as people with no character, low morals, and no respect for our women. And while this may be the case in some instances, this mentality is also shared by men in other races as well, and when we write about it in the manner that we do, not only do we exacerbate the situation in our own communities, but when these images are put upon the silver screen, then we make ourselves look like fools in the eyes of the world. I know that there are more good men in the black community than there are bad. I know that there are good husbands and good fathers in the black community. I know that there are good black men demanding respect for black women, and teaching their sons to do so as well. I know that there are good, strong black men struggling against the strong currents of this negative environment, trying to hold family and community together. And since we know this to be a fact, if we wrote about these kinds of things and promoted them as much as we promote the negative, we would eventually see more positive things come from our communities as well.

As we advance into this modern world of technology, we should reflect back on the ancestors and pick up on the value system that has allowed us to progress thus far, and contributed so much that benefited mankind. To advance technically doesn't mean that we should degenerate morally. We should not treat sex as if it's something that we live for. It seems that our every waking hour is consumed with the desire for sexual gratification. This obsession with sex leads to a total disrespect for life. Sexually transmitted diseases are killing us off and the only answer we can come up with is to use a condom. It seems that in almost every ill that society suffers from, there is a Band-aid solution for it. That is to say that instead of addressing the root of the problem, which is moral degeneration, society comes up with these shallow solutions, which in reality are no solutions at all, such as condoms, designated drivers, drug rehab, etc. These, in fact, leave society still a victim to the negative influences that put them in the adverse situation in the first place, and so we as a society become a nation of people knitted together by a string of programs that really never address what really ails the people.

When we address the worth of human beings as Allah has created them, we realize a level that is higher than all other forms of creation, and the fact that with the human makeup, comes all the attributes that Allah has given us to not only maintain the high position he has chosen for the human being, but to climb on up the ladder to realize all the limitless potential that the human being possesses.

When we address the excellence of the human being and bring into use words like virtue, decency, self-respect, and above all, respect for G-d, then we will see that the need for condoms, designated drivers, etc., will be of no use, because we then begin to realize the strength of the human being. If we continue to appeal to the weaknesses of the people, and then offer them Band-aid solutions to problems that are so profound that they shake the very souls of the people, society will become weaker and weaker, and the infrastructure, which is the excellence of each individual that make up that society, will become tainted and rotten, thus, society will crumble.

The whole society should consider it a direct insult on our intelligence that someone would tell us that we are so weak inwardly that we cannot control our sexual urges. They're handing out condoms at community centers, school campuses, clinics, etc. This is just another way of telling the masses that we are not intelligent enough to have control over ourselves, that we are not yet ready to accept responsibility. Anytime society tell us that a condom is stronger the human excellence that Allah has given to us, that is the highest form of disrespect. So then, in some cases, we may find that condom use may protect from disease or unwanted pregnancy, but it doesn't protect us from losing our honor, dignity, self-respect, and those other qualities given to us by Allah, that if nurtured, would bring out the best in us, such as leadership qualities and other positive attributes that would make us people of positive influence. But because of the negative influences, neither we nor our offspring will be able to realize the great contributions that might have been possible.

Other losses that we suffer from are, as stated before, the loss of many of the institutions that work to support community life, such as the Institution of the Family. Family members have become so alienated from each other that it's not uncommon to see total disrespect to their parents and grandparents from children. Our morals have dropped so low that we even disrespect the marriage bond between relatives in our family. The Institution of Friendship is also another pillar of the community that's in great danger. Friends are almost like family members, and in many cases, some are even closer. The loss of the Institution of Friendship would all but kill off the growth potential of community life. This is why if we continue to listen to and mimic the lyrics in today's music, we will become part and parcel to the spread of apathy, and the inhuman lifestyles that many of us have adopted.

With the loss of family and friends, who is there to lend a helping hand in times of need? Who is there to give a word of advice at the many crossroads we come in contact with throughout life? Who is there to help the downtrodden, whether they're known, or unknown? As a people, we have to become thinkers and realize what the lust for entertainment is doing to us specifically, and to the general society as well. We must realize that we're putting ourselves back under slavery, but this time it's even more serious than before. This time, we're becoming willing participants in the slave trade, and just like in Africa before, many of our people are instrumental in helping to promote the dreaded curriculum of the Institution of Slavery. Due to the fact that it's moral and mental slavery, as opposed to racial discrimination, we cannot see the real dangers, and so we fall victim to sense perception. That is to say, we come under the influences of our basic senses. We begin to do that which makes us feel good, go after that which looks good, consume that which tastes good, regardless of the devastating effect these activities have on us as individuals and on the community. And so we continue to remain blind and devoid of understanding.

In recent years, the term "casual sex" has been introduced to the public. Now what has happened since that time is that the last vestiges of sacredness and respect, which should be attached to love and affection, were removed. The free love movement in times gone by, the blatant presentation of sex through the media, these old men and women calling themselves doctors, appearing on the various TV and radio talk shows, promoting this loose lifestyle of sexual freedom, has helped to lead to a shameless society of people under the influence of appetites unchecked by knowledge.

The moral guard of the society was lowered, and at that moment, the term casual sex drove the death nail into the coffin of moral principle. Now, sex has become just another pastime. Since it was termed casual, it required no commitment, no loyalty, and no responsibility. The word commitment is a very big word because in it, we see stability, success, and struggle that's set in a definite direction. Commitment, when understood on the various levels of growth and development in the life of the human being, represents a new stage of maturity and vision. Everything from making words bond to completing small and major tasks is what builds character and adds to the quality of the individual.

One of the primary reasons why we, as members of the human race, make very little progress is that too many times, we fail to keep our word. That includes paying debts to companies or people we owe, or just following through on a promise to a friend. Unfortunately, too many of us see this as minor, but this defect in our character starts out small, and then spreads to other areas of our lives, and soon, the whole life is nothing but an insensitive mentality that ends in our failure as human beings. Whatever the strongest influence at that time happens to be, that will be what determines the direction our lives will take, whether it's something that starts out simply, like breaking your word to a friend or giving up on a task before exhausting all possibilities of success, we must realize that this word commitment is no small word, and so those who manipulate the thinking process of the masses have taken something that's so sacred that it's the avenue of new life entering the world and made it "casual."

The word casual means feeling or showing little concern, designed for informal use. So when we see the difference between commitment and casual, we can easily understand why society has gotten so weak morally, and in the process of doing so, has ushered in all these other ills and diseases we suffer from. Again, this is why we say that society is not a haphazard turn of events that just happen to occur in a particular way. Society is very orchestrated, and when words like loyalty, which means "unswerving in one's allegiance to a person, or cause, to be faithful, to have fidelity," And the word responsibility, which means "moral, legal, or mental accountability, the state of being able to answer for one's own conduct and obligations, to be trustworthy," when words of this magnitude are taken out of the society and words like casual are substituted in their place, it is little wonder why we have moral, economic, and political corruption. This mentality has taken root in the average individual in the society, and as we stated before, this is why the nation crumbles. The infrastructure, which is made up of the individuals in the society, has become weak in their character. And this is by design.

The first and most important word we break is our word to G-d, when we continue to say we believe in Him, and let our actions show other than that belief. We must be very careful, because if our word to Allah means so little, then our word to each other is totally meaningless.

The pop culture we live in today destroys the principles that uphold the dignity of a human being by making fun and shaming us out of our dignity. Therefore, all that is positive, all that is strong, and stable, and right, falls by the wayside, and human society continues to fall deeper into moral bankruptcy. The fact that men run from woman to woman with no commitment, is just a sign of what's happening on all levels of human society, and in other aspects of human endeavors such as business, politics, etc., and it has had a devastating effect on all society both old and young.

Again, I say the best way to curtail sexually transmitted diseases is to use the strength that we get from Allah, and that is our moral strength. The strength of the individual is the strength of the society. We already have what we need to combat the ills that the society suffer from, but we must cease to be weak. There is no substitute for moral strength, no! None! If we address these concerns in the way they should be addressed, we would eventually relieve the community and the society as a whole of the ills we now face.

Our leaders, with their high visibility, should be leading the way in these areas of concern. When a young girl has a baby out of wedlock, and the father of the child refuses to show commitment, loyalty, or responsibility, too many times, that child grows up with little or no education, no job, no money, and sometimes ends up in jail, or get shot down by the police. Then our leaders want to swing into action and condemn the police and others, but will not condemn us as a community for allowing the tragedy to happen in the first place. Again I say that with the high visibility and the respect that our leaders have, if they would address these problems in the right way, these problems would be gone overnight. In my opinion, the reason why our leaders don't speak out against the drop in the morals of our communities, and speak out against those who bring bad influences into our communities is that they've been bought off by the manipulators of the society, and if there are no problems, they will be out of a job.

At the risk of sounding redundant, we must mention the gatekeeper-of-the concentration-camp mentality again, and how we've become part of the machinery that help to create the negative influences that help to cripple the black community. That is to say that because we are African-Americans, we know that we have to struggle three times as hard to get ahead, and too many times, by the time we become successful, all that struggling we've done has forced us to pick up on the same value system of other people, and many times, these are the same people who are the oppressors and will do anything or will step on anybody for a dollar. So we see black filmmakers creating movies that depict us as gangsters, thugs, players, and drug dealers, or sometimes we are portrayed as successful businessmen who cheat on their wives and generally give the idea to the world that black men are useless. That, coupled with the way we are portrayed in the news, as well as being stereotyped by law enforcement officials, it is no wonder that we see the prisons full of our people, and the sad part of it is that we're creating much of the influence that helps to put them there.

Many of our entertainers, and other executives in the entertainment industry, as well as some of those who sit on boards of some of the major businesses around the country that help to contribute to the degenerative mentality of the society, have become gatekeepers to the mental concentration camps, or the more familiar term, The Institution of Slavery. We, more than anyone, should be ready to exhale these kinds of influences and help to raise the level of intelligence of our young people so that they will have a fighting chance in the world of tomorrow.

Even the church, where important meetings for community improvement used to take place, has turned its focus to providing a place where mostly spiritual entertainment takes place. The sermons, especially in the Deep South, have degenerated into nothing but a show. The congregation can understand nothing that is being said by the preacher, because after the scripture is read, he goes into what is known as a "whoop," where the sermon is done with a rhythm and the congregation is content to just enjoy the show and go home, having learned little or nothing at all.

Today, a visit to the Deep South will reveal that the life of the African-American community is more stagnated than before the days of the Civil Rights Movement. Even though we have more political representation than ever before, we are still weaker morally, mentally, and spiritually. We have better jobs, we live in nicer homes, and we drive new cars, but still we control nothing. Our aspirations are very low, the dropout rate in the public school system is very high, and in many cases, the public school system is staffed by white teachers who stigmatize and degrade African-American students, and show little concern whether they learn or not. Religious leaders seem not to care, so they just carry on their "whoop" on Sunday mornings and take the money and run.

So we continue to echo the cause behind our downfall. Our creativity, our imagination, our deep concern for those standards that traditionally have been the foundation of society, the value system that seems to have degenerated right before our very eyes. The glare of the bright lights, the fast-lane lifestyles, the commitment to nothing, stand in stark contrast to real human development, a stable family and community life, using our minds to make scientific, medical, industrial, and other technical advancements that will move human society to a new level of growth and development.

Further, we need to consider the fact that this plague we see in the society today is not confined to the African-American or Latino communities only. As Americans, we must realize that the nation as a whole is suffering. This is not a problem that can be identified along racial lines. This is a problem of moral degeneration across the entire spectrum of human society, and it will need everyone's help to deal with it. For the sake of our family and community, we must raise our standards. We can no longer depend on the politicians because they speak for the money that supports their campaigns. We can no longer depend on the leaders because they have to stay in the limelight so that they can still be perceived as leaders. Americans must cease letting themselves be led around by their genitals, and use their G-d-given strength inherent in all of them, and that's their moral excellence.

So now, we speak with a broader focus when we address the bold statement that said, "The black man will be extinct by the year 2000." Now, we all can plainly see that this statement is not just to be seen as a statement that's aimed at the African-American community only. The negative influences that destroy us are not bound by race or ethnicity, and to think so would lead to apathy and narrow-mindedness, thus making that person part of the problem as well. In this regard, let us view the statement, "The black man will be extinct by the year 2000," from a broader perspective. Let us view it as its creators meant it. We know that man means mind, regardless of race or gender. Black represents the origin of all life, as all life begins in darkness. We are referring to the human life. The life that is human, that keeps humanity progressing in a positive direction. The man, or mind of compassion, dignity, honor, and regard for G-d are what they want to be extinct by the year 2000. The year 2000 is just any time period, but it represents our moral and productive life. The new meaning for concentration camps is the negative influences we are giving our minds to. It's what we are given to focus or concentrate on. Today, some of us are so caught up in material gain, while others are just trying to make ends meet, and still others are overwhelmed by the pleasure principle, we've forgotten our humanity and the true definition of what the real life is all about. As a result, our fears are manipulated by others and we find ourselves living in a world of fear and apathy. "The New Cold War;" It now becomes clear that this statement of extinction is referring to the humanity and the intelligence of the general society.

So now, the whole of America must reach deep within the self that G-d created. The self that supports moral strength. The self that leads to the strength of their own family, and see that their family is part of the larger family of our society, so that whatever good they want for their own family, then their voices will be heard for the whole of America, and the world as well. That family then becomes the cornerstone of the community, and that community, the cornerstone of the state, and on into the nation and the world, and then we have goodness on the rise globally.

As African-Americans, our problems are more severe, so our striving must be harder. Whereas other groups are already ahead in some areas, we are behind in all areas. So no, we won't be physically extinct all together, nor will we be physically incarcerated all together. But we as a people must realize that we have regressed to a level where all over the planet, we're looked on as a dependent race. We must realize that we still have the creativity within us; we still have the vivid imagination. We have only to realize that we must raise our values and, regardless of the obstacles, make no excuses for failure. We need to realize that our contributions to this nation are just as valuable as anyone else's, and there is no need for us to compromise our values or give up our culture in order to assimilate with others, or even to be accepted by others.

This is another reason for us to continue to look back on history, for with every glance, there's a new and different lesson to be learned. There's a new burst of motivation to propel us forward. There's a sense of pride and dignity that will overcome us because we as a people have as much to bring to the table of human society as anyone else. So the question begs to be asked, why should we be the ones to sacrifice our identity in order to fit in?

As we reflect back on the words of the great philosopher, W. E. B. DuBois, who said: "Your country? How come it yours? Before the Pilgrims landed we were here. Here we have brought our three gifts and mingled them with yours: a gift of story and song-soft, stirring melody in an ill-harmonized and unmelodious land, the gift of sweat and brawn to beat back the wilderness, conquer the soil, and lay the foundation of this vast economic empire two hundred years earlier than your weak hands could have done it; and the third, a gift of spirit... Our song, our toil, our cheer, and warning have been given to this nation in blood-brotherhood. Are these gifts not worth the giving? Is not this work and striving? Would America have been America without her Negro people?"² **(28) So again, we see the words of our ancestors support the fact that we as a people have as much to be proud of as anyone, and as the ancestors would say, "truth be known." Most of what we see that have brought progress and prosperity to America came from the African-American community. So again, we say, why should we lose our identity and try to be like someone we're not?**

We are a proud people, and we should act like it. We must stop allowing others to dictate our values for us. We are a dignified people and we must raise our standards to a level of dignity. Just because it's legal in America to be as vulgar as you want to be doesn't mean we have to be. We must understand that if we are to progress as a people, we have to know that real freedom means shouldering the responsibility of upholding those things that make society strong, positive, and progressive.

"Remember the Ancestors!" "Rewrite the History!"

Chapter 5

"Up you Mighty Nation, you Can Accomplish What you Will"—Solutions

When we understand who the enemy is, then we know what tools or weapons to employ to deal with that enemy.

So since we know now that we're not on that physical battlefield, we must realize that the battle for human survival has become more intense and deadly serious. In Scripture, we read about the battle in the sky. Imam W. Deen Mohammed tells us in scriptural interpretation that the word sky or heaven is really representative of the highest part of the human makeup, which is the mind. So when we talk about the battle in the sky, what we're really talking about is the individual's struggle to come to terms with themselves. To make that decision, which ultimately will decide the course of the life of that person, we should be aware that sometimes, the wrong decision will bring short-term gratification, but in the long run, it will make us pay too high a price. To choose right thinking over wrong, intelligence over ignorance, and in too many cases, to choose life over death. This is the battle in the sky, or in Islamic terms, the Holy War, or Jihad. We have to decide if we're going to allow this world of false values overrule our humanity, the original nature given to us by Allah.

One of the reasons why we see so much apathy in the world, so much disrespect for education, and why one person can kill another without remorse is that we're allowing our humanity to be stolen away from us. Our attention is being geared toward an over-obsession with sex, materialism, entertainment, and in general, those things that bring us immediate gratification in life, while we disregard those elements that goes to build up a stronger and more secure life for human survival.

Again, let us go to Scripture where we read about the death and resurrection of Jesus Christ. And as before, we're not talking about the physical death and resurrection of a person, but the death and resurrection of human consciousness. Again we say that the word Christ should not be taken to be part of the name of Jesus, as many of us mistakenly take it to mean that. Christ is a word meaning anointed. it is the mind that Allah blessed the Prophet Jesus to have. So then, we have Jesus, the man, and Christ, the mind. This term becomes clearer to us when we understand the word concept, or Immaculate Conception.

According to Biblical and Qura'nic scripture, Jesus was a word from G-d, who said "Be," and he was. So not only did Allah speak, and Jesus came to be, but G-d also protected mother and child, and brought him to the level of Prophethood, with the knowledge of divine revelation. immaculate means "clean, free from blemish, spots, and stains." Concept, or Conception means "something conceived in the mind." It's more of an intellectual than a biological term. It is the act of becoming pregnant mentally. It is the sum of a person's ideas and beliefs concerning something. The Virgin Mary is symbolic of a particular society or community that was untouched by man's knowledge and so-called wisdom. Just as the physical womb shapes and molds the physical baby in birth, it is then born into another womb, and that is the womb of society, which then molds and shapes the mind. The Christ mind then is the mind that is free from spot and blemish of man's influence. So the birth of Jesus came as a result of what G-d wants the human being to be. A community, recognizing and respecting the word of G-d, becomes a broader representation of the Christ mind, and therefore becomes a broader influence on human society.

So we die to the negative influences of this society, and come alive again in our G-d-given humanity. In dignity, honor, trustworthiness, respect, etc., all the elements that form the character of the individual, will thus form the foundation of a strong society. The forty days of fasting represents the ability we all have within us to resist worldly influences, and get back the control of all aspects of our human makeup. Our moral, economic, political, and spiritual motivations come back under our control, and they are used for the positive advancement of the society, because now, our minds, our attention is taken up from the corruption of the world, and focused on pleasing G-d from whom we get our human makeup.

Satan is symbolic of our lower self, pulling on us to give in to the temptations of the world. So this kind of understanding of the scripture and its purpose in our lives is the beginning of the resurrection of each of us. What we are saying here is that we should not see this as just the trials and tribulations of the Prophet Jesus, but the example he was setting for us and what we must do to please G-d, and keep the control in our own lives so that we may prosper. Also, we're not to see this as just a spiritual awakening, because we're more than just spiritual people. We have to see G-d's word, generating power to our total human makeup. In this way, we begin to see our responsibility not only to ourselves, but to our family and community as well. So this resurrection is for the total self.

So now, we see a higher moral development come alive within us. We also see the need for economic development in our lives, as well as intellectual and spiritual growth. Understanding the importance of these entities and how they work in our lives tells us that our savior has arrived. Now, it is equally as important to know that the level we get to in each new stage of growth and development depends on how well we understood the former. For instance, our first level of growth begins with our moral development, and as stated earlier in this writing, we have to understand morality on a much higher level than just being good, and just merely knowing the difference between what's right and what's wrong, or what's good and what's bad.

From the teachings of Imam W. Deen Mohammed, we learn that when we maintain a strong moral foundation through study, work, and deeds, we see the graduation of morality into ethics, respect, integrity, logic, etc. Let us look deeper into the meaning of these words so as to gain a greater understanding of them and the impact they have on our lives. We know that these words used to be common in terms of their usage in everyday language in our society, and were used as measuring rods for the worth of the individual.

In today's society, we hardly ever hear these words being mentioned, and so we see less stability in the society. In other words, the use and application of these words helped to develop character and reliability in the individual, thus making the individual more established or stable. The fact that these words and others like them were in wide use in the environment meant that they became not only part of the language we use, but also the air we breathe, the atmosphere that surrounds us, and therefore, part of the everyday life of the people.

Today's society is built mostly on trends and fads. We live in what is commonly called "pop culture," here today and gone tomorrow. This kind of culture is what has led to the apathy and the destructive lifestyles we see in the society today, and the crumbling of our nation from within. The major concern of the masses is to stay in tune with the pop culture and to keep up with the trends. So it's important that we bring these kinds of words and their meanings back into the culture in hopes that they will bring us back in touch with the life that Allah has designed for us as human beings.

That which is moral, or of morality. We say this is the foundation of human nature itself because Allah has put it into the nature of every human being to know the difference between what's right and wrong. There is that part of the human makeup, known as the "conscience," that tells us when we're wrong even before the act occurs. Even a child slipping his hand in the cookie jar against the orders of his parents knows he's wrong. That's why they're slipping, looking cautiously around to ensure that no one is watching while the act is taking place. So even as babies and as little children, G-d in all His mercy has not left us without guidance.

So this word moral, according to *Webster's New World Dictionary*, means "capable of distinguishing between right and wrong in conduct; of teaching or in accordance with the principles of right and wrong; moral quality or character; standards of right conduct." So we see that just the basic word "morality" starts the person off in the right direction, which will secure them as a positive and productive individual in the society.

It should be noted here that even though G-d has given the human being this moral nature, still it has to be cared for and nurtured so that it will grow and mature. Saving the moral nature of a child, in many cases, can be compared to saving a swimmer who's drowning. The drowning swimmer will fight against the lifeguard who is trying to save his life, until he's finally brought to shore, where he then thanks the life guard for saving his life. Similarly, a child will rebel, and sometimes fight against the rules and regulations the parents have set up in the home for the family members to follow. Peer pressure and the negative influences of the environment in the life of the child are just like the water the drowning swimmer is caught up in, and just like the drowning swimmer, that child eventually will give thanks to the life guard, who is the parent, or that caring person from the community that refused to let go of him in the dangerous waters of life. So that child will likewise, as he begins to grow into the age of maturity, realize that those rules and regulations are what saved his life, and made him a productive person of society.

Without this kind of attention to the lives of our children, the influences of the environment will grow up around that individual and choke down the positive nature, thus destroying that person as a human being. Then we witness what is commonly known as second nature come into play. The first nature, which is obedience to G-d, has been overtaken by the negative influences of this world. The positive value system handed down from generation to generation has been discarded, and the frivolous and false values of this world have been picked up. So now that person is ruled by that second nature, thinking it's his own, but in reality, it's the false nature given to that individual by the society. So now, we can see the importance of nurturing the moral life and giving advice so that the person can become a living, productive member of the society.

We've already said that morality is the foundation of the life of the human being, but that moral life must grow if the individual is to realize his human potential and become an asset to the society he lives in. As we grow and mature, we come to understand that not everything is as it seems to be. That is to say that nothing is as simple as "black and white," or "cut and dry." This society produces many nuisances in life, that without a strong moral base to keep us on the right track, many of the decisions that we make could very well become detrimental to us.

So now, this sense of morality must grow, it has to graduate into a more mature meaning. It cannot stay on the kindergarten level. That is to say that it must mean more to us than just knowing the difference between good and bad, right and wrong. So as we witness the growth or the graduation of this moral principle, we see it growing like a tall oak tree out of the river bank. As the tree digs its roots deeper and deeper into the earth, we can see its branches start to sprout and spread.

The first branch from this moral seed we see in the original nature of the human being is the branch of virtue. Virtue means a specific moral quality regarded as good. Chastity, a beneficial quality or power of a thing. Conformity to a standard of right. A commendable quality or trait. Or in my own words, to do good simply because it's natural and right to do good.

The Holy Qur'an states in *sura* 30:31, "So set thou thy face truly to the religion being upright, the nature in which Allah has made mankind: no change (there is) in the work (wrought) by Allah: that is the true religion: but most among mankind know not." The scripture is telling us here that the nature, the character, the natural makeup of the human being is one of goodness and respect for G-d. In short, the human being is moral by nature, or the human being is naturally moral.

The word face in this *ayat* or verse comes from the Arabic root word in the Qur'an, wajh, meaning "face, countenance, personality, intent, repute," for the sake of G-d, regardless of any reward in this life. The word nature is from the root word fitra, meaning "creation, nature, innate, character, instinct, inborn, natural man, natural religion." The word upright is from the root word hanif, meaning "true believer, orthodox, one who scorns the foolishness of the environment and professes the true faith."

So from the scripture, we can see that the human being is virtuous by nature. This is the natural pattern in which every human being is created. When we see suffering or wrongdoing in the world, we try to act to be a part of the solution to these problems. We don't just allow wrongdoings to continue, because it bothers our nature. It troubles our very being to see the terrible ills of the society going on around us, especially when we witness the mind-altering influences that kills off the humanity of the individual and reduce us to people living on the level of animals.

The original nature not only of the human being, but of all creation, is one of submission to Allah, and it is the duty of all who are still in touch with that original nature to bring back that order in the society that respects the pattern that Allah has created us on.

After bringing ourselves back to the position of taqwa, which means G-d-fearing, or reverence. Respect for Allah. The kind of fear or respect that we have because we know that we are ever in the presence of G-d, and even though we know we can't see Allah, we know that He sees us, so we are always on guard against wrongdoing. So then, this kind of thinking sets our whole selves on the path of intelligent thinking. Our character, our conduct, our purpose in life becomes one of pleasing G-d by being of service to our fellow human beings. This, then, is what constitutes the personality or makeup of the Hanif, The True Believer.

In *sura,* or chapter 2:177, Allah says to us, "It is not righteousness that you turn your faces toward east or west; but it is righteousness that you believe in Allah and the last day, and the Angles, and the Books, and the Messengers; to spend of your substance out of love for Him, for your kin, for orphans, for the needy, for the wayfarer, for those who ask, and for the ransom of slaves. To be steadfast in prayer, and practice regular charity. To fulfill the contracts you have made, and to be firm in pain or adversity and throughout all periods of panic. Such are the people of Truth, the G-d-fearing." We are able to witness here the true example of virtue, which is the quality of not only being good, but doing good naturally. It is that quality that Allah has placed in the natural makeup of the human being. In my opinion, the highest expression of our humanity is when we do good, because it's right to do good. Although we know that Allah rewards all good deeds, our prayer is for sincerity, and an appreciation for the sanctity of human life. So then, our purpose in life becomes one of pleasing Allah, and that is the greatest blessing of all.

When I was a child growing up, there was a saying that helped to mold the thinking of the society at that time. The saying was, "He ain't heavy, he's my brother." And a picture of a young boy carrying another young boy on his back, who appeared to have been hurt, would always appear over the saying. It was common to see just ordinary people giving a helping hand to those who needed it, not because they expected a blessing or a reward for it, but because they were still in touch with their humanity, and they felt it was the right thing to do. This kind of attitude didn't just apply to friends or family, or to others who happen to live in a particular community, but it also applied to the wayfarer, the stranger passing through. Those who had somehow gotten themselves caught up in a situation that enslaved them financially, morally, or in some other form or another. There was always someone who came to their aid. It should also be noted that these people were not rich or affluent by any respect in so far as material gain was concerned, but they were rich in their human content, and that's what made the difference. It was that quality of character and conduct that charged the atmosphere and created an attitude that was conducive to the positive growth and development of the individual. It was virtue that brought such value to the Institution of Family and the Institution of Friendship. In fact, there were times when the ties between family and friends were so close, that the lines that separated them became blurred. This kind of thinking made family and friends into more than just people who know each other, as stated before; it made them into institutions that made up the foundation of strong community life.

When we look at the pop culture today, and on the kind of thinking it produces, we see apathy and frustration. One person can see another person being raped or robbed, or being abused in some other way, and instead of lending a helping hand, that person crosses over to the other side of the street, as if nothing had happened. This pop culture produces the kind of thinking in many of our young people today that make them commit unspeakable, horrible acts of terror that leaves the society pondering this question, What happened? What went wrong? Why are our kids acting like this? And in our quest to find answers, we have gone to putting military and police personnel on our school campuses, surveillance machinery that monitor every move of students and staff. We have a drug culture that has been debated so much that it has normalized the use of drugs. Now, in almost every aspect of life, we have to be tested for drugs. Citizens who are used to moving about freely in the society and who are aware of their responsibility to manage their own lives, and some who have even fought for that inherent right that have been given to them by Allah, are now willing to succumb to the idea of giving up that freedom, because we have been told that this is needed to protect the society. This kind of thinking eventually produces a military state. Our children become so used to seeing the military in the schools and in the community that they become desensitized to this kind of environment, and so for them, it becomes a way of life. Without our knowing it, our future leaders will produce a country ruled by martial law. Again we say, we do not live in a society that is governed by haphazard circumstances. America is a world leader, and nothing happens by chance where it concerns the thinking of the masses. This is not necessary when all it takes is the re-establishing of the moral values in the individual. In doing this, we will see that just as the individual grows up into an intelligent person, so then follows the growth of human society.

Another saying that I remember as I was growing up is, "It's not whether you win or lose, but how you play the game." In today's society, the emphasis is placed on winning at any cost, but as we can see, the cost of that kind of thinking is too great. This is not to say that we shouldn't strive to win and to always do our best, but don't let the loss of our humanity be the price that we pay for a prize that's here today and gone tomorrow. For unlike the fleeting values of today's society, the values that we establish as a result of our humanity builds a solid foundation for the future, and that's just too high a price to pay for something so meaningless. We should never forget that even those who lose, live to fight another day. This kind of thinking is arrived at when the intelligence of the society is addressed, rather than the animalistic urges. This applies to all aspects of life, entertainment, religious, economics, etc. G-d identifies the intelligent makeup as that part of the human being that separates us from the animal world. Then doesn't it make perfect sense for the society to address that when addressing the human being? When we emphasize this kind of thinking, we will soon see ourselves back on the road to safety and stability. So virtue is the first and the very important branch of this tree we find growing out of the moral nature of the human being.

Then we come to another branch of this same tree. This branch is called ethics. Ethics is the study of standards of conduct and moral judgment. It is also a system or code of morals for an individual or a group. When we consider the definition of ethics in this manner, it brings us to another very important word, which has to do with how we are structured as human beings. The word is constitution. This is a system or body of laws, codes, and rules that determine the makeup of an individual, group or nation, as well as how that individual, group, or nation operates. Let us look even closer to home and we find that the word also means the structure, composition, or the nature of something. When this definition is given to the individual, we then see how ethics, or ethical behavior, is natural to our human makeup, because this is how our Creator has made us. We've all heard the old saying, "That person has a strong constitution." This is referring to someone who has overcome major obstacles in his life. This then contradicts that old saying that we are sinners by nature. Not only are we moral by nature, but we also have within us the potential for unlimited growth and development. This not only improves our own lives, but it puts us in a position where the greater society will benefit as a result of the decisions made by us. This applies whether we are a common person, or the person in a position of authority.

At some point in our lives, we begin to hear that inner voice within us guiding us to the place where we know that we have to have organization and direction in our lives. That organization and direction has to be based on a system of moral codes and standards that we use in our everyday life if we are to be a positive force in the society in which we live. Since goodness is inherent in our nature, we obey the natural law that G-d has put in all creation. This includes even the inanimate objects. They follow this same system of obedience, from the outer reaches of space to the natural creation we see around us everyday. In the Qur'an, we read, "Your Guardian Lord is Allah who created the heavens and the earth in six days. Then He settle Himself on the Throne: He draweth the night as a veil o'er the day, each seeking the other in rapid succession: and the sun, the moon, and the stars, (all) are subservient by His command. Verily, His are the creation and the command. Blessed be Allah, the Cherisher and Sustainer of the worlds." (HQ 7:54) In the elevated minds of thinking man, ethics is seen as obedience to the Creator on a higher level of existence. This intelligent obedience applies to the high seats of authority, and to the general society as well. Ethics tells us that we must have standards in our own lives, as well as in our community life. With standards, we have a rule to live by, we have a certain criterion that keeps us from going to extremes. Standards tell us that as human beings, there are some things that we just won't do regardless of how attractive they may seem. We have grown to the level where we realize that some activities just do not fit into our system of conduct. They may appear to be positive or good, but in reality, they bring harm and destruction to the environment.

As we have already stated, success by any means is not success at all, because the costs in terms of our positive human attributes are too great. Soon, wrong thinking works its way down into our individual lives and spreads to our community lives, and soon we find ourselves lowering our standards and settling for less. Our communities become gullible, and people begin to thrive on false intelligence. That is to say that we start to look and listen at those people whom we consider people of achievement, such as doctors of psychology, sex therapists, etc. Many times, we think that just because they said it, then it must be true, regardless of how far-fetched it may seem. As thinking people, we have to understand the importance of examining this information in all its aspects and make sure that it conforms with our basic moral makeup, before allowing it into our lives and into our society.

In the absence of ethics, our thinking becomes shallow, and we begin to adopt Band-aid solutions for the soul-perplexing problems we see in the society. From the very basic violation we see of one's own moral code, to the corruption we see in business and government, nothing or no one is left out in terms of being affected by the negative influences in the environment, but still, we continue to deal with symptoms instead of getting to the root cause of what ails us as a nation. Soon, we are overwhelmed by everything from teen pregnancy to the selling of our government to big business and foreign governments for money to run our political campaigns. This was what Prophet Muhammed (SAWS) meant when he said, "We will know the last day when government is entrusted to the undeserving (those without ethics, and integrity)." Those who would allow themselves to be put into high political positions and other positions of influence so they can rule over the people at the bidding of the rich and powerful, when in reality, many of them are not even qualified to serve in those positions.

A sense of ethics has to be re-established within us as individuals, and within those who represent us in positions of authority, if we as a nation is going to survive. We continue to make excuses and smooth things over, fooling ourselves into thinking that things are going to be all right when all it takes is to bring back the first nature given to us by Allah. When we say government of the people, for the people, and by the people, we mean more than just electing people to office. Government has to be seen as a process of life that starts within the individual and spreads to the outer community. Also, it has to be seen as a process that goes on for the entire life of the person. To paraphrase an old gospel saying,

"The prize is not given to the strong and swift, but to the one who endures to the end," if business, law, and politics are corrupt, it is the common, everyday people who will suffer. We, the common, everyday people, the foundation of our nation, must cease allowing ourselves to be caught up in party affiliation at the expense of our human affiliation. *We, the People,* must be informed, and *We, the People,* must demand practices from business, law, and government that are based on ethics. Ethics must prevail even when it opposes our own sentiments.

We should not be put in a situation where we have to ask, "Who should we trust?" We must look within ourselves as the common, everyday people of America, who are ultimately responsible for keeping this great nation favorable in the sight of Allah. While we know that the big-business corporate world has its place in American society, we should never forget that the smaller community businesses mean doing business with people we know and trust, but it goes even further than that. It also means maintaining closer family and community bonds, which far outweighs being able to do one-stop shopping for all our household needs, where the big conglomerates have everything under one roof. These big conglomerates soon become household names, because we've invested all our confidence in them, and when they go bad because of a lack of ethics in the leadership, it has a devastating effect on our confidence in people, and we develop the "all of them is bad" attitude. So when the question comes up, "Who can we trust?" The answer has to be: our original, G-d-given self. Those who have been able to maintain their humanity. Those who live in the world, but because of their strong constitution, their strong sense of ethics, they're not of the world.

If we use this approach, the problems will not go away overnight, but they won't last a season either. The human being gravitates almost without question towards G-d, and the results will be lasting, not temporary.

Again, we go to the Holy Qur'an in *sura* 2:143. Allah, in addressing the whole community, tells us, "Thus have we made of you an *Ummat* justly balanced. That ye may be witnesses over the nations and the Messenger a witness over yourselves."

Here we see both the community and the individual being addressed in this passage of scripture. The word for both comes from the same word Ummat in the Qur'an, which is from the root word, amma, which is in the singular tense, and it means to lead the way, to lead by one's own example. Then we have umma, which is in the plural tense, and which means "nation, people, the community of Muhammed, or any community that follows right guidance."

The understanding we are trying to present here is that by the individual example that was set in the life of Prophet Muhammed, we find a progressive and productive life for the community, and ultimately, for the world.

Jesus said in Biblical scripture that "one will come and lead you into all truths." And as stated earlier in this writing, whereas Jesus represented the example that Allah wanted for all mankind in their individual lives, Muhammed represented that same standard on a community level. So when Jesus talked about all truths, he was really referring to those concerns that touch our everyday life, and that G-d would send someone to be the example for those concerns: our moral concerns, our economic concerns, our political and spiritual concerns. We know that through the study of the life of Prophet Muhammed (SAWS), that even before being called to be a prophet by G-d, he was known as *El-Amin,* which means "to be trustworthy." He had a reputation of truthfulness, honesty, and respect. His word was always relied on when he gave it. When people needed to find a place to leave their valuables if they were going on a trip, or for any other reason, they would leave them with Muhammed ibn Abdullah, because they knew their valuables would be kept safe and intact, and would be found safe and secure in the same manner in which they had left them with him in the first place, when they came to retrieve them.

Later in life, he married his first wife, Lady Khadijah, a well-known and respected businesswoman. He had gone to work for her, and when she recognized how good a businessman he was and the fact that he improved her business and was a man of impeccable character, she inquired about him, and they were married.

Prophet Muhammed also set up the first Islamic government. When Allah called him to be a Prophet, the people of his home city of Mecca refused to accept him, and imposed all manner of persecution upon him and those who followed him. A delegation of men from the city of Medina who had heard of him came and swore their allegiance to him and requested that he move to their city, and this he did. Prophet Muhammed had become aware that some of the Meccans had plotted his assassination. On the night when this evil act was to be carried out, he escaped, but he made sure that the valuables he had in his possession, even those that belonged to his enemies, were returned to them safe, just as they had left them with him.

So Prophet Muhammed had to flee to Medina for his safety, and this was where the first Islamic government was established. This government respected the rights of all its citizens, be they Jews, Christians, or Muslims. Their places of business and of worship were respected, and no one was treated unjustly. Upon establishing the government, the people of Mecca still sought to kill him, so now, we see Muhammed as a military leader, not one who sent his army into battle only, but who led them into battle. At the battle of Badr, the first battle to be fought between the Muslims and the Meccans, even though the Muslims were heavily outnumbered, still they carried the day, and thus established themselves as a force to be reckoned with. It is important to note here that prisoners of war were not mistreated. In fact, they were given the opportunity to learn the religion if they wanted to. Those who were educated were released if they could teach some of the Muslims to read, and all treaties were adhered to by the Prophet and his followers, even though many times, they were broken by the enemy.

In establishing the city of Medina under Islamic law, taxes were levied, laws were established, and the Islamic government was put in motion. It must be noted here that in establishing the government, it was not done in a dictatorial manner. There were the companions of the Prophet, as well as the council of those who were from among the population of the city whose advice was sought when it came time for important decisions to be made. So, we have the three main sources of Al-Islam: the Holy Qur'an, which is the pure word of Allah, the *sunnah,* or the example of Prophet Muhammed (SAWS), and consultation, the opinions and advice of council from among the people.

When asked about the private life of the Prophet, Ayesha, his wife at a later time, responded, "He is the Qur'an walking." On regular occasions, the Prophet could be seen walking in the marketplace, shopping with his wife, or helping with household chores and just being a family man.

So we see the public and private life of Muhammed, the Prophet, in many aspects, a private and public life in which we all can identify with. In every instance, he represented the personality and the leadership that G-d ordained for all mankind. We can now see by these different aspects, what Jesus meant when he said, "One will come and lead you into all truths." Now the *Ummah* or community following that example of Prophet Muhammed then becomes the model for the rest of human society.

So then, we see in the life of Prophet Muhammed ibn Abdullah a high standard, set not only for the life of the individual, but for the community as well. Again, Allah tells us in His Holy Book, *sura* 33:21, "You have indeed in the Messenger of Allah an excellent example for him who hopes in Allah and the Final Day, and who remembers Allah much." In another Qur'anic passage, Allah tells us, "We sent thee not but as a mercy to all creatures." HQ 22:107. In the life of Muhammed (SAWS), we can see a code that he lived by, a code based on the natural urge within him to do what's right. This natural inclination towards righteousness, fueled by the divine revelation of Qur'an from Allah, established a system of principles that acted to govern his life, and assured him that he would stay on the straight path as long as he followed what G-d had ordained, and this he did.

The life of Prophet Muhammed has been studied by many scholars around the world, from a political, economical, and military standpoint, and many have attested to the fact that his life is the example for any who desires justice and righteousness.

The fact was that he, as an ordinary human being who was able to live a righteous life among the people, meant that he was a witness to the strength of human character, which we all have been given by the Creator. "We have indeed created man in the best of molds." HQ 95:4. Those who follow his example become a witness for the rest of human society in today's environment. A community that is justly balanced. The word balance is from the root word wasat, which means "middle, center, heart, medium, mediation, intercessor, agent, or intermediary." So here is a community of people not caught up in the extremes of the society. Not in religious fanaticism or worldly trends and fads. Not only that, but a community who is able to give justice, make peace, and help to arrive at decisions that will be of benefit to the whole. The heart is the seat of the mind, and thus, in most cases, is able to keep the mind in a position of justice. Not too far to the left, and not too far to the right, but is able to make balanced judgments in all aspects of life.

Allah speaks to us again in His Holy Book. "Let there arise out of you a band of people inviting to all that is good, enjoining what is right, and forbidding what is wrong: they are the ones to attain felicity."

HQ 3:104. This is a community which is not only being good, but by word and action, calling others to the right way of life.

Another branch growing out of the natural moral makeup of the human being is that of logic. Logic, or logical thinking, according to the dictionary, is "the science of correct reasoning, dealing with the criteria of valid thought; valid induction or deduction." Necessary or expected because of what has gone before.[9] (441) One of the greatest gifts G-d has given to man is that of reasoning. To be able, through logical deduction, to arrive at a logical conclusion that makes sense to the intelligent mind.

Again we go to Allah's Holy Book, where He tells us: "Glorify the name of thy Guardian-Lord most high. Who has created and further given order and proportion; who has measured. And granted guidance." **HQ 87:1-3.**

Again, we bring our attention to the two words in the above sentence, "Guardian-Lord." The Arabic meaning for these two words is "Rabb." *Rabb* means "Lord" or "Master, to have control, to raise up, or bring up, as in a child." Imam W. Deen Mohammed uses the term "Guardian-Evolver. One who watches over creation from its earliest existence until it reaches it's fullest potential." (9) This reference is to all creation, because G-d not only gives life, but He nourishes and sustains that life as it develops.

Now, because the human being has been given the faculty of reason, he has the potential for unlimited growth and development. Allah continues to give guidance and thus allows the human being to have dominion over this great creation so that it can be put to use for the advancement of mankind. The word evolve refers to the development of those mental faculties that Allah has given us so that we can grow from a lower state of human existence, to a higher state of human existence.

The Arabic root word for order and proportion is sawiy which means "straight; right, correct, proper, unimpaired, intact, sound." The root word for measured is qadr which means "to decree, ordain, decide, to possess strength, power, be in a position to do something, quantity, measure." The root word for guidance is hudan, which means "to lead on the right way, to guide or show, rightly guided, divine guidance."

Allah is telling us here that He has created the nature of the human being and has made integrity a natural part of our human makeup. The words sawiy and integrity are one in their meanings. So now we see that not only has Allah given us a most excellent nature, but He has given us the natural strength to resist the negative influences of society. Allah already knows what we as human beings need, and just how much we need in terms of strength and power, and as such, He has already measured it out to us. We know that we will get weak and run short of this power as we go through the trials and tribulations of life, but Allah in His mercy has not only also given us the guidance we need in our own selves in terms of our conscience, which tells us when we're going wrong, but we also have access to our Lord through the five daily prayers that is a part of the Islamic faith, so that we may ask for the divine guidance that we need, and to keep on giving us the strength that we need to meet the challenges of life, regardless of how difficult they may get. And then, we also have the human example in Prophet Muhammed, who has kept the nature given to him by Allah, intact, sound, and unimpaired.

In another *sura,* G-d tells us that the creation of the sun, moon, and stars are a bigger creation than that of man, and they obey the command of their Guardian-Lord. But since G-d has given man the faculty of reason, man is allowed to use his intelligence, his sense of reasoning and deduction to study the creation, and man has found that as a result of his examinations and deductions, he has found that all creation is one. That is to say that all creation is made from the same substance. The objects we see in space, the plants we have here on earth, the animals and mankind, all are created from one creation. But the human being has been made to not only fit in that creation, he has been given the potential to be the "crown of creation." (9)

Man has reasoned that because all creation is one, then all creation is interdependent. In understanding this term "interdependency," we need only to reflect on how the moon, with no light of it's own, reflects the rays of the sun, and how the plants depend on the sun and the rain for growth, and the animals, including human beings, depend on plants and animals for life. So we can see that all creation is dependent on each other for its continuance. The vitamins, the minerals, proteins, etc. we get from our consumption of these things are not foreign to our bodies, but they fit right in, and help to sustain us.

Only Allah stands clear of needing anything for His survival. "Allah! There is no G-d but He,—the Living, Self-subsisting, Supporter of all, no slumber can seize Him nor sleep. His are all things in the heavens and on earth. Who is there can intercede in His presence except as He permitteth? He knoweth what (appeareth to His creatures as) Before or After or Behind them. Nor shall they compass aught of His knowledge except as He willeth. His Throne doth extend over the heavens and the earth, and He feeleth no fatigue in guarding and preserving them: for He is the Most High, the Supreme (in glory)." **HQ 2:255. Allah, free of all wants, worthy of all praise.**

We arrive at this Logic because if everything else is interdependent, then naturally, the force that created it was already existing before its creation. And since all creation operates in an orderly manner, the rising of the sun in the east by day, and the moon by night, the changes of the seasons during the course of the year, the habits of the wildlife, the signs we see in our own human makeup, and other changes in the natural phenomena, these things tell us that there has to be a life force behind it. The orderly manner in which the universal creation operates on tells us that there is intelligence behind it, and so by induction and deduction, we arrive at the logical conclusion that that intelligence is G-d.

We have a good example of Prophet Abraham in *sura* 6:7479. We see how he came to use his sense of reasoning to arrive at a logical **conclusion in his belief and worship of the one G-d.** "Lo! Abraham said to his father Azar: Taketh thou idols for gods? I see thee and thy people in manifest error. So also did we show Abraham the power and the laws of the heavens and the earth so that he might with understanding have certitude. When the night covered him over, he saw a star: he said: "This is my Lord." But when it set, he said, "I love not those that set." When he saw the moon rising in splendor, he said, "This is my Lord." But when the moon set, he said: "Unless my Lord guide me, I shall surely be among those who go astray." When he saw the sun rising (in splendor,) he said, "This is my Lord; this is the greatest (of all)." But when the sun set, he said: "O my people! I am indeed free from your guilt of giving partners to Allah. For me, I have set my face firmly and truly, towards Him who created the heavens and the earth, and never shall I give partners to Allah." **So we have an excellent example in the Prophet Abraham in the study of the natural creation, and how it brings us back to the Creator through** reason **and** logic. **All creation, regardless of how magnificent it may be, comes and goes; only Allah is ever present.** "And call not, besides Allah, on another god. There is no G-d but He. Everything (that exist) will parish except His Face. To Him belongs the command, and to Him will ye (all) be brought back." **HQ 28:88. So again we say that everything is relative, or dependent; only Allah is independent.**

According to the dictionary, in a brief overview of the theory of relativity developed by Albert Einstein in two theories, we find that as it relates to physics, the fact, principle, or theory of the relative, rather than the absolute character of motion, velocity, mass, etc., and the interdependence of time, matter, and space: the theory includes the statement that: 1) motion is relative, not absolute; 2) the velocity of light is constant; 3) the mass of a body in motion varies with the velocity; 4) space and time are interdependent and form a four-dimensional continuum.

We see the abstract and the apparent being addressed here in terms of light and its impact on objects. The motion of the earth as a mass, as well as of other heavenly bodies, are dependent on the rays or the light of the sun. That light must be constant in terms of time, speed, and amount at all times in order for that balance to be maintained. That is to say that different heavenly bodies, according to their distance from the sun, get varying amounts of light; but what is important is that, whatever amount of light it is that they receive must remain constant at all times, so that each body travels at its own speed. To say that space and time are interdependent is to say that they both exist at one and the same time in the same place. The four dimensions of the continuum form the motivation of that continuum, and keep it moving forward.

In an attempt to explain Dr. Einstein's theory in simple terms, as it relates to the human being, thus making the law of relativity even clearer, we must remember that the law of physics tells us that no two objects can occupy the same place at the same time. The light of the sun is the intelligent understanding we get from revelation of G-d through His prophets. The light is always there, thus, it is constant and, like the heavenly bodies, some of us are a greater distance from that light, thus our speed in terms of our understanding is not as great in some of us as human beings as it is in others. But unlike the planets, however, we are thinking human beings, and we are able to change our circumstances because we can get closer to the light, thus increasing our speed or human worth.

The word "continuum" means something that is absolutely continuous and homogeneous, of which no distinction of content can be affirmed, except by reference to something else. Something in which a fundamental, common character is discernible amid a series of insensible or indefinite variations. In this explanation, continuum represents the human mind or intellect.

Now we know that the brain waves of the mind are continuous, but in the absence of creative or critical thought, nothing worthy of being labeled "productive content" can be distinguished, and so not only is that mind lifeless in terms of productivity and the advancement of real human development, but it becomes subject to manipulation, thus losing all its individuality and just becoming part of the "melting pot," which means all citizens who, although are of varying languages and nationalities, are of like minds because many have gotten caught up in the trends of the society, or the series of insensible or definite man-made variations.

In today's environment, we are overwhelmed by this pop culture that takes us from one extreme to another, from meaningless religious rituals to self and community destruction. It is this kind of thinking that keeps the masses under the control of those who wish to maintain material and political control of the society. This can only happen to those whose minds are a blank space, with time on their hands, just waiting to be used by someone else, for if you don't use yourself, someone else will use you. The only thing that will be on your mind is keeping up with the next fad or trend, finding the next sexual encounter or party so as to unleash your wild emotions, and to generally go with the flow.

But unlike the brain-dead individual, the conscious person who is aware of the confused state of affairs surrounding him is still able to travel under his own G-d-given light without much difficulty. We know that the four primary motivations that make up the nature of the human being are our moral, economic, political, and spiritual nature. Progress in these areas is the distinguishing mark that affirms the content of our productive human life.

As we get closer to the light of revelation, we begin to see how we are supposed to use our intellect in the advancement of humankind. In other words, just as we see the light of the physical sun strike the inanimate objects and put them in motion, so then, man must look at his inner self, which is a bigger creation than his physical self, and as the light of intelligent understanding impacts the mind of man, then he is put in motion for human progress. All creation is in a state of inertia, except the human being. Those parts which are not, such as animal life, are governed by their instinct.

And so the inner life, the higher life, the moral and spiritual life of the human being begins to develop as we accept G-d's word and take on His attributes. We then become more intelligent, compassionate, rational, etc., because we then understand that just as Allah created the outside world, that same process takes place within the person. The, more or less, light or knowledge received by that person determines the speed of that person's growth.

The stronger that person becomes in his relationship with his Creator, he realizes that he is not contained by anything, except the word of the Creator. Therefore he is able to grow to his full potential in all dimensions of life, morally, economically, politically, and spiritually.

So this is logical-rational thinking, the understanding that all things are relative, the seen and the unseen. The existence of all life is dependent upon the Creator who is independent, absolute, and eternal. "That is Allah, your Lord! There is no G-d but He, the Creator of all things; then worship ye Him; and He has power to dispose of all affairs. No vision can grasp Him, but His grasp is over all vision; He is above all comprehension, yet is aquatinted with all things." **HQ 6:102103.**

There is a law for human progress and that law is moral law. Logic tells us that when we follow immoral, unintelligent thinking in an environment of relativity, we should know that the only results that will come back to us are negative results. This law is already clocked into the universal order of things and it was put there by Allah not to punish us, for we punish ourselves. It was put there for the guidance of human beings, for the purpose of helping us to maintain our humanity, and guide us back to our Creator. So this is logic, the faculty of rational thought given to us by Allah, and when used right, it makes man the "Crown of Creation."

We now come to one more branch growing from the tree of moral stability in the nature of the human being. That branch is called integrity. Integrity, as stated before in this writing, has the same meaning as the Arabic word sawiy, which is used for the order and proportion that's put in the natural human makeup by Allah. According to the dictionary, the word integrity means "that which is unimpaired; soundness, uprightness, honesty, and sincerity; wholeness." Again we go to Allah's Holy Book, where He says in referring to His Prophet Muhammed, "And surely thou hast sublime morals." HQ 68:4. And in another verse, Allah says of His Messenger, "We have not sent thee but as a (Messenger) to all mankind, giving them glad tidings, and warning them (against sin), but most men know not." HQ 36:28.

We see here that this very high elevation of character and moral development puts us right back in touch with the very foundation of our original nature given to us by Allah. The word Muslim, in it's literal definition, means the "willing submission of one's will to G-d." This tells us then that the whole of creation is Muslim. The sun as it rises in the east and sets in the west, the on-time changes of the seasons, the beasts of the fields as they carry out the various lifestyles given to them by the Creator. All do what G-d has ordained them to do, so all creation is Muslim. So it goes then that Muslim is the nature of all creation.

Special reference is made to the human being because the human being has been given his own volition. Unlike all other creation, the human being is the only one that has been given a choice in the matter. The better human being we are is determined by the degree we submit our wills to Allah. We may call ourselves Jews, Christians, Catholics, atheist, or some other name, but we are Muslim by nature, and other than Muslim by orientation. This type of character was present in the nature of Prophet Muhammed when G-d revealed the Holy Qur'an to him. After its revelation and application, we see Allah refer to him as a mercy to all mankind. A beautiful pattern of conduct for any whose hope is in Allah and in the final day. One who has sublime morals. To be a mercy for all mankind is to teach the word of G-d, as well as to be that example, and Prophet Muhammed was both. So we grow and we struggle to keep the nature whole, intact, and unblemished. In our struggles, sometimes we make wrong decisions and many mistakes, but as long as the nature is inclined toward Allah, it is still unimpaired. This speaks of mercy of Allah, for He is oft returning, most merciful.

In the book by the Christian author, Michael H. Hart entitled, *The 100—A Ranking of the Most Influential Persons in History,* he cites Prophet Muhammed as being number one.19 *(Hart 4)* His reason for placing the Prophet in the number one position is based mainly on two principle decisions. First of all, Prophet Muhammed played a far more important role in the development of Islam than Prophet Jesus played in the development of Christianity. Although Prophet Jesus was responsible for the main ethical and moral precepts of Christianity, it was St. Paul who was the main developer of Christianity theology, its principal proselytizer, and the author of a large portion of the New Testament.

It was Prophet Muhammed who was both responsible for the theology of Islam and its ethical and moral principles. It was Prophet Muhammed who spread the faith and set the example for its adherents to follow. 19 (39) As a matter of fact, the two primary sources of the Islamic faith are first, the Holy Qur'an, the pure revelation from Allah, and secondly, the life example of Prophet Muhammed. In other words, it was Muhammed who received the revelation, and it was Muhammed who set the example for how it was to be carried out. As the revelations came to the Prophet, it was revealed on his heart, and committed verbatim to memory. It was also written down, and has never been changed. Therefore today, the Holy Qur'an is intact, just as it was during the lifetime of the Prophet. No such compilation of the teachings of Prophet Jesus has survived. It is probable that the relative influence of Muhammed on Islam has been larger than the influence on Christianity of Jesus and St. Paul combined. Muhammed, unlike Jesus, was a secular leader as well. In fact, as the driving force behind the Muslim conquest, he may as well rank as the most influential political leader of all times.[19] (39)

In today's world, those who continue to follow ethical business practices follow the standards set by Muhammed, the Prophet. It was Prophet Muhammed who set the standard for the total life of the human being all over the world. He not only brought the spiritual teachings of the Holy Qur'an, but in fulfilling the prophecy of Jesus Christ, who said in Biblical scripture, "One will come to lead you in all truths," he established the standard for a successful family and community life, the moral life, the business, political, and spiritual life, and even set the example for right conduct in the military. He became the model for progress in all aspects of human development. Again G-d says of him in His Holy Book, "Thou standest on an exalted standard of character." Qur'an 68:4

So we see the life of the Prophet as the example for anyone who wants to see decency and care for real life established. From a child, with his basic moral instincts intact and unimpaired, he grew into a man of flawless character and integrity, and was chosen by G-d to be the leader of the world. He was not chosen for his education, for he was unlettered, nor for his wealth, he had none, nor for his military might, for he had no army. He was chosen because he kept his original nature from G-d whole. Thus, Allah found a solid foundation for His revelation, and it was that revelation that kept the nature intact and evolved it to the level of the "Crown of Creation."

And just as Muhammed, the Prophet, was that example, that same responsibility falls on all of us who say we believe in G-d. We all have the same nature as Prophet Muhammed. "Muhammed is no more than a Messenger: many were the Messengers that passed away before him." HQ 3:144 In another place we read, "Muhammed is a man just like you." So again, we see that we all have that same human potential, and as stated before, even though we make mistakes, as long as our nature inclines towards G-d, we remain unimpaired. We all have the seed; it just has to be cultivated, nurtured, and cherished, as our Lord has cultivated, nourished, and cherished us so that we may grow to our fullest potential and be of service to mankind. That is the duty of us all, to serve mankind. So then, Allah has blessed us all with not only the example of the Prophets, but we also have our own conscience to warn us against wrongdoing, and if we follow it, we keep the nature whole, and the negative influences of the society will have little effect on us. Thus, every human being can grow from having a childlike mentality to being a person of influence and responsibility. Our vision becomes broader as we grow in the direction intended for us by Allah. Virtue, Ethics, Logic, Integrity, these are just a few of the examples of the branches growing out of the tree of Morality. As it says in the words of that old Christian spiritual, "Just like a tree that's planted by the water, we shall not be moved."

So then, now we see the source of the motivation behind the great rulers of Africa as they established sound governments and educational systems, and raised Africa to the highest position of excellence it had achieved before slavery. Likewise, we see the source of the inspiration behind the progress of Spain, where the epitome of democracy was established. The arts and the sciences were brought back to life. The study of the heavenly bodies, poetry, literature, agriculture, mathematics, medicine, and all that makes life worth living, were brought back to life and spilled over into the broader European civilization, and thus we have the European Renaissance. The whole world has come alive and is now on a steady path of progress.

We can better understand now why the Christian author chose Muhammed as the number one most influential person in the history of mankind, because he was the man whom G-d chose to bring enlightenment to the world because he kept his character intact.

Now with all these aspects of our lives intact, we find ourselves on a new level of consciousness. No longer are we seeing with just the physical eye, we now have a sense of moral vision. That is to say that now, we just don't see, we also see into. Now we see the need to extend ourselves, because all the levels of moral excellence we've grown into is now applied to other aspects of our lives. Our moral foundation has graduated to all these different levels of growth and development, and we now see the importance of developing other aspects of our lives. Economic and political matters now come into our new mode of thinking.

It is considered a sin and a moral flaw in the character of a people to stay in the position of a beggar and a protester, especially when we know that our ancestors have already set the example we need for us to make progress for ourselves. We must understand that an economic foundation is vital for any people who want to maintain their own self-respect, as well as have the respect of others. It is shameful for a man to ask another man to feed and clothe his family, and that's exactly what we're doing, as long as we remain outside the world of commerce. We're not talking here about the faddish, trendy type of business mentality that we see in the entertainment world that's fueled by the influences of this pop culture.

When we look around, we see the role models that are held up in the media before our children, and the devastating effect this pop culture has had on our communities. Even though those who are involved in it are making money, they are doing it at the expense of our future generation. The mentality that we see in much of the entertainment world is, for the most part, much to blame for the downfall and the degradation of the African-American community. Many of our young people, following the example they see in the music and movie industries, have lost all sense of responsibility. They have no desire to work in any real employment, and those who dream of getting into the entertainment business and can't usually end up trying to mimic the lifestyle by dealing drugs, or getting into other negative activities. At any rate, their lives are virtually lost because it's too hard to get back.

We have determined that the kind of business activities that we see many of our people getting into the entertainment world, which is based on the pop culture mentality, can only hurt our people more because of the images and role models they present. There is no foundation or stability in it, and enough of that kind of life is enough. Let me stop here and say that this is not a blanket condemnation of the entertainment industry, because that same industry can be turned around and made to work to uplift the people of the communities they claim to serve, and in many instances, they have done so, as in by highlighting the disenfranchisement of the black community during the Civil Rights Movement, documentary films on the plight of other people around the world, support for environmental causes, and generally sponsored and supported good and positive causes around the world. And there are people in the entertainment industry who do great and wonderful things to uplift fallen society. Actors, actresses, playwrights, singers, producers, comedians, etc. So this critique is not a blanket condemnation of the media, for indeed, the media has played life saving roles in terms of human advancement. My point is that African-Americans must also realize it's power and importance in terms of the positive influence it can have on the thinking of the people, and as a result, start to control our own. As stated before, if we want our story to be told right, we have to be the ones to tell it.

Since it is the African-Americans and Latino communities who have been most adversely affected by these images in that business, those who are already in the business should, either in their own communities or wherever possible, come together with each other, and pool their resources and start or buy their own television and radio stations so that they can become the primary influence for their own people. They should, however, realize that if their goal is just for profit, they may as well continue on doing what they are already doing. But if the intent is not for profit only, but to raise the level of dignity and pride in the people as well, they should realize that projects with a positive spin on them in a world of negative relativity will take a little time, but they will be successful. The concern cannot be for winning an Oscar, a Grammy, or a Music Award, for these awards are based on the value system designed by those who are already a part of the current trend of things. The concern has to be for saving the lives of our future generations. Our history is much too rich and we have too much to draw from to present to our youth nothing but contempt, in the form of vulgar expressions of dance, language in music that is based entirely on sex, violence, and disrespect, and movies that have absolutely nothing redeeming about them at all. What is so tragic is that we're doing it to ourselves. But then, this is the natural results when we take on the values of others.

Now as we say, we can't blame it on the white man, for we must look within ourselves for the cause and the solution to the problem. Like anybody else, those who start these kinds businesses may have to start small and grow big, but the concern has to be the preservation of the next generation. As stated before, in looking back on the history of the African-American community, some of the greatest heroes of all times can be found, and in any aspect of life. Western, comedy, drama, documentary, whatever you want to make a movie about, you will find a life or an event in black history to base it upon.

We don't have to use this garbage they give us in this society, and we don't have to adhere to their standards. We don't have to adopt their values. Oh my G-d! Why have we stooped so low and still come away with nothing? We don't have to beg and force our way on others to make them accept us in their movies and in their sitcoms. When we do this, we leave ourselves at the mercy of those in control; therefore, we are forced to accept just what we are given. Most of the times, we are depicted as thugs or drug users or dealers, as gays, or some brother trying to play a game on his woman for sex or money. Our women are presented in such a way that they are looked upon with total disrespect in the eyes of the world. Even those of us who are depicted in positions of authority have no authority at all, and our presence usually end up being of no positive or significant influence at all. Those African-Americans who do produce movies have taken on the values of others to the point that they even depict us as thugs and drug users, shooting and killing each other. Our only concern is to be *Juiced* and *Strapped,* which makes us more of a *Menace to the Society,* and those of our youth who watch this junk can never get *Above the Rim* of the negative environment they're in because they are too busy trying to become what they see on the silver screen. Our idea of *Higher Learning* is to be a member of *The Players' Club*. This is *Foolish,* because we become *Caught Up,* and too many times, end up in no-way-out situations. The real *Poetic Justice* would be if we could stop *Waiting to Exhale* this degrading kind of thinking that helps to keep our people enslaved, and give them the kind of entertainment that will not only entertain, but would add to their positive growth and development. It can be done, and we must do it!

Any leadership that continues to degrade us as a people through a campaign of begging, protesting, and dependency has to be rejected if we are ever going to be counted as a people of worth. What we've become as a result of our participation in today's entertainment puts us in a position that is worse than the days of *Amos and Andy.* At lease in those days, the whole community wasn't encouraged to act like a fool. Any leader that encourages his people to get into something they have no control over is no leader at all. If those who are recognized in business and those who we call leaders would talk loud enough, and often enough, putting the onus on us for the determination of our future, we will begin to see a change in the thinking of our communities, in both young and old. From there, we follow up the talk with productivity, and in this way, we will truly become the driving force in the minds of our next generation.

When we do for self, we're not forced to play degrading roles that take away our dignity. To the contrary, we're able to exercise our own creativity, and our own imagination. We will be successful because our goal will be different, to wit, save and preserve our dignity, not win an Oscar. Soon, this kind of positive thinking will catch on. All we need to do is promote the positive as opposed to the negative, and success will soon come. The same instrument that lead society away from dignity can be used to lead society back to dignity.

We hear the expression that the music and the movies are expressions of real life. I say that they are about a life that has been imposed upon the African-American community in particular, and on the broader society in general. What we call life in the streets today is an imposed lifestyle. There has never been a time in the history of the African-American community or in the general society when life has meant so little. Although we know and realize that there has always been crime, it has never been to this level. Our communities and places of learning have never been flooded with blood, as what we're seeing in America today. We have never had to deal with incurable sexually transmitted diseases on a scale of what we're dealing with today. There have never been so much widespread apathy and selfishness in the common person as we are witnessing today. The reason is that the media, through its promotion of this pop culture, has made sex the topic of most conversations, and the lifetime goal of the masses, and our value system has become so blurred that we have begun to place material accomplishments over our concern for real humanity. There are other reasons as well, but we keep saying that the media is a good place to start in setting society back on the right path for positive human growth and development. So no, we say that music and movies do not imitate life, but rather they influence much of what we see in the society today.

We must get our own life back, and it's going to take more than just playing positive roles in music and movies. When members of our communities, both young and old, know that there are brothers and sisters who own their own television and movie properties and they are promoting that which is good for the society, and our leaders begin to push and promote that endeavor, then we will see progress come.

We have to cease making movies based on the mentality we get from others. As stated before, we are the most creative people on earth, and we must trust our own talents and imagination. Let us look into our own history and find the heroes we need. Not just in slavery, but in independent life as well. Even in today's world, we have heroes. The brother or sister who is living a positive life and contributing to the positive growth and development of human society. Those who are in the forefront of space travel, economic and community development, or just the everyday brother and sister who are struggling to raise their families and be a positive example in their community. We have had our fill of these programs that do nothing but depict our communities as dope-ridden areas to live in, when this is just not the case. We are just fed up. We must realize that we have to take charge of our own future. It's our story, so who can tell it better than us? The entertainment industry can be good to us because it gets the attention of our young and old members alike. Those who are in it and own a part of it can make a world of difference, but as stated before, the goal has to be more that just profits, and "living down" to the standards of today's society.

Many of our African-American entertainers are very rich. The question is, how much money do you need before you realize that it's time to turn the thinking of our youth around, and that you are a key in that effort? Please allow me to propound something here in terms of a direction. We start small, but we think big. Make our own movies using the major black entertainers on the scene today. Get the support of our ministers, community leaders, and others. These projects can be shipped to our churches, mosque, and community centers around the country, as opposed to the movie houses. Charge the usual fee to get in, and with good advertisement as we do in other projects, in time, this will grow, and the thinking of our young will changed from negative to positive. These movies should be exciting and entertaining. They don't have to be exact history, but they can be based on historical events, such as Brother Spike Lee's *Malcolm X,* with Brother Denzel Washington, the *Gladiator,* with Brother Russell Crow, or *The Patriot,* with Brother Mel Gibson. Again, everyone involved should remember that the goal is not for profits alone; the goal is to save our future generations. Documentaries can be made based on the real lives of the ancestors. The main street in our own communities can be the Broadway that our young playwrights will aspire to. Just like we march and protest against police brutality and other issues, let us use that same energy and participation to support these kinds of positive projects. Again, we say these projects must be free from profanity and vulgarity, etc.

As we continue to look in the direction that we as a community should go in order to achieve true dignity and respect, our attention should be focused on other aspects of the business world as well. Those kinds of businesses that provide employment not for African-Americans only, but which will represent stability in the community as a whole. It is time we got on with the more substantial types of business investments that will produce the kinds of products used for world consumption. Sound business investments and developments will produce strong families and stable communities and schools. We will begin to see a new respect for life take form. The problem of racism as we know it today will begin to fade because not only will others begin to see us as a people with strong moral principles, but also as a people who are in control of our own neighborhoods. They will see us not only providing jobs for our own people, but for many of them as well.

When we as African-Americans become job developers and job providers, we open up a whole new outlet for the progress of the society. That is due to the fact that instead of being a people that's always looking for work, we have now become a resource, sharing in the responsibility of bearing the burden of the society, instead of being a part of that burden. We need to see ourselves establishing manufacturing plants for the many needs of the society, the imports and exports of goods and services. Construction companies, educational centers, hospitals, clinics, pharmacies, banks, credit unions, law offices, grocery stores insurance companies, and other types of businesses that add to the upliftment of our communities. Now some may say that we already have some of these types of businesses, and this is true, but we have nothing even remotely close to what we should have to achieve true freedom and respect, and as a community, we must support these businesses, just as we support those we see in existence now.

And just as equally important, those who become successful in business have to, in turn, give back to the community that raised them. We must remember that just because some of us are able to become successful, we should never forget that we didn't get there on our own. We must see the community or the environment that we came from as the womb that shaped and molded our thinking, our character, our being, some good and some bad, but all being a part of what pushed us along the road to progressive human development. Never ever forget that we owe the community we come from.

It is also imperative that we keep in mind that establishment must come based on the seed of moral principles. Those branches that we discussed earlier in this writing; Virtue, Ethics, Logic, Integrity, etc. must be the foundation of any successful movement.

When we look at the accomplishments our ancestors made, and when we understand the fact that regardless of the obstacles they faced, they still maintained their dignity. "We must Rewrite the History." This means that we are not just to settle for high-paying jobs in other people's businesses, but we are to be the owners and operators of our own. This kind of thinking will establish us as a respected people in the society of man. We must see ourselves as a participant in every aspect of the global economy. Now we can see what Booker T., Carter G., and Mary McLeod were talking about. We can now appreciate the advice given by Madam C. J., Malcolm, and Elijah. We see ourselves participating in sound economics not just for profits only, but just as important, to establish a value system that respects the nature given to man by Allah.

This economic development also has other far-reaching advantages. Not only are we able to employ ourselves and others, but now we can see a reduction in crime in our communities. The financial burden on all levels of government is lessened because now, we have a whole new nation, contributing to the stability of the economy. Inflation and interest rates are reduced; businesses do not have to have as much security installations so the price of merchandise shouldn't be as great. So there are all kinds of advantages that work for the good of the whole when we see a whole segment of society become part of the employers, whereas in the past, we were the employees. Many of the moral dilemma that we find society faced with, such as abortion, gun control, stress, homelessness, and the general day-to-day routine of survival begin to disappear.

This is because people are now seeing themselves in a new light. A new self-awareness has come into play. Standards of dignity are being set that will never again be reduced. The human potential is able to grow in an atmosphere that is conducive to positive growth and development. Racial conflict is now reduced because we are no longer filling up the nation's jails and prisons. Instead, we are viewed as a people of power, respect, and dignity, on the same level with others. This will be the case wherever we go as individuals or in groups; people will know that we represent a community formed in dignity. The same respect accorded to others will be accorded to us, and in cases where it's not, we won't have to protest, march, and demonstrate. We won't have to employ outdated tactics of the sixties because we will be in positions of influence and authority, but these high positions we occupy won't be just token positions where, even though we have them, we're afraid to act with justice, because someone else has put us there. Rather, we will be in a position that came about as a result of our own skills and merits, and we will act without being afraid of anyone, and so we will be able to deal in a meaningful way with injustice on any level.

Also, our influence becomes global in terms of our being able to deal with the injustices done to our people, as well as to others.

Our lobbying power will be as great as anybody else's, but our rise to moral, economic, and social dignity will speak for us also. This is what our ancestors fought and died for, and this level and beyond is what they want to see in us.

Again we hear the words of the great Liberator, Frederick Douglass: "We must become mechanics as well as ministers; we must build as well as live in houses; we must make as well as use furniture; we must construct bridges as well as pass over them, before we can properly live or be respected by our follow man. We need mechanics as well as ministers. We need workers in iron, clay, and leather ... To live here, as we ought, we must fasten ourselves to our fellow countrymen through their everyday cardinal wants. We must not only be able to black the boot, we must make them."[2] **(30)**

So again, we hear the words of our ancestors urging us on to greater levels of growth and independence. Just as others have studied us and determined our wants and needs, so like wise, we have to get into the race for productivity and wealth as they have. The ancestors don't want us to just memorize their words and deeds, they want us to put them into action. We must establish the economic life, free from all the pulls of the negative influences that we've suffered from in the past. Those who keep crying out for affirmative action will get more positive results if they turn their attention inward to their own abilities to do for self. Not only should the cry be for economic establishment in our own communities, the cry also has to be just as loud for support of those African-American businesses. Black people will pass right by black businesses and travel twice as far to spend their money on others, and that's not only a sin, it's a low-down dirty shame. We can always find an excuse not to patronize self. The price is too high or it's too far to travel to; any excuse will do. We are the only people that think with this negative mentality towards our own people.

I remember on several occasions when I was a door-to-door salesman selling fish in San Francisco. I would knock on the Chinese door, and they would refuse to buy my fish because they shop in Chinatown with their own people. I remember one lady who didn't have a car, so she had to use public transportation to get downtown to Chinatown; she lived in the Mission District, which was quite far from where she needed to go to shop. Also, my fish was only 99 cents a pound. Even though I offered her the convenience of bringing the fish to her door, as well as selling it to her for less, she still chose to inconvenience herself by catching the bus, going out of her way to shop with her own. Now when I thought about the situation, I couldn't get mad. I was just amazed as I realized that this was just a small showing of the pride in a people in their rise to economic dignity, and I longed for the day when my people would exercise that same loyalty to our own.

I remember reading story from a book, and I'm not sure of the title, but I think it's *Why We Declined*, or something to that effect. I forgot the name of the author also, but the story was about a master who had sent his servant to buy some oil. He gave the servant the usual amount of money for the purchase, and the servant set off to make the purchase. Upon his return, he gave his master not only the oil, but also more change back than usual. So the master inquired of him the reason for so much change. The servant replied that he found out about another store that sold the same oil at a cheaper price, so in seeking to please his master by saving him more money, he bought the oil at the new store. At this news, the master became very upset and told the servant to return the oil, get his money back, and go and spend it with his own, for saving money is not the most important objective, but supporting each other was, for this is what keeps us strong as a community. Now in my own opinion, this is the epitome of affirmative action. We have people that will bus their children across town to attend another school, which is probably not going to do any more for them than the school they are leaving, but won't drive across town or even around the corner to spend their money with a black business establishment. This is one the primary reasons why we stay weak as a people. Dear people, we must realize that if we are ever going to rise as a people, it must be from our own exertions. This theme must be echoed by those of our people who are in positions of visibility, whether it's in church, political, media, or community leadership. All those who are in positions where our masses look up to should be shouting not only the "Double Duty Dollar" slogan, but that dollar should pass through the black community hundreds of times before leaving it. Now please, let me be absolutely clear on this point. I am not by any means advocating the boycott of any other people's businesses. What I am advocating is that the best way for us as a people to rise is to encourage positive business development, and for us to support those business developments. That's affirmative action in its best form.

The Honorable Elijah Muhammed gave the command years ago in a public speech to the African-American community. He said, "Up, You Mighty Nation, You Can Accomplish What You Will!" So again, we can see the responsibility for our success is being put squarely on our shoulders. The operative word in this statement by the Honorable Elijah Muhammed is "Will." This refers to the ability of the people to think and reason. It's telling us that we can use our creativity just like others can, and with the right resources in place, we can WILL ourselves to levels of respect in this society. We must come out of inertia and put our WILL power to work, to put our intelligence to work. In today's society, there have been such a gross lack of vision in the leadership that it has left the people wandering in the dark as to what direction we as a people need to take in order to raise ourselves to a new level of dignity and respect, not only in our own eyes, but in the eyes of the greater society as well.

The mark of enlightened leadership is to impart real knowledge to the masses so they will be in charge of their own lives. For a leader to continue to use outdated tactics while blaming others for the downfall of our people in this age of education and opportunity is to keep the masses in a mentality of slavery so that leader can maintain his position of recognition in the eyes of the public. This is one of the great flaws we alluded to earlier when referring to W. E. B. DuBois' idea of the Talented Tenth.

The dire condition of the African-American community, and indeed that of the total society, has to have leadership that emanates from a flawless and selfless character. That is to say that the leader has to have the concerns of the people genuinely at heart. Since we as a society have been brought away from G-d and are suffering from a famine of knowledge, then just like when G-d blessed society centuries ago with enlightenment for its own survival, so leadership have to come from G-d today as well, and even more so, because the times we live in today are far more serious than in times gone by.

We now stand at the epoch of a new leadership that's speaking to the concerns of the people, both locally and globally. The message is plain and simple, based on the revelation of scripture received by all the prophets of G-d and made applicable to problems we see in the society today. We're not talking about someone staying in the lives of the people, telling them what and when to do things, but rather a voice that's recognized as a voice of wisdom and knowledge and those who hear it will be able to apply it in their own situation. Imam W. Deen Mohammed's wisdom has on many occasions been accepted by many heads of state, and he has not only brought respect to his own faith, but he has also reawakened the leadership of other faiths, thus reawakening the consciousness of the masses.

The mark of a true leader can be seen in the growth and development of a people who, before, didn't know they could be master over themselves. A people who, after being under the teachings of that leader, are now able to find their own way in the world by the light of their own vision. Imam W. Deen Mohammed is the only leader today where the message of both the ancestors and the prophets can be heard in his voice. At a glance, you will be able to realize that he condones what Allah condones, and condemns what Allah condemns. He teaches that regardless of what the popular opinion in the society is, the word of G-d has to be the motivating force in the life of the individual. People have to be trusted with the knowledge and wisdom to be able to manage their own lives. Once knowledge is given to a person, and that person has been brought into the knowledge of their own relationship with Allah, then that individual becomes responsible for himself. So then we say that the job of a leader is to build leadership in the individual and then that individual is to become responsible for the positive advancement of his communities by bringing enlightenment, thereby giving everybody the right to the tree of life.

The mark of a true leader is to tell people where they are wrong as well. Many of those who we call leaders seem to make excuses for the people, even in some situations where the people are wrong. As leaders, we cannot support an idea simply because it's popular with the people. The people have to be told that they're responsible for themselves, especially in the black community, and the way to make ourselves responsible for ourselves is to identify the weaknesses we have within ourselves. We can no longer continue to blame others for our continued regression. As we have heard in the message of the great Frederick Douglass, to wit; "Our destiny is largely in our own hands, others may clear the road for us, but we must go forward, or be left behind in the race of life."[2] (28) Let us understand that America promises her citizens nothing but opportunity for their productive lives. The Ku Klux Klan, Jim Crowism and the like are no longer factors in terms of being obstacles for our progress. We even see those who committed crimes during the Civil Rights era being brought to justice, not only in those states where these crimes were committed, but by the people from those states as well. So the road to true Freedom, Justice, and Equality is wide open. All we need to do is step on it and go forward.

When we hear the language of Imam W. Deen Mohammed, it is the message of the ancestors being repeated. We see no other voice on the American scene today articulating the same message as the ancestors', a message that is appropriate for all times and generations. The message is one of moral stability and independent thinking. It is a message of selfhood connected with an unshakable bond with the Creator. It is a message that is calling us to a responsibility to do for self. Also along with that message of self-responsibility, the voice of moral reasoning is coming back to life, not only for the sake of America, but also for the world. Now because of that great leadership in America, not only for the African-American communities, but throughout various communities in America, that same message is being echoed, not only by Muslims, but by others who have heard the message; therefore, we see a new awakening of people of all faiths, and slowly but surely, we see a return to those values that has brought us thus far as a nation.

Let us again stress the point that leadership is not about someone coming into a community every time there's a crisis, or a report of some police brutality, or a problem in the school system, stirring up the emotions of the local people and grabbing the attention of the media, and then leaving the area in worse shape than it was before they came. Leadership is more about making the people aware of the knowledge they already possess within themselves, and what they need to do to effect change that will make the life of the community better. It is time out now for us to keep making excuses for ourselves. It is time out now that we stop telling ourselves that we don't have the intelligence that others have, so we are doomed to a life of protest, dependency, and begging.

So again, we hear the echo of the ancestors as they urge us, push us, force us on to productive life. Telling us that though they made great strides and achievements in their own lifetimes, we are to view them and their accomplishments as signs of what we can do. They are telling us that we are to surpass them. They were and still are the greatest. But we are greater in terms of what we can do, and those who come after us will be greater than us in terms of what they can do. "We Must Rewrite the History." In the words of the great playwright, Sister Lorraine Hansberry, to us; "Perhaps we shall be teachers when it is done. Out of the depths of pain we have thought to be our sole heritage in this world.—O, we know about love! And this is why I say to you that, though it may be a thrilling and a marvelous thing to be young and gifted in such times, it is doubly, so doubly dynamic to be young, gifted, and black."[2] (30)

Here again, we hear the ringing voice of our ancestors calling out to us to remind us that we have to put our creativity and our imagination to work to make progress for ourselves. Some of the most progressive ideas in the history of the human race have come from the minds of the black community. In the areas of medicine, inventions, art and literature, agriculture, space technology, etc., we find that history is replete with shining examples of success in all areas of human endeavor. So when Sis. Hansberry talks about being young, gifted, and black, she is encouraging our young to get into the race for all that is good and beneficial to mankind, for we can see today how all mankind has benefited thus far from the creative minds of our ancestors. We must pass on to the younger generation the gift of high expectations for them selves in the future, and the dignity of a strong value system from the past. Again, we say the memory of the ancestors must be more than just shallow celebrations at a certain time of the year. Their words must dwell in us, and be materialized in us through our productivity in life.

"We Must Rewrite the History."

Imam W. Deen Mohammed said in a public speech; "There exist a need and a desire in the souls of the survivors of slavery..., as slaves lost the sense of responsibility... we will not be comfortable with freedom or satisfied in our souls, until we can reflect on the condition of our people and not be sadden by it." (9) So we can see that we hear the same message here as we hear in the language of the ancestors. We must view this society we live in today as an extension of the Institution of Slavery, for in doing so, we will see that it has given us such a sense of false values that even though many of us have materialistic comforts, there is still an empty void in our essence. We still feel a need or we lack something that is more akin to the nature that G-d has given us. While it's true we need and like these material things, still they cannot take the place of the real responsibility of deciding not only our own destiny, but indeed, the destiny of the world. The false values created by this society are designed to replace that responsibility, and this will just not do for us.

Also, we must realize that although we never want to forget the history of slavery, we must learn to look back on it as something we will never allow to happen again. This will automatically mean that we know we must educate ourselves towards coming into moral and economic independence. We have a bittersweet recollection of the past. The bitter is the memory of the brutal chains and torture of physical slavery, and the sweet is the memory of the giants who stood up tall and strong in the face of the physical oppressor and refused outright to accept to be treated any less than human. So then, we build for the future on these two aspects from the past. The former we never allow to happen again, and the latter tell us that we must stand tall and strong in the face of psychological oppression and refuse to allow this society to strip us of our humanity. In doing this, the world will recognize us as being a people created and designed by G-d.

We are a people who, although reduced to the lowest of the low, still came back standing on high standards of dignity. We were able to take whatever they put on us in terms of oppression and still maintain our humanity. So no, we cannot continue to look back with hurt. We must move forward with a knowledge of the past, and our eyes on the bright future. Also, it tells us that those who live among us today and have chosen to live a life less than human are not the ones that we as a community or society in general should use as a measuring rod for the African-American community. These are some of those in the political and entertainment business who have lowered their dignity and have been part of the cause of so much violence and the moral degradation so prevalent in the black community. They are, and will continue to be, the exception to the rule. The rule stands regardless if that person has wealth or not, for material wealth alone is not the determining factor in the real life of a people.

As we stated earlier in this writing, the African-American community should take a personal interest in the area of education. This is because the ancestors fought so hard to make education a reality for all those who were not within access of it. I believe that even though America has the opportunity to have it, we as African-Americans should view it as our personal legacy, left to us by our ancestors. Therefore, we should strive with all our heart, soul, and mind to get as much as possible to bring ourselves up to the standards that G-d intended for all His servants. Education has always been a part of the African past, especially with those who came from an Islamic background. The Muslims who were among the slaves brought from Africa were known as Mandingo which means "book man."6 (9) This came about when Islam moved to Africa. The already civilized African governments moved to even higher levels of achievements by developing some of the greatest institution of higher learning in the history of mankind. The advancements in the areas of arts and sciences, wit and poetry; the advancements in medicine, and the study of the universe, and all that was responsible for the

European Renaissance were made possible because of the dedication our ancestors had to education. I believe that those who stood for education, as well as those who raised their voices and lifted their hands against slavery, came from an Islamic background. People like Benjamin Banneker, Phillis Wheatley, Gustavus Vassa, George Washington Carver, Mary McLeod Bethune, Nat Turner, Fredrick Douglass, and all those African-Americans who fought hard for the establishment of a public education system during the period of Reconstruction, came from an Islamic background. We can see it in their belief in the unity of G-d, and in their belief in the strength of the human spirit.

The great warrior, Brother Malcolm Shabazz, stated, "Education is our passport to the future, for tomorrow belongs to the people who prepare for it today."[2] **(30) In a public address by Imam Mohammed, he said,** "The more education we get, the more freely we can exercise our freedom. Many of us are half slaves right now. We have been free for more than 100 years. But many of us are half slaves and have freedom right now. It is because we don't have the education to know how to exercise that freedom." **(9) Prophet Muhammed said,** "Seek education even if you have to go to China." **Even in times of war, Prophet** Muhammed would set free those who had been captured in war if they would educate some of his people.

So we see much emphasis being put on the educational process. Since we know that knowledge and development is the result of the educational process, and we take notice of the circumstances of the African-American community, we see this question begging to be answered, "What kind of an education have we been getting?" This question covers all aspects of our learning institutions, whether it's academic, religious, from the streets, or whatever the source may be.

Wherever we go, we see the African-American people on the bottom of society, and it isn't because we're not going to school, because we are. And it isn't because we do not have intelligence, because we have some of the most brilliant minds on the planet in our communities. So then we say that it is primarily because our focus is on just being able to get along. And when we do get into decision-making positions, by the time we get there, we're thinking with the same value system as others. Consequently, we are free because we're no longer bound physically by the chains on our ankles and necks, but we are still slaves because not only are we still bound to others to provide a livelihood for us, but many of us who are successful have adopted the values of others. Nor has the education that we've received taught us the importance of having the control over our communities, thus putting us in a position to help shape and mold the minds of the youth in the areas that we live so that we will be the major influence in their lives, as opposed to the negative influences from the media and other sources. It seems that the two major sources of education in the black community, the school and the church, are ill equipped to give us as a community the kind of knowledge we need to go forward and be real leaders in the world.

To revisit the already mentioned *hadith,* or the sayings of Prophet Muhammed, in more detail, as narrated by Abu Huraira, the Prophet, (May G-d's peace be upon him) was saying something in a gathering, a Bedouin came and asked him, "When would the hour (Doomsday) take place?" Then the Prophet (May G-d's peace be upon him) said, "When Al-Anamah (the trust or moral responsibility or honesty) and all the duties which Allah has ordained is lost, then wait for the Hour (Doomsday)." The Bedouin said, "how will that be lost?" The Prophet, (May G-d's peace be upon him) said, "When the government, or the power, or authority comes in the hands of unfit persons, then wait for the Hour (Doomsday)." (Bukhari) 20 *(Abdul Alfahim* 145) This tells us that knowledge and education in and of itself is still not enough. As human beings, we still must be grounded on moral principle and regard for Allah because anything else would just make us people without vision, and a puppet for others to use for their selfish desires. So then, what is it that make us fit? It is a genuine desire to please Allah and Allah alone, thus being able to render genuine and honest leadership to mankind. So we have to see an obligation within ourselves to seek to educate ourselves, not to be in a position to have a better-paying job so as to earn more money to party every weekend, or even to realize the "American Dream" only, but to be of service to humankind as well.

I remember back in the day listening to a song performed by the talented group, the O'Jays. The title of the song was "Living for the Weekend." Although the song has a very good rhythm and the O'Jays performed it very well, it was the lyrics to the song that caught my ear. If the listener can refrain from getting caught up in the beat, you will see that there's a "Message in the Music" (another song performed by the O'Jays). Although this is just another recording for the multi-talented O'Jays and is meant for the enjoyment of their fans, the message is a description of the way the world views how the black man thinks.

The song starts off by saying, "I'm dead on my feet, most of the time, too tired to eat, try to read the paper, and fall fast asleep." Even though we as a people are physically alive, we are seen as the walking dead. We have no appetite for intellectual food, or intellectual growth and development, and when we try to read about the issues or someone tries to talk to us about something we should know about, we have no desire to hear them. We're always too busy to talk about anything but foolishness. So we're physically awake, but we're mentally asleep.

Our entire focus is on the fun we're going to have once Friday rolls around. In fact, our attention is so fixated on the weekend and on the good time we're going to have that sometimes. we take off of work early, even though it will cost us some of our paycheck. But even the loss of some of our income doesn't matter, because we've taken as much of this job as we can bear. This is because we look at it as a grind, or something we're doing for someone else, as opposed to being a means to an end, something for our own benefit if we use it right. Finally the weekend rolls around and we put on our "glad rags" and hit the town. We travel all over town, the east side, the west side, north and south sides, to find a party so we can "get down." We're so used to getting down, until we don't know how to get up. Any place will do so that we can squander all our precious resources on foolishness. And this is why we as a people find it so difficult to achieve here in this land of plenty. By squandering all our valuable resources, we remain weak and dependent, going from one job to another, depending on someone else to provide for our livelihood. "Living for the Weak End." This kind of thinking keeps us "weak" as a people, and it will mean the "end" of us as a people of productivity.

The American Dream as seen in society today is not, or does not, have to be the African-American dream. That is to say that although we are Americans living in America, we must have the ability to chart our own course through life. The values of others do not have to be our values in terms of how we identify ourselves as a people. Our culture, our heritage, the great dignity and high standards handed down to us from the ancestors, must be kept intact. In this way, we can progress materially as a people, yet maintain our self-respect. If we analyze the methods by which many here in America have gained their material wealth, we will find that in too many cases, they have had to use unscrupulous means. This not only denied them their self-respect, but the good that they may do in the future as a result of their wealth will always be under a dark cloud, because they will always be rooted in unscrupulousness.

Also, many times, those of us who do make our gains in ways that are honorable, still trying to "keep up with the Jones," to stay up on the trends and fashions, and generally go with the flow of whatever the mentality happens to be at that time. So again, we say that the American Dream does not have to be the African-American dream. We are the ones to decide our own value system, as we make progress in this world.

We have to be educated into the true definition of freedom. Since we now know that a great number of our ancestors were Muslims, we should rethink our definition of the word "freedom." Freedom and education are part of each other, and to know one is to know the other. The reason our ancestors were able to excel in the field of education, and why mathematics, science, and knowledge in other areas came so naturally to them was because their nature was still intact, as Allah had intended.

In Allah's Holy Book, sura **2,** ayats **30-32, we read,** "Behold, thy Lord said to the angles; "I will create a vicegerent on earth." They said: "Wilt Thou place therein one who make mischief therein and shed blood ?—whilst we do celebrate thy praises and glorify Thy holy (name)?" He said: "I know what ye know not."

And He taught Adam the names of all things; then He placed them before the angles, and said: "Tell Me the names of these if you are right."

They said: "Glory to Thee: of knowledge we have none, save what You have taught us: in truth it is Thou Who art perfect in knowledge and wisdom."

In the above verses from the Qur'an, the word vicegerent is from the root word in Arabic, khalifah, which means, "to be the successor, the substitute, to appoint as successor, caliphate, office or rule of the caliphate." So now we can see the very high position that Allah has given to the human being, not to just be in the earth, but to manage the earth for our own productive life, as well as for the life of others. So G-d has created us to be rulers in the earth. We are the khalifah. But we should always remember that we should not make the mistake of thinking that we're G-d, or that we're all powerful and that we rule on our own merit. We should never forget that all we have, everything is only on loan to us from Allah, and it's our decision whether we will use it for the advancement of mankind or cause mischief and shed blood.

Allah tells us in His Holy Book to travel through the earth and see what was the end of those who came before you. A true ruler, whether it refers to his individual life or the life of the society, rules with intelligence and humility.

When we study the history of mankind, we will find that there have been many powerful nations that have left their mark on the earth. Those who rose up in might and thought they were all-powerful can be seen to have a very short life span. The two most recent examples are Russia under communism and Germany under Hitler.

Not only did they fall, but also the entire civilized world was glad to see the kind of mentality that was ruling gone from the face of the earth. This was because not only did they deny G-d in their way of government, but also they denied G-d in the individual lives of the people. I believe that the reason Allah allowed them to be so noticeable while they were here was so that the world would not only witness their demise, but the reason behind their demise. The khalifah that Allah puts in the earth studies the language of the prophets, and understands that regardless of how powerful they become, it is only by the grace of G-d.

The word taught is from the root word alima or 'ilm, which means "to know, have knowledge, be informed, cognizant, to teach." To have knowledge, such as in the sciences, bacteriology, sociology, arithmetic, zoology, ethics, nuclear physics, etc., a distinguishing mark, a distinguished, outstanding mind. World, universe, cosmos. So all these definitions are from the word alima or 'ilm. So when the Holy Qur'an tells us that Allah taught Adam the names of all things, it is telling us that G-d has given the human being everything that we need to be productive in this world. Allah has put this knowledge in our genes, in our own human makeup. This is why the scientist is able to make the discoveries that they make. This is why we're able to come up with mathematical solutions to difficult problems. This is why man has a yearning to go into outer space, because G-d has put this desire in our nature by clocking the knowledge of these things in our nature, and this makes us anxious to cultivate that knowledge and bring it to the surface so that it will be of a benefit to mankind.

Now we can see why the human being has been given this lofty station. Allah has placed the human being even above the angles, as we read in Allah's Holy Book in verse 34, where Allah commanded the angels to bow down to Adam.

The human being is distinguished from the rest of creation in that he has been given rational thought and intelligence, therefore all creation is placed before the human being for him to use for his productive life. And since we are all children of Adam, we are all entitled to this same station in life, but the influences of this negative environment must not be allowed to distract us. Also, let us understand that the revelation of the Holy Qur'an came to Prophet Muhammed; so when we talk about the mark of distinction, then we should understand that no matter how much knowledge we acquire, his example is still the one we strive to emulate. As stated earlier in this writing, Allah tells us that Muhammed is the most excellent example for any whose hopes is in Allah and in the Last Day. Let us remember that the knowledge comes from Allah and not from ourselves. This remembrance will keep us humble and progressive.

In understanding the true meaning of freedom, all we need to do is reflect on the high standards of the lives of the ancestors, then we begin to make the connection. This word "freedom" comes from the Arabic root word hll, and it means "to unbind, unfasten, abolition, freeing, and liberation." It also means "that which is permissible, or lawful. That, which is legal, legitimate, respectable, decent." So we find that the Islamic definition of freedom not only means to be free to move about or to exercise free speech, etc., but along with that freedom comes a sense of responsibility. That is to say that freedom means to be free to establish a society that is conducive to the positive development of the people who live there. The definition that this present-day society has given us for freedom is to just let it all hang out. Do anything you're big enough to do and say anything you want to say where you want to say it, and as loud as you want to say it. This kind of freedom, when presented to us through the media and made to appeal to our sexual appetites, will eventually lead society to slavery, so in reality, it's no freedom at all.

As we see in today's society how those who are in the entertainment world use the First Amendment to the Constitution to spew all types of poison and vulgarities in the atmosphere without regard to who gets hurt, or what child gets aborted in terms of their intellectual development. Those who call themselves "artists" and go out of their way in the name of free speech to desecrate religious symbols, as well as other types of symbols that have stood in the past as a source of strength for the society. What is so tragic is that their only concern is for their free speech, and not for the hurt they're inflicting on others as a result of the reverence others hold for these symbols. And as a result of the mixed-up bowl of confusion, we are witnessing everything from sexually transmitted diseases, for which a cure cannot be found, to small children committing heinous acts of murder and being tried as adults, with many spending years and years of their young lives locked up behind bars. So we can see that with this sick definition of freedom that we have, it will eventually kill off the whole society from a moral standpoint, thus, we as a nation will collapse from within.

We're not saying that we should not have free speech; what we are saying is that this word freedom carries with it a great responsibility. It requires a sense of moral refinement, with an eye to the establishment of a strong society with a strong community life. For this, we should appeal to the responsible part of our human makeup, as opposed to our lower desires.

When a sister speaks about being young and gifted, she means with knowledge of the experience of the black past. Not with a sense of hurt, nor with shallow concerns. It is only when we are able to look back on the trials and tribulations we came through, and still survived, that's what makes it doubly, so doubly dynamic to be young, gifted, and black.

We must see ourselves as being the soul of America, by virtue of the fact that we have experienced in America what no one else has, or ever will. This is the significance I see in the leadership of Imam W. Deen Mohammed. He represents a people that have experienced the very lowest of the low. His message, and therefore the message of the people he represents, speaks to the best in all of us as Americans, and as humans in the world of mankind. We must remember the hurt of the past so as to never allow it to happen again, and we must remember the best of the past so that we who live here in the present can do better, while keeping in mind that the present doesn't belong to just us only, It is the springboard for the future of the next generation. It is the proof, the evidence that G-d is the Creator of the human spirit, and not man. The human spirit is that connection that all mankind have in common that makes us be concerned with each other.

"The ultimate measure of a manis not where he stands in momentsof comfort and convenience, butwhere he stands at times of challenge, **and controversy."**[21] *(Dr. Martin Luther King, Jr.)*

No financial or political influence, no popularity or public opinion, no fear of anything, will sway the man of sincere principles from what he knows to be right and just. Even if he has to standalone against the winds of immoral and unjust reasoning, he will stand his ground, because his ultimate accountability is to G-d.

We Must Rewrite the History!

Chapter 6

New Leadership

Throughout this writing, we have talked about the soul and its victory over the abuses inflicted upon it by the Institution of Slavery, and those who worked in the dreaded camp to try to keep it alive. We now are trying to bring this understanding about the soul into more of a concrete form. Traditionally, we've always been taught that the soul was something separate from ourselves, something that we have, but is never in possession of. In our religious services, we would make statements like, "Where will your soul spend eternity?" Or we would say, "I don't care about the world, I just want to save my soul." It is because of this kind of understanding that we as a people remain at the bottom of society. That is to say that in too many cases, our religious understanding keeps us in a world of suspended spiritualism. We don't see the material world and our success in it as being part of our duty to Allah. We must understand that our spiritual success must be tied to our material success if our lives are to be of any consequence in this world. The objective here is not to say that we are only to strive to be rich or wealthy, but more importantly, our religious understanding should show us our responsibility in all aspects of our lives, whether it be morally, economically, politically, or spiritually. So when we think of the soul, we're not to see it as something separate from ourselves, but we must see it as being the self. Because of our traditional misunderstanding of this very important word, let us revisit its meaning once again.

The word for soul in the Holy Qur'an is nafs. It means "the self, the psyche, spirit, mind, inclinations, life." It also means "precious, valuable, priceless." From this same root word, we get "struggle, fight, compete, desire, sorrow, frustration, appetite, breath, aspiration, nature, essence," etc. So we can see that the soul is the person. We can also see from this definition the understanding the Muslim Moors had about themselves and their relationship with Allah, and how that understanding enabled them to make great progress in advancing the life of the society. By the same token, it is also clear why the slave master tried to destroy the soul of the human being by attempting to reduce him to a level below that of animal existence by killing off all human aspirations and intelligent thought. Kill off the will to compete in the world of mankind. Kill off the moral and spiritual self, and have us exist only in the physical self. The fact that many of our people before the Civil War, and on up through the Reconstruction period were able to maintain their humanity and become successful in life is in itself a great testimony to the resilience of the soul.

This present-day society with its pop culture and its emphasis on sex and glitter keeps the human being on the physical level and thus, hinders his ability to realize his greater self. There is something very important about the soul, or the person that must be known, and that is the fact that there are various levels or stages of growth and development that we go through, and we must qualify ourselves in each stage if we are to go on to the next.

This first stage of growth for the soul is known as ammar, HQ 12:53, from the root word, amr, which means "constantly urging, always demanding, inciting, and instigating." The baser side of man that incites to evil. This is known as a stage of immaturity. We're just like a kid in a candy store, and everything looks good to us. As human beings, it is in our nature to want nice things and things that look good. And this is the part of our human makeup that the world of commercialism and entertainment appeals to. We like the shine and the glitter, and so we are deluded into thinking that this is what the real life is all about. We begin to think that these are the "finer things in life," and too many times, this leads to irresponsible activities and destructive lifestyles. In this stage, we are motivated by appetites unchecked by knowledge. Our desires outweigh our responsibility, and unless we can muster enough control to come into a higher form of knowledge, we will be forever doomed to be of little or no consequence, except to be used as a tool for others to manipulate.

As we continue to make ourselves more acquainted with ourselves, we come to another level of development for the person, or the soul. This level is called lawwaamah, from the Qur'anic Arabic root word lama, HQ 75:2, which means "to blame, censure, rebuke, chide, reprimand, reproach," etc. Here we have the conscience of the human being coming into play. We have managed to grow to a level where many of the decisions we make are decisions of consciousness. When we commit acts that we know are beneath us, we tend to think about it, and it bothers us that we would participate in such low activities, even if some of these activities are considered okay by society's standards. So our conscience rebukes or reprimands us. This is good because as long as we have a conscience, we have a chance to get back. It is when we don't have a conscience that we stand in danger of being lost to the influences of the environment. Allah has blessed us with a conscience to be a warning to us to help keep us straight. So this word lawwaamah, or the self-reproaching spirit, gives us a fighting chance to resist or struggle against the vicissitudes of society.

We now come to a final stage of development for the nafs, or the soul, or the person. This level is where we find complete rest and satisfaction for the nafs, or the soul, HQ 89:27, and it is from the Qur'anic Arabic root word, tam'ana, which means "calm, quite, to be secure, confident, assured, trust." We understand this definition from the perspective of those who have been striving to not only make society more conducive for the positive development of themselves and their families, but who also work to improve the environment for others as well. They see their lives as one with a lofty purpose that is unselfishly dedicated to pleasing G-d.

So this idea of rest and satisfaction is not to be seen in the same sense of retirement, for those who are aware of their purpose in life are not satisfied unless they're working in the service of Allah, be it politically, socially, morally, or whatever. They know that their fight is not over until the physical life is over. These are people who have overcame the obstacles in their own lives, and now see their lives as a service to all mankind, and this is their heaven. This is their preparation for the greater heaven or paradise in the afterlife, in nearness to their Lord. This is the supreme felicity.

Now as we reflect back to ammar, the first stage of development of the soul, we find another word that comes from the same root word as ammar, but which has a complete and opposite meaning, and that word is amir, which means "commander, one who has authority, or rule, or power; a ruler." The knowledge of our relationship with Allah, and our regard for that relationship, qualifies us as the amir over ourselves. Jesus tells us in Biblical scripture; "You have been faithful over these few things, now I will make you master over many." Allah says in the Holy Qur'an, "You must gain self-mastery." This tells us that Allah has given us the power to have authority over ourselves, and by exercising that power, we disassociate ourselves from the gravitational pull of things irrelevant to human growth, and thus we become concerned about the society we live in, thereby becoming assets to that society. We become stable morally, economically, politically, and spiritually. We have the power within us but we have to struggle to prove ourselves, and this struggle is what makes us the masters, the amir.

Imam W. Deen Mohammed teaches us that "Life is a contender, even your own nature, or your own soul, especially if you're trying to be right." **He goes on to say that,** "Allah chooses that life for us, and now that we understand it, we should welcome the challenge." **(9) This is what makes us champions. How can we call ourselves champions if we don't have a contender?**

When we talk about leadership, we must remember that the mark of a true leader is first, one who has regardfulness for Allah. We know then that this leader has set him apart from the corruption of society and has the genuine concerns of the people at heart. Secondly, the leader must possess a unique kind of knowledge that sets him aside from the rest of those that society looks at as leaders because they may have wealth, education, or is favored by the media. Just a very shallow glance at history will tell us that G-d never chooses His primary servants from the ranks of these people. That is to say that the knowledge that was brought to free the people of Moses, Jesus, and Mohammed was revealed knowledge. Not knowledge from the schools and universities of man, but revealed scripture from G-d.

When a people sinks to the depth of moral degradation such as we see in the society today, and in the times of the prophets, we must understand that we need revealed knowledge in order to not only achieve true freedom, but to understand what true freedom is. This is the purpose of the revelation of Qur'an to Prophet Muhammed. It is not only G-d's last revelation to mankind, but it also bears witness to the truth of those scripture that came before it, and it represents the kind of freedom that advances the life of humanity in all its aspects.

The progress that we have in the medical professions, all the modern conveniences that we enjoy, all came about as a result of the fact that Allah revealed the Holy Qur'an to Prophet Mohammed, and he taught it to his people. It was through the stimulation of the minds of men by Allah that man was inspired by this great scripture to take charge of this great creation given to him by Allah and work for the progress of the life of all mankind. In highlighting a portion of the Qur'anic text regarding these concerns, Imam Mohammed says, "Mohammed the Prophet is a mercy to all the worlds. Prophet Mohammed is our leader, so that means our concerns are for the entire human family. G-d has made us from one soul, one nafs, and from it male and female, our original parents, the parents of all people, of all nations, of all races. All from the family of Adam. G-d has made us to know in Judaism, Christianity, and in Islam that the human family is one family, and we will return to Him one day in unity together." **(9)**

So we see in this kind of leadership from Prophet Mohammed, a genuine concern for all mankind, and with that concern, a revealed book of scripture to follow so that mankind will be able to live up to the best of his potential. This kind of teaching speaks volumes about the leadership of Imam W. Deen Mohammed because it tells us that we are servants of the one G-d, just as the prophets were. Our service then becomes due to no one but G-d. This kind of knowledge builds leaders in all of us, both male and female. We are not to worship other men or have others to worship us. We are not to use positions of leadership to get the attention of the public, and to glory in the things we have not done.

Our leaders must inspire people to do better, to take control of their lives, and to move on up the ladder of human development. We must have a determination to live the best of our lives, to respond to the best of our motivations and aspirations. A people coming from under the evil yoke of physical and mental slavery, being able to realize what has happened to us, and because of the depth of the soul, we didn't allow it to destroy us. We are able to move on with our humanity still intact, following the example of Prophet Mohammed, as a mercy to all the world. The message is this, "We are not to use the past as a reason to fail, but a reason to succeed."

Again, the question is asked, "How do we identify the true leader?" We identify the true leader by the fact that he doesn't compromise the principles given to him by his Maker to satisfy the desires of man. Also just as important, he gives freely to the people the knowledge that will create the ability within them to lead themselves. This is the message of Imam W. Deen Mohammed, and this is what makes him the greatest leader since the time of Prophet Mohammed of 1,400 years ago. In my opinion, just as Prophet Mohammed was the culmination of all the prophets sent to mankind by Allah, Imam Mohammed is the culmination of all the righteous leaders that came to the people since Prophet Mohammed.

By the grace and the mercy of Allah, not only has he opened the eyes of America and the world to Al-Islam, but he has also brought a people who descended from the slaves, a people who were considered morally, mentally, and spiritually dead in the eyes of civilized society, and placed them in the forefront of positive change in America. As stated before, not using the past as a source of hurt and an excuse for failure, but instead, using it as a source of strength that beckons America and the world to success in human development. For indeed, if a people that have experienced that peculiar Institution of Slavery, as has the African-American, can rise with the absence of malice and the presence of brotherhood, this is indeed a mercy to all the worlds.

Another aspect that's equally as important in Imam Mohammed's leadership is that he has brought life and respect back to religion, not just in his own Islamic faith, but in his call to Christians, Jews, and other people of faith. We are now witnessing not only a revival of faith, but a genuine respect between leaders of different faiths.

We have seen Muslims pray at synagogues and Jews pray at mosques. We have seen Christians and Muslims come together and fight against ignorance, the common enemy of all, both in religion and society life. We have seen the world's religious organizations come together and take a stand for real peace in the world. We have seen Imam Mohammed address the Vatican at the invitation of Pope John Paul II, and we have seen Pope John Paul II visit Egypt, Palestine, and Israel, calling for peace, love, and brotherhood.

A very brief profile of Imam Mohammed is as follows: He was born on October 30, 1933 to Elijah (Poole) Muhammad and Clara (Evans) Muhammad. Imam W. Deen Mohammed succeeded his father as leader of the Nation of Islam on February 26, 1975. He is leader of an estimated 2.5 million American Muslims and is recognized as spokesman for the American Society of Muslims.

Imam Mohammed has met, conferred with, and/or advised many prominent leaders, including heads of state and Muslim and non-Muslim religious leaders. His extensive travels throughout this country and abroad, often at the invitation of heads of state and religious leaders, have taken him to China, England, Kuwait, Saudi Arabia, Denmark, Malaysia, Mexico, Palestine, Iran and Italy. He has built and maintains strong alliances and relationships with Muslim, Christian, Jewish, and interfaith groups. Some of his affiliations have been: appointments as president to the World Conference on Religion and Peace; appointment to the Executive Committee of the Religious Alliance Against Pornography (RAAP); and elected as president in the U.S. for the World Conference on Religion and Peace Assembly VII (W. C. R. P.).

Imam Mohammed has also hosted prominent leaders, such as Mufti Abdullah Muhtar, leader of an estimated 60 million Muslims, on his first visit to the U.S. He has met with Pope John Paul II. In February, 1992, he was the first Muslim to deliver an invocation on the floor of the U.S. Senate and he has toured the Pentagon and addressed Muslim chaplains and other personnel there. He delivered the first address by a Muslim on the floor of the Georgia State Legislature in 1992; he has addressed the World Affairs Council, which serves as host to outstanding figures of this nation and the world. Forbes Magazine officials hosted an address Imam Mohammed gave in Florida in 1995 on the topic "How Do We Save Our Youth?"

Imam Mohammed has been featured in newspapers such as the Wall Street Journal (July 1999) and the Chicago Defender (September 2001). He established the Collective Purchase Conference (CPC) in 1996, a member organizing for strengthening the economic status of the poor community through a collective purchase program. So we can see that this is not media-made leadership, or the traditional type of leadership that we're used to seeing placed before us by other people. Rather, we see leadership that starts out at home, building a strong foundation based on faith in G-d and self-responsibility. Then we see its influence on the rest of society as unity and love, and brotherhood once again becomes the cry that unites humanity.

Today, as a result of the climate being charged by the voice of Imam Mohammed, we can hear the voices of tomorrow's young leaders as they rise, calling for an end to the dusty old voices of hurt and protest that continue to beg others to do for us what we can do for ourselves. This new leadership is stepping up to the challenge of not only guiding the African-American community to a new level of independent thinking, but also instilling within them the fact that it's not enough to just say "I'm equal," nor will we make progress by begging to be equal. The fact is that we must become producers in the real sense if we as a people are ever going to have self-respect, and get genuine respect of others.

A new voice is telling us that not only do we have the same potential as others, but when we reflect back on the ancestors, we can see that they had far less to work with than we have, and they, despite all the dangers that they faced, were still successful, so that tells us that we have no excuse. We must understand that it won't be easy, but we must start now to chart our own course for progress here in America. We will face obstacles, but we must be steadfast.

If we heard more about the excellence of our moral character and the fact that we should maintain that character, if we could hear more about using our own creativity to produce for self, then protesting because a company won't hire us, if we would call on ourselves to stop doing injustice to ourselves, if we would stop being stagnated over affirmative action and begin to affirm our own action, in the period of just a few short years, the world would see a totally new African-American.

Our aspirations must be higher and our patience must be greater. We must see ourselves in a battle for our very lives, and we are our own worst enemies. We must come up from the lowly position in life that we are in, and see ourselves as the salvation of America and the world, instead of always struggling for the very basics just to stay alive.

Mrs. Jimanna Sumrall, who was a strong, outspoken critic of society's wrongs, and who was responsible for raising many of the young people that came along during my generation, leaned out of her front door one day and yelled at a brother who had fallen victim to alcohol. She said; "That ain't you, that ain't your essence, that ain't what G-d made you." So here, we see Jimanna Sumrall appealing to the soul or to the conscience of the human being, calling on him to summon the strength of the excellence given to him by Allah.

This is the task of the new leadership: a call for dignity, respect, and responsibility. We must not enter the new century with the same problems, and use the same tactics to solve those problems, as we did in the past century. True leadership must put the onus on us for our success in life. Again, we say the mark of a true leader is one who creates leadership in others because leadership in the individual creates within them the ability to chart their own individual courses through life, while at the same time, providing direction for family and community.

To paraphrase a statement made by Imam Mohammed in a public speech he gave, he said that slavery could happen again in America, even in these modern times. (8) That is to say that when we're not connected to the essence of our human makeup, as Allah has created us, we become vulnerable to other influences in the environment. We can easily see how these negative influences in the environment have enslaved the minds of much of the society today. We don't see these things as slavery because they are things that we like to do. Drugs and other kinds of intoxicants. Our loose attitude about sex, the lack of respect for responsible authority, and generally, almost a total disregard for G-d. Because of this kind of attitude in the people, negative influences, primarily by way of the media and through some other sources, seem to have taken manipulative positions in the minds of the people by appealing to their base desires. When we become slaves to our base desires, we take ourselves out of the race for positions of leadership, influence, and a successful life. So we continue in a seemingly never-ending struggle for a meaningful life, while blaming others for our problems, when we really have the power within ourselves to cure whatever ails us.

This kind of thinking has been especially devastating for the African-American community because of our pre-occupation with entertainment, loose lifestyles, squandering of our valuable resources on frivolous things, party life, and listening to the negative messages in the music that bombard us on a twenty-hour-a-day basis thus playing a major role in killing off our value system so that our total concentration is focused on our next point of excitement.

So slavery today comes in the form of negative influences we have in the society today. We don't see it as such because these are things that we like to do. Even our culture has become a subculture that causes much of the pain and hurt we're experiencing today. What we should understand is that this is not the true life and culture of the black community, but rather it is one that has been imposed upon us through influence, and because it is one that appeals to our pleasure principle, we find it hard to tear ourselves away from it, to our own detriment. Some of the magazines that are published by African-Americans adorn their covers with hip-hop entertainers, movie actors, sports stars, and dub them as our leaders of tomorrow. This is wrong and this helps to aid in the downfall of our people. Just because we have people who are tops in their particular field of entertainment does not qualify them as leaders. Instead, it acts to pull our young people's attention away from the more important avenues of life, such as medicine, law, education, real business development, etc. and in too many cases, they are lead down the road of self-destruction as a result of trying to emulate the image they have been given on the cover of a magazine. I do believe that the black magazines are the only ones that carry on that practice, and it should stop.

As new leaders in the coming millennium, we are calling for total responsibility from ourselves, for ourselves. As new leaders in this society, we will not allow the media, black or white, choose our leaders for us. Those who still advocate marches, protests, demonstrations, and sitting on the corner, shouting "What do we want?" "Freedom!" "When do we want it?" "Now!" We demand that you move on up out of the way because that is not leadership. That kind of activity doesn't bring dignity to us, it only makes us look like spectacles in the eyes of civilized society. Anytime you see a leader standing before a crowd that number into the thousands or hundreds of thousands, and still talking affirmative action as opposed to pooling resources, that leader is either getting paid by someone else or lacks the vision to lead the people to real freedom, justice, and equality. In either case, he needs to get out of the way, because that's no leadership at all.

New leadership means having the courage to blame ourselves for our own shortcomings. We know and understand that there is a reason for us to be in the mental shape we're in today. We know that today's mental condition dates back to the days of slavery. But just like we know the reason, we also know that there is no excuse for failure. There is too much opportunity, too much knowledge, and other advantages at our own disposal to find excuses.

This is not a new kind of thinking that we're bringing to the public, for it's the same message of the ancestors in times gone by, and while it can be found in the thinking of many of our people across the country, it's found primarily in the mentality and the language of the emerging youth leadership under the tutelage of Imam W. Deen Mohammed. The reason for this is that this new leadership for the African-American community and for America is the focus of the youth in the Muslim American Society, and as a community, their voices will be loud and clear, "We Must Rewrite the History!"

There can be no compromise of the moral principles. The adherence to strong moral principles is the beginning of successful leadership. This new leadership puts the burden squarely where it belongs, and that's on our shoulders. We must remember that when we allow others to chose our leaders for us, that leader must be doing something they like, and their method of leadership keeps us in a position of inferiority. The ones who choose the leaders are, in reality, the real leaders.

Just like we have a past of hurt, we also have a past of dignity, and this is what must be emphasized and used as a springboard to bigger and better achievements. We must reconnect with the essence of the human makeup given to us by the Creator, and realize that everything we need for success we already have.

Imam W. Deen Mohammed is the only leader I see from the African-American community on the scene today who puts respect for G-d first in our efforts to bring ourselves as a race up to a level of achievement and respect in human society. This is as opposed to relying on the politicians, the private sector, etc. Allah is the source of all our blessings, and we must not only say it and believe it, but we must act on it. I think the highest compliment a person can receive is that they respected G-d as the source of their success, whether it's in politics, economics, community, or whatever the case may be. If we don't depend on G-d, then we depend on man, and I think that too many of our leaders seem to think that when it comes to the affairs of man, our belief in G-d does not apply.

Imam W. Deen Mohammed has set aside from that kind of thinking, as can be seen in his independent thinking, his independent leadership, and his sincere desire to advance not only his own race, but the whole of mankind. As stated before, the example of Prophet

Muhammed can be seen in his life, and the voice of the ancestors can be heard in his words.

As we witness the new leaders of the twenty-first century emerge on the scene, they are also saying that we must cease to view ourselves as a special-attention type of people who need special programs to make it in the world. We should be in a strong enough position that when these programs are needed, we should be the ones doing them for others, because now, we've reached that level where we can be on the giving end, as opposed to being on the receiving end all the time.

New leadership into the twenty-first century must be the kind of leadership that will put us in a position of true independence and give us the kind of knowledge where no one will ever be able to enslave us again. Freedom for the African-American community means freedom for the world. We want to appeal to the intelligence of the human being, and to encourage them to begin using their creativity, their imagination, and all that they have that's positive to help to advance society for the good of us all.

This new leadership has to address the issue of freedom from a new perspective. That is to say that whereas from the beginning of the slave trade and on up to close to the end of the twentieth century, the issues of equality have been based on race, or black-and-white issues. In other words, whatever the issues were that came up, whether it was voting, public accommodations, housing, employment, etc., it was dealt with from a black-and-white perspective. This is because the two parties who were mainly interested were black folks and white folks. In today's society, the issues have very little to do with color, although there are some white and black racists out there who still push this issue, but then, they are just tools and fools of a larger mentality who, in order to maintain political and material dominance over them and the masses, uses them to do the ignorant things they do. The issue of freedom has to be addressed from the perspective of adherence to principles and standards so that the society can grow in dignity.

So then, as we have stated before, after physical slavery, we still remained psychologically tied to the slave master, which we use to identify as the "white man." In today's environment, we find that slavery has been elevated to a level so high that we can only call it "influences." Imam Mohammed said in a public address that while he was on a visit to Washington, D. C., someone from a high position approached him and said to him in private, "Everybody is on the same bus now." This statement expresses what the new leadership of the twenty-first century will be faced with in the future struggle for true freedom for mankind.

We don't have just a black-and-white situation anymore. In other words, we're not dealing with just a personality, we're dealing with a mentality, and in its abstract presentation to the masses, only the well informed will be able to identify it. This is because too many of the masses just live their lives on a day-to-day basis, with their focus more on providing for themselves and their families, as opposed to the cares of the world. Taking life as it comes and dealing with it the best way they know how. The mentality has no boundaries in terms of race, therefore, we are all susceptible to its influences. "We're all on the same bus."

Many of us are caught up in a matrix, or the manmade womb of society. We feed on the influences of this society, therefore, we develop our value system from the influences we feed on. As we have stated before, most of the things we see in the environment are trends and fads that are presented to the masses as the objects of life, and so we get caught up, dedicating much our lives to the standards of man rather than the standards that Allah has set for us. Most of what we see change with the seasons, so we're never stable or established, we're never in a position of strength where we can make real contributions.

We continue to live in a virtual reality, which is an effect, not a fact. The fact is that we continue to chase after dreams that others have created for us.

When we look at all the different communities of the society, we see that the black community is in far worse shape than any other. That is to say that while others are showing some signs of life, we're still begging others to do for us what we can do for ourselves. What happens in these kinds of situations is that other people take advantage of the opportunities America has to offer, and soon we see business development and other kinds of productivity in their communities, while ours stay in their degraded state. Their future generations are provided with hope for a productive life, while too many in the black community are faced with a no-way-out situation.

Today, we must realize that we're caught up in the worse kind of slavery. While many of us think that we're chasing the American dream, which incidentally is someone else's interpretation, in reality, we're tightening the chains of moral, mental, and spiritual slavery around us; and so the beat goes on for us as a people to continue to fall victim to the forces of negative influences in the face of our magnificent past. To continue to be ruled by our senses means that we will forever remain a shallow people. That is to say as long as it tastes good, feels good, looks good, etc., we will remain slaves to our appetites, our base desires. We will never be able to ascend the ladder of true creativity and imagination so as to put ourselves in position to further advance human society, as we saw in times gone by in the lives of our ancestors.

This is not to say that we won't be contributors, because as African-Americans, we have made huge contributions to this great society, today as well as in times gone by. But we're doing it in the name of others, so our youth never get to know the great advances and contributions our people have made. As a consequence, we remain consumers in the eyes of the world, and non-contributors in the eyes of our own communities. With nothing to look forward to, our future generation gets caught up in a false world of trends and fads, and a life of no significance. So again, we say; "Oppression is the negative influences we enjoy." "The American dream is genuine freedom from oppression so that the human potential can grow to it's fullest."

So then, the emphasis is on the simple essentials of human development that get us ready to establish community life, which is our interpretation of the American dream. In the establishment of community life, there must be foundation, there must be standards that are set high to guard against those influences that seek to destroy the excellence of the human being. This foundation is already a part of the life of the human being at birth. That is to say that the human being is born into the world with his nature already intact, as Allah has ordained it to be, and as caring parents, we have to be careful, or societal influences will take that original nature given to the child by Allah away, and we will find ourselves with a burden almost impossible to handle.

I remember back in the day when I used to listen to a song by that magnificent singing group, Earth, Wind, and Fire. They sang a song entitled, "The Way of the World," and one of the lines in the lyrics said, "Child is born with a heart of gold, the way of the world, makes his heart turn cold." The message is this: The minds of our future generations are our own responsibility. No one else will watch over them as we will. We have to watch over them as a mother hen watches over her young. We must view this world as a fight for the life and death of our good community life. In order to ensure that the minds of our young will be safe, it is important that we understand that after they are born from the biological womb of physical development, we have to create a womb for their healthy psychological development.

Again, we go to Allah's Holy Book, which says, "By the Fig and the Olive, And the Mount of Sinai, And this City of Security, We have indeed created man in the best of moulds." **HQ 95:1-4**

When young minds are born into the world, in most cases, they are viewed as consumers for the commercial establishment. Studies show that the world of commercialism will spend large sums of money on demographics in order to know how to target a particular community with a particular product. Then there are the illegals, the gangbangers, the dope pushers, the liquor stores, etc., all in competition for the minds of our youth. So the fig is symbolic of the vulnerable minds of not only the youth, but of the grown-ups, who fall victim to the negative influences of the society. The fig is a soft and sweet piece of fruit that contains many tiny seeds. But because of its sweetness, if it's not harvested in time, the parasites of the environment will ruin it. Also, the tiny seeds must be viewed as tiny fragments, or figments of the mind. As long as they remain separated and scattered, they are open for destruction, and will find it difficult to prosper.

The olive is not sweet, as is the fig, and it is symbolic of a certain stage of maturity. The skin of the olive is tight and more secure. The seed of the olive is solid and cannot be chewed, as can the fig seeds.

So the olive seed is symbolic of the unification of those fragments, or figments of ideas. The word Mount is from the Arabic word tur, which not only means mount, but also means "to evolve, to develop, to advance, to promote." So what we're saying here is that as we come into this life, if we as a people continue to remain disunited, it will be the cause of our demise. The mount or mountain represents stability. Growth from the innocence of the fig, or a people who were fragmented, to a people who has evolved to a position of stability in the world.

The word for security here is amin, which means "loyal, faithful, upright, trustworthy, peace, security, protection," etc. This word amin is the character and the personality of those who are members of that society. They are the protectors of the property and the minds of the society in which they live.

The word for best is hasan, or ahsan, which means "more handsome, more beautiful, better conduct, more excellent, more admirable." All these qualities are in terms of character and conduct. The word for mould is waqa, or taqwa, which means "to safeguard, to protect, to fear G-d, for the sake of G-d, piety, G-d consciousness, to be regardful of Allah." To know that we're always in His presence, and though we can't see Him, we know that He sees us, etc. So the reason that we have a community of safety and security is because we have a community respecting G-d. The human being is created with this attitude of regardfulness clocked in the nature by Allah, but the negative influences of society will rob us of that, and society as a whole will suffer.

So this new leadership of the twenty-first century will be concerned with the establishment of a good community life. This means to be on guard for anything that might act to pull us into activities that will make us end up in wrong situations. This regard for Allah also acts to ensure that we never lose our humanity by keeping us humble and compassionate toward other human beings because regardless of how affluent we may become, we are also human beings. The technical advancements will get ever so complex, but the human being will remain simple in his attitude towards other men by realizing that a simple smile, a handshake, or a good morning greeting goes a long way in keeping the society human. The requirement that Allah has given us to remain human never changes. That requirement is a simple reading from the Bible in the words of Prophet Jesus, to wit; "Love the Lord thy G-d with all thine heart, soul, and mind, and thy fellow human being as thy self."

In the establishment of our community life, we must never forget the contributions of the ancestors. Our greatest mistake is to lose our history.

When we realize that there is nothing new under the sun, we then understand that we can always refer back to the ancestors for advice and guidance for the future. To reduce the accomplishments of our ancestors to mere academic expressions, I think, is the greatest crime that we ourselves can commit. The greatest tribute we can pay our ancestors is to make our accomplishments excel over theirs.

"We Must Rewrite the History"

We should never forget family. Family should be adhered to in the traditional sense. We should not accept this society's idea of what a family should be. One of the strongest pillars for holding up the community and the society is the family, and included in that definition of family is friendship.

What has happened to families across the entire nation, especially in the black community, is that the family has fallen by the wayside. What is so tragic is that it's getting to the point where the only place we see family as it relates to the black community is on TV commercials, and the only reason for that is to appeal to our sentimental nature so we will buy their product. It's just so tragically ironic that the institution that we cherished so much to keep us together as a people; we have gotten so caught up in the vices of this society that all we care for is the next dose of drugs, the next party, or the next fad, and so the family is just torn apart.

Friendship is almost as important as family. As we have said earlier in this writing, it seems as if the institutions of family and friendship are being attacked so as to make us weaker still. You can hear it in the lyrics of the music that many of our young people listen to. It's all about one friend getting together with their friend's girlfriend or boyfriend. While this may seem small to some, when we see our youth mimic the lyrics, and the spread of mistrust in the community, then we witness the community life getting weaker still. So family and friendship must be guarded as if they were priceless treasures, because that is exactly what they are. We must also see ourselves as an intricate part of the world community, being contributors as well as consumers, using our economic and intellectual strength to advance the world of mankind. Allah tells us in His Holy Book, "Live for the life in the hereafter, but don't forget your share of this material world." So we must look to have a balanced life.

New leadership into the twenty-first century must put us on the level of contributors to the society of man morally, economically, politically, and spiritually. This is known as universal growth and development. We should no longer just accept society's definition about anything, unless it agrees with what we know to be right. We can set our own standards as to what we know to be good and bad.

What we see as bad may not be bad in the sight of others, and so it may act to undermine the healthy growth and development of the community. So it goes then that just any definition of good has to meet a certain standard for us to accept it as such. In this society, anything can be considered as good. We cannot accept this world's definition of good. Being good but disconnected from G-d leaves society to the interpretation of others as to what good is, and this acts to take us away from the guidance of G-d.

We are being led to consider what is good for the individual, as opposed to what is good for the society as a whole. We are told to accept anybody regardless of what kind of example, good or bad, they may be setting for the society. And as stated before, many of those who are in political and other positions of authority have sold themselves to the highest bidder, and so their leadership is really no leadership at all.

Our concern for a value-based individual that sets the example for correct conduct has been diminished to the point that the very stability of the society is threatened. That is to say that we live in a climate that affects the thinking of the general masses. Words like "integrity," "honesty," "morality," etc., and the people who practice them are becoming fodder for the joke circuit. The values that have been the stuff for the advancement of human society have been pushed aside for whatever gratifies us the quickest and the most. We have the best example in the life of Muhammed, the Prophet, as it relates to morality, integrity, honesty, and above all, his willingness to live up to the standards set by Allah, that has made him the model for the human being to follow regardless of what walk of life he may come from.

The new leaders of the twenty-first century must be able to stand up for moral excellence as well as for economic development. They must be willing and able to stand in the face of a counterculture that goes against all that is good for a strong society. The vision of this new leadership must be able to look into the environment, regardless of what aspect of life it may concern, detect what is needed, and be about the business of making things right. This does not mean that these leaders have not had flaws in their own lives as well, but what it does mean is that they have been able to meet and overcome those obstacles, which is in fact what makes them leaders.

The message of these new leaders, unlike the hollow and shallow messages we're hearing from our so-called leaders of today, who would want to see human life brought down to a level of instinct rather than lifted to a higher level of intelligence, must be sound and unimpaired. When the level of intelligence is raised in the people, we begin to not only see G-d as part of our lives, but see Him as very much involved in the affairs of man instead of someplace we go after we die. When this level is reached, then never will anyone be able to pull the wool of slavery and servitude over the eyes of the people again.

To see G-d logically is not to be misunderstood with seeing Him physically, or even understanding Allah. It only means that we are to use the faculties given to us by the Creator, to study His creation for the purpose of giving direction to our own lives. Our goal is to bring ourselves, as His servants, more in touch with His reality as opposed to our own, so that we may realize our purpose in life.

Although the world today is more complex than the world of yesterday, one necessity continues to stand out, and that is the need to be able to search the scriptures for the answers to what ails us.

True leadership does not deviate from the guidance of G-d, because we know that just as Allah gave guidance to the prophets in times gone by, then, that same guidance is here today. It is the scripture that holds the answers to whatever problems, however small or great, human society may be dealing with, but it takes one who uses the light of intelligence to search the scriptures and give right guidance to the people.

Imam W. Deen Mohammed has profound insight in Biblical and Qur'anic scripture, as well as in other ancient knowledge, and knows how to apply that knowledge to today's complex situations. He is the best example of Prophet Muhammed we have among us today. This means that the standard for leaders in today's world has suddenly been raised, and for those who are fed up with the destruction we see going on in society at all levels, then this is the best example to follow, and the best message to copy. The standard for true leadership cannot be lowered. On the contrary, in today's highly technical and psychological environment, the standard for real leadership for human advancement has to be raised, but one thing will always remain constant, and that is that leadership must always be based on insight in the scriptures, for although everything else is always changing, the word of G-d is eternal.

So we have to know that it's not good enough just to be good. Allah has set standards for human society to live by, and if society is to advance in the proper fashion, it must follow the guidance of Allah.

To revisit the statement made by Imam Mohammed upon his assuming the leadership of the Islamic community after the passing of his father the Honorable Elijah Muhammed, he said, "Words make people." He then issued a challenge to the Islamic community to "Remake the World." That is to say that we're not influenced by just the spoken word in the environment only, but all the images and influences that come into our psyche from the environment in which we live. These influences act to determine how we think, and therefore what type of person we will be.

So then, our job as Muslims, and all other people who want to live in a society that is conducive to the healthy growth and development of ourselves and our families in all aspects of life must work to get the ear of the public and bring them back to intelligent thinking again.

So then let us re-emphasize the gigantic task that lies ahead of the new leadership for the twenty-first century. First we must realize that our progress in this world does not lie in the halls of politics, on the stage of entertainment, or the fields of the sports arena. We must establish belief and obedience to the one G-d. Not just belief, but it must be belief and obedience, for these are what govern our conduct in these and all other affairs.

We must also establish ourselves as an economic force that is able to supply the needs of not only just the African-American community, but the world community as well. In doing so, we are not to see ourselves as successful business individuals only, but more importantly, as part of a broader community, beginning with our own and then spreading abroad. We have to understand that the employees are just as important as the employers, and we're obligated to each other. As stated before, we will see that what we call racism today will change forever, because we then will have gained the respect of the human society, because now, we have become contributors to the world of mankind, instead of asking them to do for us what we can do for ourselves. Now we can give them a job as well as them giving us a job. Plus a whole new economy will have developed that was not there before, and this will improve the life of the whole.

Along with that economic development, we must establish the community life. In doing so, we then are able to provide a womb that will nourish the young minds of our children so they will grow up healthy and be positive contributors to the advancement of the society as a whole. The establishment of business in the community will mean unlimited growth for that community because the dollars will stay in that community for a longer period of time. Educational institutions will grow and the black community will take its place, along with other societies, as a respected community in the world.

As new leaders into the twenty-first century, we cannot be afraid to speak out against those of our own community who would continue to lead us down the path of dependency, and continue to provide excuses for our failure. We can no longer afford to look back on the hurt and suffer because of it. Instead, we must look back on the success of the ancestors, and exceed their excellence. We must look back on the hurt to remember it, and succeed in spite of it.

G-d has blessed the human being to be the crown of creation because He has given the human being something that He did not give the rest of the creation. Allah has given the human being intelligence, and rational thought. New leaders have to speak to the intelligence of the people, and realize that the people have the ability to govern themselves once they come into the knowledge of themselves. This new leadership for the twenty-first century must realize that the strong moral foundation that Allah gave us from the beginning is now, and will always be, strong enough to hold us to our principles, and not only welcome new technical advancements for the progress of the future, but indeed, use these advancements to help improve the real life of human society.

"We Must Rewrite the History"

Chapter 7

Spiritual Application: A Summary

We have often heard the opponents of religion use language that would make the average person think that religion is the primary cause of the world problems we have today. I remember during the days I was active in the Black Revolutionary Movement, we used to hear statements like, "Religion is the opium of the people," which is a statement that has been attributed to Chairman Mao Tse Tung, one of the past rulers of China. We have also heard people talk about how much blood has been spilled in the name of religion. And still others would say that if you want to get a good argument, try discussing religion and politics. Many people say they believe in G-d but reject organized religion. So we see there have been an onslaught of criticism as it relates to religion. In fact, it seems that the only role that religion has ever played in the lives of mankind is that of a destructive nature. However, what we as the general public need to understand is that man, in his quest to rule and enslave other men, did not use the word of G-d for this purpose, because religion, when understood right, condemns man's unjust actions against another human being. A brief study of history will show us that those who stood in the forefront of justice for the human family were people who had a strong belief in G-d as their foundation. Although there are accounts that date back further, we'll just note a few examples beginning with the period of slavery to the present.

Beginning with the abolitionist movement whose origins are rooted in religious circles, we see strong, anti-slavery voices rising using religion for their reasoning. The Quakers and the Methodists played a very important role in the anti-slavery movement. Theodore Dwight Weld's The Bible Against Slavery (1837), and American Slavery As It Is (1839), influenced public opinion against slavery. Elijah P. Lovejoy, a Presbyterian, argued that the slaves were human, created by G-d with the same inalienable rights. He argued that G-d was the master of all human beings. He called slavery a moral evil for the usurpation of those rights. He was murdered in 1837 for his views. Fredrick Douglass declared that slave holding religion of the United States bore no relation to Jesus Christ and should not be labeled "Christian" at all. "Revivals of religion, and revivals of the slave trade," he said, always went "hand in hand."

In the decades preceding the coming of the Civil War, the three largest denominations were disrupted by issues concerning slavery, as have been mentioned earlier in this writing.

In 1837, the Presbyterians split into the "New School" and the "Old School." The former referred to the revivalist methods of evangelism and political reform, while the latter insisted upon conservatism in matters of doctrine, worship, and politics.

At the Methodist General Conference in 1844, the Northern section of the church adopted an anti-slavery position, forcing the departure of the Southerners and the formation of the Methodist Episcopal Church South in 1845.

Finally, a firm stand by the Northern Baptist against appointing slave holders as missionaries angered the South. The Virginia Baptist Foreign Mission Society issued a call for a Consultative Convention, and in 1845, in Augusta, Georgia, the Southern Baptist Convention was organized.[22] (Prothero 3-4)

The abolitionist, John Brown, who in his study of the scriptures could not find any justification for slavery, and so he gave his life for the freedom of all mankind.

As we move on up past the nineteenth century, we see the Honorable Elijah Muhammed, in his quest to bring honor and dignity to his people, use religion as a motivator. I believe that the two strongest desires the Honorable Elijah Muhammed had was for the moral and economic growth of the African-American community.

Although many people may try to highlight the separatist philosophy, I believe that his real focus was on our moral and economic developments, which in itself, when accomplished, would set us aside as a community, not geographically, but that we would be a community practicing genuine religion that would make us the example for others to follow.

We saw Sister Fannie Lou Hamer, Sister Annie Devine, of the Mississippi Freedom Democratic Party, try to unseat those who would use their political positions to try to deny the dignity to the people that G-d intended for them to have. Sister Jewel Williams and Sister Annie Pearl Spears-Nichols struggled tirelessly and courageously to bring justice to the brotherhood of mankind. All were driven by their strong faith in G-d. Rev. J. C. Killingsworth, perhaps one of the strongest forces of the day on the local level, was motivated by his religious convictions to aid in the fight for the freedom of all mankind. Mrs. Jimanna Sumrall, whose care and concerns for humanity extended farther than the boundaries of her own home, was not only instrumental in the personal growth and development of her own family members and those others whose lives she personally touched, but her positive influence is well documented throughout the broader community as well.

Dr. Martin Luther King Jr., Brother El Hajj Malik Shabazz, and other leaders who stood for the cause of human dignity were motivated by their strong belief in Allah, that all mankind is equal in the sight of Allah, and that given the chance, we could all tap into our own human potential, and our growth and development would be limitless.

On a broader and more general level, we see organizations like the Red Cross and the Red Crescent who, while not being religious groups, are made up of volunteers from the G-d-fearing masses.

Delivering blood, helping those who have been caught up in floods, earthquakes, war, and other kinds of disasters. They provide help worldwide to people regardless of race, creed, or national origin, many times at the expense of their own lives.

And then there are the unsung heroes who most of us just don't hear about. They make it their business to do random acts of kindness on a daily basis. There are those who are busy helping the homeless, and those who are establishing other kinds of aid for the less fortunate. Most of these people are motivated by a strong belief in G-d, and these are some of the ways they express that belief.

The YMCA and the YWCA were established by those who professed a belief in G-d and in doing so, sought to provide a safe place for the wayfarer.

Lastly, as we have already discussed, the modern conveniences we enjoy today came about as a result of man's strong faith in G-d, his insight on the holy scriptures, and his being blessed by Allah to develop this creation for his own progress.

These are just a few examples of some of the things we already knew. Today, we hear so much negativity as it relates to religion that soon, we begin to associate only negativity with it. We should understand that what has caused the confusion; bloodshed has not been the word of G-d, but rather man's deliberate misinterpretation of G-d's word for his own selfish use.

Politics and other areas of public service is to be seen as an extension of our religious beliefs in terms of being in a position where we can legislate laws, and influence the society in ways that will benefit mankind, as opposed to hindering mankind. This is not to be misunderstood as someone being in a position to force their own religious beliefs on others. To the contrary, it means simple and practical application in that which we know and do that is of righteousness. In other words, it is the magnificent exercise of one's own humanity for the good of others, whether politically, professionally, or personally.

The inertia we see in the masses of the people, especially the African-American community, is because of the way religious instruction is given to us, as it is evident by our actions that many of us, including some of the ministers, are devoid of knowledge and understanding. As stated before in this writing, much of the understanding we as African-Americans, and some others have as it relates to religion is spiritual belief only, and some of that is misunderstood. That is to say that our religious understanding is so spiritual that it disconnects us from the day-to-day activities of the world. We see G-d or heaven as some place we go after we die. This is because the sermons we hear and the way they are presented have nothing to do with the reality that we as a people live in.

Recently, a young lady came into my place of business, which is a clothing store. She looked around and found a beautiful red suit that fitted her very nice and modestly. She placed the suit on lay-away. A few days later, the same young lady came back in the store and exchanged the suit for something different that didn't look as good on her as her previous choice. When I inquired as to her reason for the exchange, she told me that her pastor had preached vehemently on the subject of Jezebel in the Bible. He talked about how she painted her face and wore red, so the pastor forbade the congregation to wear red, or wear makeup. Or in another case where we're made to think that we can go out and commit as much sin as we're able to do, all we need to do is bring it to Jesus because he has already paid the price for us with his blood, thus rendering us not responsible for the sins we commit.

It is in my opinion that these are the exact kinds of teachings that keep us in an inferior position in this society. While others go on to develop this creation given to us by Allah for their own progress, we continue to protest because they have, and we have not. So much emphasis is placed on the life of Jesus, and that is the exact opposite of what he taught. Jesus placed the emphasis on us, and on what we need to be doing. The commandments brought to us from G-d by Jesus are designed to bring dignity to us, but they will require that we work and exert ourselves. These commandments help us to maintain a sense of morality, without which our communities will become cesspools for just any old dirty bird to nest in. When we look closely at the African-American community, we will notice that we have fallen to last place in terms of respect, even when referred to in connection with other morally illegal groups, such as the homosexual community. In

TV sitcoms, and just in general language, whether it's political or otherwise, we usually hear the statement lesbians, gays, and blacks.

At one time, the gay community used the Jewish and the African-American communities to associate themselves with, but the Jews quickly and quietly disassociated themselves. Then they used the Latino and the African-American communities, and like the Jews, the Latinos disassociated themselves as well. As a people who have suffered more trials and tribulations than any other people in the history of mankind, and still standing and maintaining our humanity, we should be too proud, and have too much dignity for ourselves to allow such a group whose lifestyle we know is wrong to use us as a springboard for the purpose of getting their lifestyle to be accepted as legitimate.

So then, we can see that religion, in the way it has been presented to the African-American community for the most part, has become nothing but a soothing salve, rather than a body of knowledge that the masses can put to use so that they can free themselves. Let me stop and say right here that we are only attempting to bring more clarity and emphasis to some points we've already referred to earlier in this writing. So at the risk of sounding redundant, our point is this, in order to understand scripture and apply it in a practical manner in our lives, we have to see ourselves in the scripture. We have to be able to see the parallels both in the scriptures and in our own lives.

The reason why others can come in and take advantage of us as a community is because we are devoid of the understanding of the knowledge we think we have, and while we have been able to maintain our humanity, others will come into our communities, take our innocence and our humanity, and use it to take advantage of us. The answer to our problems, and to the problems of the general society lie in the revealed word of G-d and its application to our lives. So then, let us give some examples as to how we are to see human society in the scriptures, and thereby make it more applicable to our everyday life.

We find that in the twelfth chapter of Exodus, Allah speaks to Moses and Aaron concerning the Passover. Allah says to them, "Speak ye unto all the congregation of Israel, saying, in the tenth day of the month they shall take to themselves every man a lamb. Your lamb shall be without blemish, a male of the first year. You shall keep it until the fourteenth day of the same month. And they shall take of the blood, and strike it on the two side post of the upper door post of the house. And they shall eat the flesh in the night roasted with fire, and unleavened bread, and with bitter herbs they shall eat it. Eat not of it raw, nor sodden at all with water, but roasted with fire. For I will pass through the land of Egypt this night and will smite the first born and against all the gods of Egypt. And the blood shall be to you a token upon your houses where you are; and when I see the blood, I will pass over you, and the plague shall not be upon you to destroy you." **Exodus 12:3, 5-9, 12-13**. G-d instructs Moses to each take a lamb on the tenth day. The lamb is to be without blemish, which is symbolic of the unspoiled innocence of human nature before it's exposed to the negative influences of the world. The tenth day is symbolic of a new beginning, since there are only nine numbers in the numerical system. The fact that G-d instructs them to allow the lamb to grow for four more days is telling us that we must grow in all aspects of our lives, in our moral, economic, intellectual, and our spiritual lives. So we're humble, but strong and wise, and we are not to be preyed on by others. Just like the physical blood that runs throughout our physical bodies, carrying out the impurities we have in us and providing for our physical life, then the blood of the lamb is the pure word of G-d that brings life to those who accept it, and apply it to their moral life. The house is our own human makeup, and the two side posts of the house is the highest part of our humanity, which is the mind, and our ears, where we receive the knowledge for our salvation.

The unleavened bread is symbolic of pure knowledge. We know that leaven is a substance like yeast or baking powder, that when used in baking bread, causes it to rise because of the fermentation it produces. So the gas lightens the dough. In reality, much of the bread we think we have is just how it has swollen from the gas produced from the yeast. It's the same with knowledge. The unleavened bread is the pure knowledge without the yeast, or as we know it in today's society, all the emotionalism, the whooping and hollering that some ministers do, and all the yelling and shouting that go on in some of our church services, are nothing but hot air, produced from the yeast put into the message, so the people who went to the service desiring a full meal, came away with nothing but some emotionalism. And we're still not free. The bitter herbs are the fact that this truth is hard to bear, especially when we're so used to doing things our way. But we must realize that if we are to make progress in this world, we have to give up our will and obey the will of Allah.

To eat the flesh in the night, roasted with fire, is symbolic of our spiritual growth tempered by our rational makeup. The moon is our spiritual life, and the sun is our rational life. That is to say that in receiving the word of Allah, some of us tend to get too spiritual or lopsided. G-d wants us to stay balanced, not too far right or too far left. We don't want to get so spiritual that no one wants to be around us, or we distance ourselves from the real world, nor do we want to be caught up in the world so much that G-d's word will have no effect on us. When we accept the word of G-d as truth, it acts for our moral, mental, and spiritual life, just as the physical blood acts for the physical life. We come into this world committing no sin. Our human nature is intact, just as Allah created it from the beginning. So our good human nature, our moral human nature, is our firstborn. Morality comes before anything else, so this is our firstborn. When we accept G-d's word and apply it, our firstborn is saved.

Egypt is any society that strays away from its moral base, and loses regardfulness for Allah, and many times, think that they are self-sufficient. So whether this happens to us as individuals, or on a national level, we begin to crumble from within. So as we see ourselves in this scripture, we can see that as we take on knowledge and the wisdom to use that knowledge, the angel of moral, mental, and spiritual death passes over us. That is to say that because of the mercy of Allah, we have grown to a level of high standards so that we refuse to participate in activities that are below us.

Many of us are walking around here, physically alive but morally dead. We're not a productive people, and we have allowed teen pregnancy, gang and drug activities take over our communities. As we witness our youth of today and the people they take for role models, we can see our future generations slipping deeper and deeper into slavery. The tragedy is that this kind of slavery we are witnessing today is the worse kind, because it's mental slavery and we can't see it tightening it's grip around our minds as it lowers our standards of decency, and destroys the value systems that have been handed down to us from generation to generation. In this mental slavery. We think we're making progress, but all that is happening is that we're getting caught up in the trends of the environment. Some of us are making lots of money, some are making little or no money, but none of us are establishing a moral and economic foundation for the future.

Too many of our youth refuse to take interest in the arts and other professional endeavors. When we reflect on the past in the days of physical slavery where our men and women were stripped of their physical clothing and placed on the auction block for the perspective slave buyers to come by and purchase them for slave labor on the plantation, so we see today how the entertainers strip themselves, not only of their physical clothing, but of their moral consciousness, their pride, their high standards, and above all, their respect for Allah. They have stripped themselves and put themselves on the auction block of society to the highest bidder. The brothers parade themselves up and down the stage and on their music videos, with muscles flexing to the waist, while the sisters dress so scantily that they are less than a step away from a striptease act. They think it's trendy to perform these kinds of acts, but all they're doing is appealing to the sexual desires of the youth of the society, thus helping to contribute to the vicious cycle of an inferior position in the society for our future generation.

How can our youth raise their aspirations when day in and day out, twenty-four seven, they're bombarded with a constant barrage of naked men and women singing about sex, or how they would like to get with the friend of their girlfriend or boyfriend, or how dirty one has been to the other. How do they expect to grow in a positive direction when that's the kind of garbage we feed on on a day-to-day basis. Telling the parents to control what their children watch is out of the question because most of the time, the parents themselves are nothing but babies who have become victims of the same negative influences, and so the beat goes on. We see many of our youth getting into this subculture of a lifestyle, and many of the entertainment groups they follow are adopting the names of criminals, mobsters, animals, and penal code violations on the law books of various cities around the country. We see very young rappers come out, making big money and being given high status in the media, so then the generation of their time follow that example down the road of failure, and no productivity for us as a people. And so yeah, the beat goes on.

It's no wonder why we see so many of our young people locked up in jails and penitentiaries because they are trying to mimic the lifestyle of the person they saw on the music video. Our sense of decency has fallen so low that we think nothing of pissing on the street in public with no sense of shame, like an animal would do. It's as if the slave master has finally succeeded in reducing us to below the level of an animal.

Our focus is so strong on our sexual appetites, our interest in real business, the arts, and intellectual growth, are minimal. So the world of life and productivity moves on while we as a people continue to fall farther and farther behind. Instead of addressing these kinds of issues, the average preacher continues to appeal to the emotional makeup of the masses with a whoop and a holler that does nothing for the people but give them a good feeling, and satisfy their conscience for all the wrong they may have done during the week. The sermons, for the most part, have nothing to do with the reality that the people are facing everyday, so we leave the church, feeling good from an emotional outburst, but without an inkling of direction for our lives. And it's not because the knowledge isn't in the scriptures, but because either the preacher doesn't know it, or he's continuing to keep the masses in the dark so that their allegiance will continue to remain with him, and he will be the major influence in the lives of the people. So then, he becomes another one of the gatekeepers to the Institution of Slavery. I say this because real knowledge is supposed to free the people, and it is evident that we are not a free people, not because we're black or because the white man is hindering us, but because we are devoid of knowledge.

I think it's important that we make note here that this is not a blanket condemnation of all preachers, because there are many,

many ministers who are making great progress for the masses, and bringing knowledge to the people. There are many ministers who are very active in the lives of the people they serve, and who do their utmost to bring enlightenment to those who follow them. But sadly, we know there are too many who get into the ministry just for the prestige and the paycheck. Now we know the meaning of the term, "The harvest is ripe, but the laborers are few." It means that not only are we, as ministers, supposed to teach the truth to the people where they can use it or apply it to their lives for their own self-improvement, but we're also supposed to speak out publicly against those things that hinder the growth of our people, and be instrumental in the communities in which we live to insure that we help promote a healthy and strong environment for our future generations to grow up in. The people will follow the truth if it is given to them.

We now come to another scripture, this one from the New Testament, and one which, I think, will bring us more in tune with what our responsibility to G-d and each other is. In the New Testament, we find that at almost every turn in his mission, the scribes and Pharisees were confronting Jesus. These were people who sought to put stumbling blocks in front of Jesus, or try to hinder him in some way by criticizing his method of teaching the people. It seems that there was always a challenge from them to him. In the fifteenth chapter of Matthew, we see again the scribes and Pharisees addressing issues that have little or nothing to do with improving the lives of the people they're supposed to be leading. When we understand it, it's much the same scenario described in the above reference to Jezebel. The scribes and the Pharisees wanted to condemn the disciples for not washing their hands before eating. Jesus told them that while they were putting so much emphasis on things of little concern, they themselves were guilty of committing much greater sins. Jesus said unto them, "Why do you also transgress the commandments of G-d by your traditions? For G-d commanded, saying, Honor thy father and thy mother: and he that curseth father or mother, let him die the death. But you say that it is a gift, by whatsoever thou mightest be profited by me; and honor not his father or mother, he shall be free. Thus have you made the commandments of G-d of no effect."

In teaching the people, Jesus said, "Not that which goeth into the mouth of man that defiles him, but that which comes out the mouth that defiles a man." **In reference to the scribes and Pharisees, Jesus said,** "Every plant, which my Heavenly Father hath not planted, shall be rooted up. Let them alone, they be blind leaders of the blind. What ever enters in at the mouth goeth to the belly, and is cast out into the draught. But those things, which proceed out of the mouth, come forth from the heart; and they defile the man. For out of the heart proceed evil thoughts, adulteries, murders, fornication, thefts, false witness, and blasphemies. These are the things that defile a man." **Matthew 15:3-6, 11, 13-14, 17-19.**

To have honor and respect for the father and mother is one of the greater commandments given to man by G-d. In the Holy Qur'an, Allah tells us, "Thy Lord hath decreed that you worship none but Him, and that you be kind to your parents. Whether one or both of them attain old age in thy life, say not to them a word of contempt, nor repel them but address them, in terms of honour. And out of kindness, lower to them the wing of humility, and say, "My Lord! Bestow on them Thy mercy even as they have cherished me in childhood." **Holy Qur'an 17:23-24.**

So we can see why Allah saw the need to raise Jesus up at that time. The religious leaders thought more of the traditions of man than they did of teaching the word of G-d. To have children brought pride and honor to the family, and when that child went on to make a name for himself, this brought more honor to the family, but instead of the child giving honor to the parents, the parents were made to feel obligated to the child. It is apparent then that according to the language that Jesus is using, the religious leaders were more concerned with keeping themselves as the focus of the people as opposed to teaching the people to have faith in Allah. And as a result, they continued to remain at the bottom of society.

The reference to any plant not planted by his heavenly father tells us that once the people hear the real truth from someone who is truly representing G-d's commands, they will no longer want to hear the weak and meaningless teachings of those who are rooted in shallow traditions. Just as we said about some of the so-called leaders who put themselves up before the people today, they are blind or devoid of knowledge, so the question begs to be answered, how can someone who is mentally blind himself lead someone else? Just because someone says they are called to preach or they say they represent G-d, does not make it so, and they will be rooted up.

The food that goes into the physical mouth is just that, physical food, and it comes out as waste. But that which affects the minds is what does the real damage. So then we see Jesus putting the emphasis where it really should be, and that is on the mental food, or the negative influences that continue to plague the society. When we look around society and we see that it is based on all the things that Allah has outlawed, what we are truly witnessing is the imagination of the human being at work. The ideas that we get from the media, the music and all other forms of communications are ideas that come from the hearts and minds of men, and they have an effect on the hearts and minds of other men. Jesus is telling us that these ideas don't leave us, and we begin to act out whatever negative messages we've gotten from the negative influences in the environment. This is what defiles us as human beings. So the concern then is not on dirty hands and physical food, but rather on the manipulation of the minds of the masses. We must see that the hands only manifest what the mind thinks. We need a society that produces good and positive thinkers.

We don't come into the world committing these horrible acts of murder, adultery, thievery, etc. We are influenced by the environment we live in, and man brings about whatever influence we see. When we look into the society, we see the negative influences robbing the people of the life that G-d intended for them to have. We look a little further and we see our leaders selling themselves out to business groups and getting caught up in scandals, losing their credibility, thus rendering them ineffective against fighting the ills of the environment.

New leaders must use their positions to unify the people and make the people see that our position in life depends squarely upon what we do as a people. Even though a person maybe of a different faith, still, the goal of us all is to Allah, so unity between us all should be urged. We have to realize that the glory is for Allah, not for ourselves. Our communities are suffering so bad because too much emphasis is placed on what Jesus has already done, instead of what we need to do. Therefore, our children don't read as they should. Their biggest aspiration is to be an athlete, a rap star, or some other profession that will make their lives insignificant in the future progress of mankind.

The problems that we suffer from, while they may be many, and take some time to deal with, they are relatively easy to solve. All it takes as a start is to get back to our basic value system. Our parents and grandparents worked so hard to keep their children on the right path, but the influences we get from media and other sources are literally killing us off. Parents find themselves having to compete with TV, radio, wild magazines that appeal to the minds of our youth, and at the same time, parents try to provide for the welfare of the family. These influences are all around us and we consume them in our every thought, so most of the time, the parent is fighting an uphill struggle. When our children go outside of the home, they are bombarded with so much garbage that the parents don't even know them when they come back home. So it's not the fact that the parents are not trying to do their job in raising their children, it's just that the environment is contaminated with so much garbage that it reaches right up to the nostril of G-d.

Again, we say we are victims of the environment we live in. As we observe the lives and the lifestyles of our youth today, we can see that the hip-hop culture has a huge influence in the way they think, dress, and the activities they participate in. The name "hip-hop" is a play on appealing to the sexual nature of the human being, especially our youth. In fact, when we think about it, it's taken directly from the bunny rabbit. We know that its mode of travel is to hip-hop, as we say. But we also know that the rabbit is known for its high sexual nature, and the high nature of fertility. So whoever it was that came up with the name "hip-hop" for this kind of music that our youth are caught up in must be a devil of the worst kind. By appealing to the sexual and the violent nature of our youth, we can see that the real goal was to destroy them, generation after generation, until we wake up and put a stop to it. We can also see this same trend in the so-called adult music as well. It's all about sex, that's all. So we suffer from both ends of the spectrum.

Now I know we've already mentioned this before in this writing, but the problem is so serious that it bears mentioning again. Also, as stated before, the music industry is not the offender here, but it is a good place to get started. The only reason we have a political and an economic problem is because we have a moral problem. The same energy we exerted against racism in the days of the Civil Rights Movement should be exerted against the moral breakdown in the society today. The masses need to put a check on their biological desires, and begin to demand better and more quality programming. The kind of programming that influences the society to a higher level of thinking, rather than the jungle-type lifestyle we see that is so prevalent in society today.

Our lives shouldn't have to hang on a computer chip to keep out the negative influences. Allah has given the human being the moral strength needed to stand against the bombardment that's pounding the society today. At no time should we allow technology to be a substitute for the inner strength inherent in the creation of the human spirit. We want always to be in control of our own lives. **So again we say, this at least is a start. When we begin to redevelop our value system, then we are on the road to getting our lives back.**

Now, we know how people look up to and respect the religious leadership, and the political leadership. It is because of this respect that they carry a heavy influence among the masses. This tells us then that four things must happen in order for that leader to be successful: First, that leadership must have the concerns of the people genuinely at heart. Secondly, that leadership must be moved by inspiration from G-d, as opposed to the popular opinion of society. Leadership without understanding and conviction shall be rooted up, for they are without foundation. They are just as blind as those they try to lead, so they all fall into the ditch. Third, that leadership must have knowledge of the scriptures, not from memory only, but more importantly, from understanding. Fourth, the best way to tell the worth of a leader is to notice the progress in the lives of the people they claim to lead. Not only on an individual level, but also on a community level as well. In far too many cases, we see the material progress in the life of the leader, while the lives of those that follow remain under the control of those who manipulate the masses.

When we look at the context of the life of Jesus, and the times in which he lived, we can see that he stood outside the leadership of that day. We know that at the time Jesus was born, the Jews were in pretty much the same inferior position under the Roman government of that day as the African-American community find themselves in on the bottom of society today. So they were looking for a hero, or a messiah, to come in and save them from the oppressive rule of the Romans. But when Jesus arrived on the scene, instead of condemning the Romans, he began to teach on the shortcomings of the Jews and the weak leadership of the scribes and Pharisees, who represented the religious law, and the aristocratic Sadducees, who valued their material accomplishments more than helping to bring true direction to the lives of the masses. Jesus cautioned the people not to follow the example of these people whose works were done only to be seen of men.

When we study the leadership of Imam W. Deen Mohammed and the Muslim American Society, we see the same attitude of resentment from some of those African-American leaders, and others that influence African-American thought today, as Jesus experienced in his day and time. Instead of jumping on the bandwagon and blaming others for the plight of the black community, Imam Mohammed puts the responsibility right on us, where it should be. The Imam began to tell us of our own shortcomings, and that our success or failure in this life lie in our own hands. And it's because of these kinds of teachings that encourage us to look inside ourselves to improve ourselves, that not only made some of the African-American leadership turn their backs, but also the African-American media as well. Because of the fact that the African-American media put so much emphasis on the entertainment world, and in many cases, even sanctions the way they influence the society, many of our people take this as a sign that this is the accepted way to go.

This is not to say that the African-American media is not a valuable part of the African-American community, because they do bring valuable and much-needed information to the black community. But it seems to me that a leader who is from our community and is respected by heads of government the world over, including here in our own country, and whose words even influence government decisions in some cases, a leader of this caliber should get more attention from a press that claim to represent the same people.

In reflecting on religion once again, we are to realize that it is not to be used in praising someone in the past for what they did, but rather it has to be about using the example and the advice given by those heroes of the past to make life better for the future. In Mark 6:4, Jesus tells us that he is a prophet of G-d. Jesus represents the individual or the type of human being that G-d wants us all to be. He is the type of man to whom gave G-d the credit for everything he did, even for his own being. So as stated earlier in this writing, we are not to put so much emphasis on the physical birth, death, and resurrection of the Prophet Jesus, but we are to pay more attention to keeping the commandments that he brought to us from Allah. We then come into a new birth, which means we die to the influences of weakness and corruption in the society. In dying to the corruption of the world, we are resurrected with a new mind. When we understand that the birth, death, and resurrection of Christ is meant to be used by us as an example for us to follow in our own lives rather than to keep our minds back in history over 2,000 years ago, then we begin to make the Scriptures more applicable to our own lives.

Now let us understand that this new mind is not the kind of mind that keeps us in church everyday of the week for prayer meetings, choir practice, men's night, ladies' night, or some other function that requires your to spend time in church. This is not what the new birth represents, because when you study the Scriptures, you will find that Jesus spent very little time at the temple. If we stay up in church all day and all week, we have no time to practice what we've learned. Our resurrection is to be in the form of moral development first. Hold on to the strong principles that we learn in church and family so that we will be successful in meeting the challenges in the environment.

Now that we have our morals intact, we are now ready for economic development. We are tired of being sub-contractors, who only got in on an affirmative action bid. NO! We should never be satisfied with special treatment. That in itself tells us and the world that we are a people that needs special treatment because we're not as well equipped as others to step up to the plate of responsibility on our own. We have to come into a mind that if we're going to be truly successful in this world, we're going to have to do it on our own merit. Our black business people must come together and build shopping malls, like other people do. We must build the home, not just live in it. And we should look for dependable African-American contractors to do the primary work. This is another advantage of community establishment because we can build the homes, the roads, the streets and bridges, etc. This is how we get on top and how we become a respected people, because now, we're seen in the same light as any other respected people who are doing things not only for self, but helping others as well.

Let us give one word of caution here. We are not to hire people just because they are black. No! We want the black contractor to know that we demand first-class work from them, just as we demand it from others. If a black contractor develops a reputation for giving inferior service, then they should be rejected by all. It has to be known that when we talk about making it on our own merit, that quality applies with the African-American community as much as it applies with anyone else.

So yes, we want to build buildings, sub-divisions, freeways, etc. We want to own chains of supermarkets, have hospitals that we own and operate for the good of the whole of the community, and be known as the best in providing the best service. We want to be the manufacturers, importers, and exporters of merchandise, pharmacies, doctors, lawyers, dentists, scientists, explorers, etc. Everything that makes the world move for the advancement of mankind, we want to be a part of it, not just on the receiving end, but on the spearheading end. We want to be among the initiators of all that's good.

When we reflect back on the history of the ancestors, we see that we were builders of great empires and civilizations in our motherland of Africa. We were kings and queens and rulers, a fact that any of today's modern civilizations would envy. In conquering Spain, we were able to bring about a renewal of life to the arts and sciences. The study and development of new medical techniques, optics, the study of space and the universe, etc. It was our ancestors who were responsible for the enlightenment of the world. After being brought to America in chains, the creativity still continued. Some of the greatest inventions that the world has ever known were created by our ancestors and are used today the world over for the progress of human society. What country do we know that doesn't use the traffic light, or the electric light? Where is it that blood plasma is not being used? The answer is there is nowhere that these inventions are not being used. Everything, from the soles on the shoes we wear, the telescopes scientists use to study outer space, the aspirin we take to make us feel better, the zero we use to balance our check books, were brought to the world of mankind by our ancestors, who had practically nothing to work with except faith in G-d, desire and determination to not only show they were as good as anybody else, but they worked with a sincere desire to advance the society of mankind.

So then, when we begin to see ourselves in this manner as contributors to human civilization, then the whole world will witness our resurrection from the dead. A people who were known to be morally, mentally, and spiritually dead has now taken their place, along with others, as partners in the world of human advancement. As it says in the Bible about the resurrection of Jesus, "All eyes shall see him." We are to see ourselves as that great resurrection, for truly, all eyes will be on us. And just like Jesus did, we give ALL praises to Allah. We never forget where we came from, and just like other ethnic groups, we keep our history alive, and we continue to pass it on from generation to generation.

"We Must Rewrite the History"

In John, the twentieth chapter, when Mary Magdalene went looking for Jesus at the sepulcher, he had risen. When she looked around and saw him, she did not recognize him because he appeared to her as the gardener. We know that the duty of the gardener is to cultivate the garden, to keep out the dangerous weeds and insects that will do harm to the plants. When we apply this same principle to human development, we understand that to cultivate is to bring a thing to a level of refinement. Culture is also related to cultivation. So we're talking about being culturally refined through moral, intellectual, and spiritual development. We then pick up the dignity of our ancestors.

We begin to recall when men really knew what it meant to be a man. We cease having fatherless sons and daughters growing up in broken homes. The wretched idea of family life this society gives us fades into oblivion. Gangs, drugs, liquor stores, obscene acts on the streets, are replaced by positive activities. Parents are not afraid to let their child outside the house anymore. Life and productivity abound to the level that not only do our youth not have to go to others for employment, but we will be able to employ others as well. The money will remain in the community longer, thereby adding to the strength of the community.

No, they will not recognize us at first. They will ask themselves the question, "Can anything good come up out of Nazareth?" Nazareth is representative of any negative environment. Then they will see this "New Jerusalem" or "model community" "descending from the sky, or the minds of men," and everyone will proclaim the glory of G-d.

Let us once again revisit the word leadership. A leader is chosen by the people; a leader is another person of rank who is to be out front so as to guide others. The suffix "-ship" refers to quality or proficiency. Hence, the word leadership has to do with how well the person who is in that position advances those he or she is leading. As stated before, Allah tells us that He has made man the vicegerent, or the khalifah in the earth. We have said that this word khalifah is similar to the word leader, but it carries more responsibility. Not only does it mean "to be out front," but it also means "to be the successor, to follow, to take the place of someone, to come behind."

So when Allah says He's going to put a khalifah in the earth, the meaning is one who comes behind G-d with the permission of G-d.

One who G-d has appointed to have dominion over the earth to make it productive for the whole of mankind. As human beings, this potential is inherent in the nature of all of us, and with the freedom of mind that the human being has, we can be as productive as we want to be, or as destructive as we want to be. Our rise and fall are done by the choices we make as individuals and as a nation.

Again, we say that wealth and technical advances are not the only signs of a nation's progress. America is the leading nation in the world today. There is no other nation that can come against America militarily and survive. But we must be careful not to be the cause of our own destruction from within. Just as it was patriotic to go and fight wars for America in other lands, how much more important then is it to fight for the real survival of this great nation. Our position as khalifah, or world leader, has to be of such that those who come after us will have the best example to follow. And those who are on distant shores will not fear us for our military might, but rather for our human achievements.

So this new leadership moves into position with a sense of G-d consciousness. That is to say that having the knowledge that we rule by Allah's permission only means that we are to take care of this great planet. The khalifah is one who follows the will of Allah and leads by the most excellent example. This new leadership will be followers and leaders. They come from behind, following the guidance of G-d, making sure that the dangerous influences in the environment doesn't rob the society of the good life that Allah intended for it to have, and they also go out front, clearing and pointing the way to true Freedom, Justice, and Equality for the whole of mankind. A mercy to all the worlds. These new leaders, while working Locally, will have to think Globally.

In the African-American community, we must realize that our concerns must grow beyond the issue of race. As stated earlier in this writing, when we become a more productive people and share in the power of the world, not on the basis of race or because of being appointed by someone in a position of influence to a position of influence. That will not do when looked upon in the situation of our people, and of the whole nation, for that matter. We must get to a position where we are truly equal to others who have a share in the real power of this world. To do this, we must get beyond the small sins that hold us down. "If you want to be successful in a career, develop your life so that your life is dead to that which takes you down and alive only to that which takes you up or helps you to get up. This life is a trial, and no matter how much academic knowledge you have or how much you have acquired as a student in college or as a professor, a little small thing can take you down."[23] (Mohammed 13)

I remember, growing up as a child, the old gospel song that had a strong message in it: "Yield not to temptation, for yielding is sin. Each victory will help you, some other to win." This tells us that just as we have physical muscles that get stronger as we exercise them, so then our moral muscles grow stronger the more we resist wrongdoing. The foundation of life is a strong moral principle.

"Remember the Ancestors!" "We Must Rewrite the History!"

The following is a hadith or saying of Prophet Muhammed (May G-d's peace be upon him), and some quotes by Imam W. Deen Mohammed on Leadership and Trustworthiness. They are taken from the Leadership Training and Development Study Guide of Imam Mohammed and compiled by Imam Qasim Ahmed.

From the sayings of Prophet Muhammed, we read; "Everyone of you is a shepherd and everyone is responsible for what he is shepherd of." **(Bukhari-Muslim)**

*In order for anyone to be a leader, he has to learn how to be trustworthy. G-d wants us to be leaders. Men and women are going to become leaders if they have children. They become leaders over their families. The method that uses is through loyalty. To be loyal is to keep your word, to keep your commitment to each other, and to protect each other's rights.

*The married couple must learn how to share what they have with each other. Likewise for the good leader, he must learn how to give his love to his people, and he has to learn to share what he has with his people. If he sees the people need his mind, his good thoughts, his intelligence, his strength, and even his life, he would have to give these things to his people.

*Here is how G-d makes the good leader. He puts the man and the woman together, and they have to share love with each other, and trust each other. They have to give and take. When the baby comes, they already know how to be loyal, how to suffer, and how to be honest. Now they are fit to be leaders. G-d established a partnership that demands trust, loyalty, giving and taking. The subjects for this partnership are the children.

*The job of leaders is to create new circumstances, to have a role in shaping circumstances so that the future is better than the present. Muslims must be responsible for our circumstances. It's not just the mayor or president's job; it is firstly our job.

*Allah wants leaders to come forward with a desire to live and work for a better world, to influence the many and who will be a great factor in bringing about better conditions for people to have a better life.

*The role of the leader is to care for the Muslim life and to give advice and to help people in matters of religion. If we respect the charge of authority in the local people, we will be successful. This is the obligation of the shura. Our most urgent instrument is Muslim democracy.

*Leaders must accept the responsibility for our children today and generations to come. God didn't give this to one certain race to shoulder the responsibility for man's existence now and in the future. This responsibility must now be accepted by the African-Americans, because now they have been called again to accept God and to accept the life that God has planned for them.

*We have been able to achieve what we achieved because we trusted Elijah Muhammad. Don't let anybody tell you to give up the idea of trusting leaders. And we have been taken many times. We have been fleeced, robbed, and sent down the deadend road. We have had all kinds of bad experiences with African-American leaders, but let nobody discourage you. The answer is to build trust among us. If we don't have leadership strong enough to carry us, to carry the load of leadership, then let all of us together work on bringing about leadership that can carry the load for us.

*How do you work on grooming leadership or bringing about strength in your leader? By showing in your own behavior, by showing in your own determination, with your own actions, that you would not tolerate weak leaders who cannot bear the burden of leadership. Bearing the burden of leadership is faithfulness, loyalty to what they profess. They must remain loyal and faithful to what they profess. They must have your interest at heart and work for your interest.[24] (Mohammed 4-5)

Chapter 8

The Rise of Moral Intellectualism

To be a leader these days takes a person that not only has courage, but willing to risk whatever the corruptors of society has to throw against them. Bodily harm as well as harm to their reputation. This is because they see that the world is being enslaved and brought under darkness under the guise of freedom. Truly the darkness here is that of the mind, the mistake of allowing immoral causes to usurp those that are moral.

There is a process in the destruction of the moral nature of society that happens over a period, until society comes to accept the idea that that's just how things are. But there are still those in the society who do not accept these ideas but are unable to speak out because they have no platform. The media is the primary vehicle for transporting immorality, so it does everything to keep the voices of those who see the trick from being heard by the public. The media is used as a tool to dumb down the minds of the people reducing them to mere mush, and shallow minds. The mind of the average citizen is preoccupied with trends, fads and sex, while those who are considered intelligent are news pundits who appear on the major cable news channels as guests speaking on issues as opposed to solutions to the issues, and many make a living at this game. The politicians have checked the pulse of the local electorate and speak to the issues that ignite them, even though those issues have no place in the political arena.

The great leader and reformer Dr. Booker T. Washington said, "A lie doesn't become truth, wrong doesn't become right, and evil doesn't become good, just because its accepted by the majority." (Booker T. Washington. Internet, 10/25/22.) When we reflect on the history of the Civil Rights Movement, we get an idea of why the struggle for human dignity took an abrupt turn that limited its success. Before it was called the Civil Rights Movement it was known as the Struggle for Human Rights, and the focus wasn't about integration or segregation, but as Malcolm X or El Hajj Malik Shabazz stated, our struggle is to be recognized as humans in this society. We weren't trying to move in with white people, or sit next to them at a lunch counter, we had those same establishments in our own neighborhoods, so we weren't lacking for business to spend our money with. Our struggle was for human dignity.

From Human Rights to Civil Rights: How the direction of the movement was changed!

I remember sitting in a meeting over on Lynch Street in Jackson, Mississippi, I was still kind of new to the movement, so I didn't know everybody personally, but I do remember Lawrence Guyot who was the director of the Mississippi Freedom Democratic Party was present, another activist named Mo, short for Mohammad, an adopted name. Unita Blackwell who served as head of the Student Non-Violent Coordinating Committee (SNCC) which was one of the organizations that had joined forces to lead the movement at that time. The others were, the National Association for the Advancement of Colored People (NAACP), the Congress of Racial Equality (CORE), the Southern Christian Leadership Conference (SCLC). It was these organizations that joined forces to form an umbrella group called the Council of Federated Organizations (COFO), the group that I worked for and was charged with leading the state-wide voter registration initiative across Mississippi to register black folks to vote. It was also at this time that hundreds and maybe thousands of volunteers came to Mississippi and to other parts across the South to work as volunteers in the movement.

These volunteers came from all part of the country and was comprised of all ethnicities, black, white, Asian, Mexicans, Jew and any other ethnic group you can think of. The FBI kept close watch on the activities of the movement monitoring its direction. In fact, some of the volunteers who came to work were FBI agents, and all volunteers lived in the black community with the local people. But not only were there FBI agents among some of the volunteers there were also many Jews who worked as volunteers in the movement, and there were some from among them who came with a specific agenda to thwart the progress of the struggle for human dignity for black folks. Now let me stop right here and make clear that my reference to Jews isn't a blanket condemnation of all Jews, but rather its aimed at the ruling class that seeks control over the minds of the masses and uses every tool at their disposal, including the media for that purpose. Most Jews are just like any other people seeking to live in harmony with others, but the ruling class of Jews those who Jesus Christ condemned in Biblical scripture where he said, "You are of your father the devil, and the lusts of your father you will do. He was a murderer from the beginning, and abode not in truth, because there was no truth in him. When he speaks a lie he speaks of his own; for he is a lier and the father of it. Bible: John 8:44. In the Holy Quran we read, "Strongest man in enmity to the believers will you find Jews and pagans; and nearest among them in love will you find those who say "we are Christians" because among these are men devoted to learning. And men who have renounced the world and they are not arrogant. HQ: 5:82.

The discussion centered around making the primary focus political reform as a means of achieving equality for the masses. This decision in and of itself changed the entire trajectory of the movement. We went from demanding recognition and respect for who we are as dignified human beings, to using white people as a measuring rod for our own self-worth. Suddenly the goal became integration, political power, material gain, and all that were attached to these kinds of concerns. While it's good and necessary for any community worth its worth, it isn't good to be tricked into being sent in a false direction thinking you're headed towards freedom, when in reality, you're under the control of someone's influence. Those white people who sat in on that meeting were Jews who had infiltrated as volunteers working on the voter registration project, but really their goal was to gain control of the Human Rights Struggle, thus taking the vision and the focus away from human dignity and placing it on the material things they already had control over. This was the plan, and this is what happened.

Even Stokely Carmichael in his Black Power speech placed the focus directly on material accomplishments. Stokely, who later changed his name to Kwame Ture, seemed to have played right into the hands of the colonizers. During the Meredith March Against Fear from Memphis to Jackson Ture's emphasis in one of his speeches was 'we want the same thing you have,' referring to white people's material gain. He saw black power as material gain, and in a sense, it is material gain, but not when you don't control it, and when you don't accomplish it on your own terms. Jews came into the Human Rights Movement and changed the focus to civil rights and material wealth. The danger here is that when you don't have control of your own resources, you lose your dignity, and you won't ever control anything, including what goes on in your own community. We don't control the politics, so we compromise to participate in politics. We don't control the economics in our own community, so we must beg others for help to fill our needs, and so the trend continues. And this was the goal of those Jews who infiltrated the Struggle for Human Rights in changing the focus and the purpose.

Suddenly, sexual perversion has been elevated to a right. The LGBTQ+ movement has co-opted the struggle of the black community by identifying their immoral movement with ours. This was done with the control and use of the medial. Radio, television, news, every form of media is controlled by the ruling class of Jews. This is what happens when we were tricked from putting our focus on human development to material gain. It opens the door to all kinds of foul players who want to elevate immorality to acceptability by society. When we fall this low as a people, and as a society, we also fall from grace with God losing his protection leaving us at the control of satan, the evil mind that wants to rule humanity, as Jesus Christ identified in the Biblical verse above. The language has been changed in the name of inclusion, while at the same time, devaluating the high morals and value system of the people so they can be manipulated into accepting this immoral lifestyle as same as the struggle for black folks. The Jews are the ones who control all these so in our effort to obtain equal rights through integration and politics, we stopped supporting the black owned businesses in our own neighborhoods and began spending our resources with the very people that was oppressing us.

As I mentioned earlier in this writing, most people when they hear the word intellectual, they think of someone with a college or university degree from some institution of higher learning, but a study of history will show that most of the intellectuals that are known by the common masses, because they are the ones from among that class, didn't come from that upper crust or class, but were themselves, part of the common masses. Again, as I mentioned earlier, the Prophets themselves were part of the intellectual class, and from among the common masses.

Most people may not recognize Adam of the Bible as an intellectual, because we've been taught that he was the first man God created, and that he committed the great sin that plunged humanity into darkness. This is not the true meaning of that account. Adam was not the first man to be created, as he was already living his biological life. The Adam that we understand that God created as the first man took place in Genesis 2:7, where it says God formed man from the dust and blew into his nostrils the breath of life and he became a living soul. But before this event took place, in the first chapter of Genesis, 1:27, God had already created humanity, male and female created he them, in his image. Since we know God is a spirit therefore he has no image, we understand this image we were created in were the attributes of God, honesty, uprightness, ethics, integrity, etc;. So humanity was already here and Adam has to be seen as part of that humanity. Adam became a new mind when God formed him from dust, the dust means an unstable mind, clinging to everything it touches. But when the rain, or moral conscience came down and mixed with the dust, and God breathe into his nostril the breath of life, Adam became a new soul, or spiritual being, a Prophet to the people. Of course, much of this is allegorical but it's designed to show the growth of the human being through intellect and start his journey from the darkness to enlightenment. We see this in Greek culture as well as in religious scripture. As highlighted earlier, the Greeks studied the celestial bodies as well as the earth and found oneness between them. Socrates and other well known philosophers have been studied and reverenced for their contributions to the advancement of the human intellect. We call this, the human being finding himself and coming into his own. Finding himself and his purpose for existence.

The allegorical story about Adam and Eve, the tree of good and evil and the apple are all symbolic of man's desire to rule over his fellow human being through deceit and appealing to our weaker desires. It is unfortunate that this has been made to be seen as an actual event and the woman have been made to take the blame for the downfall of the society. If history is to be viewed correctly, the female greats of those times including Jochebed the mother of Moses, as well as the wife of the Pharoah at that time, Queen Aasiyyah who rejected the ways of her husband and prayed to Allah for a home in the Jannah. Hagar and Sarah the wives of Abraham who both birth the linage of two great Prophets both receiving revelation from Allah. Hagar gave birth to the first son, Ishmael through whom the bloodline of Prophet Mohammed Ibn Abdullah is traced, and Sarah gave birth to Isaac, the second son through whom the Prophet Jesus, or Isa as he in known in Islam bloodline is traced. And we know Mary the mother of Jesus. History is replete with strong women who helped bring the world from darkness to light, many dragging men along the way kicking and screaming. Abraham, Noah, Idris, Hud, Salih, Lot, Jeremiah, Isaiah, too many to name but all were Prophets of Allah and of the intellectuals.

Every era has produced the needed voice for that time. We see during the times of slavery, as mentioned earlier in this writing, the voices of the past could be heard speaking to the conscience of the leaders in the society.

Perhaps the two most powerful and influential leaders at that time were Dr. Martin L. King leader of the Southern Christian Leadership Conference and the Civil Rights Movement, and the Honorable Elijah Mohammed leader of the Nation Of Islam which taught self-sufficiency, independence, and respect for self and kind first. These are basic teachings that all communities espouse to their people, but when the Honorable Elijah Mohammed taught it to his people, he was accused of teaching hate. Actually, the truth of what he was teaching was that most everyplace we travel on the planet we see disharmony, disunity, war and bloodshed, and puppet governments influenced by western powers at that time, so the Honorable Elijah Mohammed call white people devils, he described their actions as actions of devils. Now this wasn't meant to be seen or taken to mean all white people were devils, but those who wanted power, wealth and influence over the masses and worked to keep the people divided against each other so they could stay in control. The news media seized upon some of the language used by the Honorable Mohammed and tried to use it against him. They did this through radio and t.v. interviews with Malcolm X the then spokesman for the Honorable Elijah Mohammed. Malcolm X was from the streets of New York and Detroit where he made a living at hustling as well as some honest work, but primarily, he was a hustler. He was finally arrested and sent to prison where he served a number of years. This is the very same tactic we saw that divided the struggle of black folks.

Malcolm X, here after, referred to as Malik Shabazz was by far the most forceful speaker and proponent of black independence of his time, and was the greatest asset to the Honorable Elijah Mohammed. In fact, it was the honorable Elijah Mohammed who set brother Malik Shabazz out front so his talent as national representative would draw more black folks to the Nation.

After the death of the Honorable Elijah Mohammed and the assassination of Dr. Martin L. King it looked like the leadership in the black community came to a standstill. It was as if direction for the black community had reached its peak and there were no other voices to be heard. Some black folks were allowed to head up huge corporate structures but again, they are not in true control. There are more blacks in political positions but even at that, the plight of the black community is in a worse situation than ever in history. With the advent of the Civil Rights Movement, the Struggle for Human Right were cut short, because we settled for what was handed to us in the form of political positions, not power, just positions, integration, some good jobs, recognition of a few blacks in higher up positions, not control, but just position, and that was about it. The rest of the black community was still powerless, and less dignity than ever before in history. A great part of the reason for our regression comes from the destruction of our culture, which was supported by strong family life, love for education and the arts, and a budging economic base that was abruptly cut short. The music we listened to and the language we used reflected our mindset and was the strength of the black community in terms of cultural expressions.

Minister Louis Farrakhan a very dynamic and knowledgeable leader stepped into the leadership role of the Nation of Islam, but he wasn't qualified. It seemed as if he had gotten away from the do for self ethic espoused by the Honorable Elijah Mohammed to accusing America of all that's wrong with our people, and while much of this is true, he offers no direction or pathway out. He looks like just another preacher holding the people in limbo. As for the civil rights movement in terms of leadership, not only has it been co-opted by immoral causes like LGBTQ groups but media made leaders like the Reverend Al Sharpton and other blacks who are well versed in current social and political affairs, they all have become part of the media landscape used to keep black folks in moral, mental and spiritual slavery.

It was at this time Imam W. Deen Mohammed the son of the Honorable Elijah Mohammed and sister Clara Mohammed rightfully took the lead of the Nation of Islam and brought the community from the narrow mindedness of nationalism to our true role of leadership in the advancement of human society. We often hear the phrase, "religion is a way of life." Under the leadership of Imam W. Deen Mohammed, we get a new perspective of what that means.

Most people in the world see religion from a ritualistic perspective, where we go to our different houses of worship and preach, pray and sing. Many time we even go outside the four walls of houses of worship to help those in need and do all the good we know to do to help others. These kinds of acts show the natural goodness of our human nature and how we truly are as human beings, and if left alone, the world would naturally return to human kindness again.

From the teachings of IWDM we get an even more comprehensive definition of the phrase, "religion is a way of life." To some people their religion is to oppress other people, they get into powerful positions in the society and use their wealth, and influence to bring hardship on the world. They not only oppress the people, but they oppress the environment and usher in health crisis on people by polluting the natural environment due to selfishness and greed. Since racism, greed, war, immoral lifestyles disguised as "rights" all these things are tools of evil doers who care nothing about people and will use these things to cause division between the people.

Because racism, greed, homosexuality, oppression and these other evils are a form of religion for the oppressor, then the new intellectuals have to see and understand this fact and address them from an intellectual view so as to effectively make intelligence and common sense prevail. We are in intellectual warfare and the very life of humanity is on the line. This is a life and death situation we are dealing with. The time for marching, protesting and demonstrations are over and done, it is time now for the next generation to came aways from the foolishness of party life, hip hop and gansta rap and realize these are some of the weapons used against us to keep us down. How can a young black man help himself when he's listening to music that's telling him to get high and kill another black man. The same racism that used ropes, whips and chains to lynch us back in the day, now uses gansta rap to do the same dirty deed but making us kill each other while they still make the money but keep their hands clean.

How you going to free yourself when you disrespect the woman who has stood by you since the plantation days of physical slavery, and today you use all kinds of vile language at her, you won't even take the position of a man, so she has no respect for you. Allah created the woman to love and respect her man, but he has to be a man, he has to earn her respect, not because she's too proud, but because Allah created her like that. As men we see that as a worthy challenge, and we rise to the challenge. It is the slave master who use rap and other forms of entertainment to cause us as men to want our women to take care of us, disrespecting them by calling the bitches and hoes thinking this kind of treatment of our women makes us look like men when in reality, we're acting like foolish and stupid little boys in possession of God's highest form of creation and not knowing its true value. The African American Woman!

The next generation of leaders will need to be created by Allah in their thinking, not by the influences of this world for they are designed to bring us under the control of Sahytan, the avowed enemy of all mankind, and the environment as well. To better understand what is meant by the statement, "the need to be created by Allah in our thinking," we need only to return to our history during the days of physical slavery for those are the times when we stood tallest, and even with the threat of death hanging over our heads, still we sought to raise our intellect, The mind is the highest part of our human makeup, through it we imagine, we create, we develop moral vision, we chart direction, we decide our own destiny! Those who seek to keep us in servitude and control our thinking know the power of the mind, especially the power of the mind of the black man, and this is why they use gansta rap, hip hop, sex, drugs, and the entire weight of the entertainment world to keep our minds on these low, immoral things so that we will never realize the higher life. It was also during those days when the slave master referred to us as "heathens," not a complete human but something just below human existence. Today we see that view they had of us as a people as what their intended goal was, for even though we were slave suffering the worst inhumane treatment any human being could put on another human being, yet we still maintained our high human standards, values and dignity. So this description they had of us as heathens wasn't how we were at that time, but their thinking was futuristic. Their goal was to reduce our people to that low level of animal life at a future time and we would still be their perpetual beast of burden, and under this evil influence we would kill each other like animals, disrespect our women leaving them with leaderless children as an animal would do, and the tool for this is the world of entertainment. The world of entertainment is the biggest slave master on the planet today, and we must free ourselves if we are to thrive as a community. The destruction we as black folks do to each other is no accident. it's by design!

There is a distinct difference between just being black in America and being African American. While we know that all black folks are treated unjustly, subject to police brutality and other systematic forms of discrimination, African Americans come from a different history here in America. As I said earlier in this writing, the Institution of Slavery was much more than just physical bondage, whips and chains. The intent was to change the very nature of our people through cruel and harsh treatment and other forms of systematic racism that was used to destroy us as a thinking person and cause us to see each other as less than human and therefore treat each other with total disrespect. To be African American in America is more than a skin color, it's the creation of another people. Imam W. Deen Mohammed in addressing this issue said this,

> "*We African Americans are a new people living in America. Before slavery and being brought to North America, there were no such people as African Americans living in the new land. We are a new social group living in America. God has created us again. The African children were emptied of their lives and put into slavery, and God restored life to the human vessel, and we became another people, a new people on this planet. Those who study psychology and the development of societies would agree with me because I am speaking with respect for my knowledge as wall as respect for science, the science of human life and nature of society. We are definitely a new people on planet Earth. We didn't exist before as African Americans. We are new thinkers. We don't think like Africans, we don't think like whites we think like US! We don't think like Asians or Arabs we think like US! We think like the people we were created*

to be. Why should the Islamic world be deprived of Islam expressed through a new and innocent vessel." Imam W. Deen Mohammed. (Raa)

When we look back at our history you will find that black men and women stood united together with each other in our quest for freedom and dignity. The black man and woman have always stood strong as a united front. The black woman has always stood beside her man, but this world and the deadly influences of media, the world of entertainment targeting our communities with gansta rap and hip hop have drove a wedge of hate and disrespect between us. These deadly influences are given to us by satan and they create the kind of mind set within us that turn us against ourselves and stop our progress.

This new generation of black leaders need to realize they have to rise above the negative influences of this world because they're designed to kill us morally, mentally, and spiritually. True leadership have a strong respect for Allah and look to Allah for guidance. They understand that religion isn't just praying and preaching, but it also covers every aspect of human life. education, economics, politics, science, everything, all created by Allah for the use of the true human being to use them to uplift their fellow human being. The next generation of leaders have to realize that these resources are needed for our advancement, but they are controlled by others. That is to say that if other people control these, they control us. Our goal is not only to seek the best from others in terms of their high character and integrity, because that's what is required for success, and we have to work with like-minded people, but as well, our goal is to seek the best from self in terms of intelligence and moral vision.

To elaborate further on the meaning of the statement, "the next generation of leaders have to be created by Allah in their thinking," tells us that they must see themselves as a higher form of God's creation. They refuse to be caught up in the deadly influences of this world. They will not allow themselves to be motivated by drugs, sex, party life, killing each other and meaningless that creates a meaningless life. The see themselves as God's chosen people, not because they think they're better than anybody else, but because they choose to obey Allah and take control of the resources that control their lives and decide their own destiny. They develop their own educational system that teach their high values and standards. They develop their own economic foundation, so they don't only become self-sufficient, but when they speak, they speak from a position of strength, not having to bow to anyone other than Allah.

This next generation of leaders need to be equipped with the weapons of intelligence and understanding of language because saten is waging intellectual warfare on the minds of the masses. The language of Imam W. Deen Mohammed equips the minds of the youth to not only have a firm understanding of scripture and its symbolic applications in human society, but it gives strength and confidence to those who employ the wisdom and knowledge that Allah has blessed him with, and he gives out so freely.

The black celebrities are among the worst enemies of the black community, and this includes not only the entertainers of music, dance and acting, but politicians, the world of academia and religion as well. These are slaves paid by those in power to use the platform given to them by today's slave master to influence our people away from those things that builds us up and instead go after the things that tear us down. If the black celebrity had lived during the times of Nat Turner, Toussaint Louverture, Harriet Tubman, or even in the more modern times of men like Marcus Garvey or the Honorable Elijah Mohammed, they would have been eliminated even before the white slave master. To be clear, this isn't an action that I recommend for or against, I only saying that we must beware of those who may look like us, but in reality, they are against us.

There's a surah or chapter in the Holy Quran entitled the Bee and talks about the bee lives in men's habitations. The way we are to understand this surah is that just like human being, bees form communities or as they are called bee colonies. There are different species of bees as there are humans who live in different communities, and it's the community we live in that influences our thinking and values. So, a person from one particular community can enter a different community and the people who live there can detect if that person lives there or not, never mind the race or ethnicity. It's the same with bees, a bee from another colony may enter a colony that not theirs. These bees give off a different odor and the home bees can detect if they belong there or not, and the strange bee is chased away. While humans are Allah's highest creation, we don't chase people from our communities, but this is just an illustration of the value of raising the level of thinking of this new generation of black leaders the importance of intelligent thought and understanding that the world of entertainment is the primary tool used by this world to kill us off morally, economically, intellectually, and spiritually.

Another passage of scripture we find this time the Bible where it says Jesus walked the water. Most of us think that Jesus actually walked on the water, and so we miss the more important message. As explained earlier in this book, there are several different meanings of water when it comes to religious scripture, including emotionalism, spiritually, morally, etc. In this case where it says Jesus walked the water its talking about being too overly spiritual which is the case with the black church. We sing, we shout, we pray and preach, but we don't change our situation in the society. In scripture Saint Peter is known as the head of the church, so in the verse whare it talks about him walking the water with Jesus, he sank. The interpretation of this scripture is that Jesus was rational, intelligent, and the winds of emotions didn't affect him as they did Peter when he tried to walk the water as the winds rose, meaning worldly influences that overshadowed his faith and he sank in the waters of spiritualism, which is the problem with the black church. We're so caught up in emotionalism and spiritualism caught up in singing, shouting and preaching that we don't see ourselves as productive leaders in the society in business and politics, so we're always economically and politically compromised. Jesus walking the walking doesn't mean he actually walked on water, but it means he was balanced and didn't allow himself to be ruled by lopsided spiritualism. In another scripture in Biblical scripture it says Peter was hung upside down. Again Peter represents the head of the church, so this scripture is telling us that our feet, indeed our entire being have been taken out of contact with the earth which is where all our material needs are fulfilled, therefore we're left depending on others to do for us what we should be doing for ourselves.

So, this is what is meant by New Leadership into the 21st Century. The black community must have an unwavering belief in God and understanding of scripture and societal language and how the world works. We live in a very orchestrated world, but if we're upright and intelligent God will guide us, and we will be the victors. We must put ourselves in a position where we control the resources in our own communities and therefore control our own destiny. Take our children out of these schools that's teaching them to be other than what Allah has created them to be. It's foolish to allow those who hate you to shape and mold the thinking of your children, your future generation. We must rid ourselves of this foolish mindset we have and stand up and develop productive community life. This is the only way we will gain respect from others.

Let us never ever disrespect our women. Let us hold them in high esteem so they will be our willing mate as Allah has intended. They stood with us through slavery, they stood with us through Jim Crow, and the trials and tribulations of racism. Let us as men maintain and protect them, love them, and allow no one to disrespect them. We will allow no one to disrespect our women, and we will not allow them to disrespect themselves. As I alluded to earlier, being black and African American in America are two different things. Our history has made us an entirely new people. The African American woman is a unique woman in her own way. So beautiful, so strong, so compassionate, the very best of God's creation. No matter the shape or size, or the shade of color, she is the very best. Y'all think about your women how you choose, but this African American woman is truly unique and she not only knows the struggle back then, she knows the struggle today, and we need each other. Never allow anyone to divide us!

We pray Allah's mercy and guidance upon us as we take control of our own destiny never again to relinquish it to anyone!

SOME CENTURIES LATER AFTER THE RISE OF CERTAIN EMPIRES IT WAS NECESSARY

After the war of 1812

References

1. Wesley, Charles H. The Quest for Equality, International Library of Afro-American Life and History. The Publishers Agency, Inc. Corn Well Heights, Penn., 1978. (Under the auspices of the Association for the Study of Afro-American Life and History).
2. Bennet, Lerone Jr., Ebony Magazine, Vol. 40, issue 4, Feb. 1985.
3. Washington, Booker T. Up From Slavery, Lancer Books Inc., 18 East 41st St., New York, 10017, 1968.
4. *DuBois, William Edward Burghart,* The Autobiography of W E. B. DuBois, A Soliloquy on Viewing My Life, from the Last Decade of its First Century, *International Publisher's Co. Inc., 1968.*
5. Marable, Manning, W E. B. DuBois, Black Radical Democrat, Twayne Publishers, Boston, 1986.
6. Romeo, Patricia W., I Too Am America, International Library of Afro-American Life and History, The Association for the Study of Afro-American Life and History, The Publishers Agency, Inc. Corn Wells Heights, Penn., 1978.
7. Muhammed, Amir Nashid Ali, Muslims in America, Seven Centuries of History (1312-1998), Ammana Publications, Beltsville Md., 1998.

8. Wesley, Charles H., Wesley, In Freedom's Footsteps, International Library of Afro-American Life and History, The Association for the Study of Afro-American Life and History, The Publishers Agency, Inc. Corn Wells Heights, Penn. 1978.
9. Imam W. Deen Mohammed. Various Public Addresses
10. Imam W. Deen Mohammed, Muslim Journal, Vol. 25, No.2, p. 11.
11. Romero, Patricia W., Afro-Americans in the Civil War, International Library of Afro-American Life and History, The Association for the Study of Afro-American Life and History, The Publishers Agency, Inc., Corn Wells Heights. Penn., 1978.
12. Robinson, Wilhelmina S., Historical Afro-American Biographies, International Library of Afro-American Life and History, The Association for the Study of Afro-American Life and History, The Publishers Agency, Inc. Corn Wells Heights, Penn., 1978.
13. Wilson, Jay Jay and Ron Wallace, Black Wall Street, A Lost Dream, Limited Edition, Black Wall Street Publishing, Dularon Entertainment Inc., Muskogee, Ok. 74401, 1992.
14. Kunjufu, Jawanza, Solutions for Economic and Community Empowerment, Black Economics, African American Images Chicago, Ill., 1991.
15. Boyles, John B., Editor, Masters and Slaves in the House of the Lord, Race, and Religion in the American South (15401870), Planters and Slaves Religion, Blake Touchstone, The University Press of Kentucky, 1988.
16. Jackon, John G. (Introduction), The Story of the Moors in Spain, Black Classic Press, Baltimore, Md., 1990.
17. The New Encyclopedia Vol. 18, 15th ed., Encyclopedia Britannica Inc., Chicago, 1998.
18. Jenkins, Timothy L. and Om-Ra-Seti, Black Futurist In The Information Age, KMT Publications, San Francisco, Ca., 1997.
19. Hart, Michael H., The 100—A Ranking of the Most Influential Persons in History, Hart Publishing Co. Inc., 600 Madison Ave., New York, 1978.

20. Alfahim, Abdul Rahim, The 200 Hadith, Makkah Printing and Information Est., Makka, Saudi Arabia, 1988.
21. King, Dr. Martin L. Jr.—Public Speech.
22. Prothero, Stephen R., The Encyclopedia of American Religious History, Proseworks Facts on File, Inc., 11 Pen Plaza, New York 10001, 1996.
23. Imam W. Deen Mohammed, Muslim Journal, Vol. 28, No.4, p. 13.
24. Leadership Training and Development Study Guide, Muslim American Society, P.O. Box 262309, Houston, Tx. 77207, 2000.

Dedication

On one occasion, I was home for a family reunion, and I remember my friend Robert James Lewis (Duck) came up to me and said, "Man, you ought to write a book." So this work is dedicated to my childhood friend, Robert. Also to those who gave so much, for a cause so great.

Greg Kaslo
Pat Hanson
Joe Morse
Nancy Sowers
Mary Schaffert

Yahya Shabazz was born John Otis Sumrall, the tenth of twelve children to Otto and Jimanna Sumrall in the city of Quitman, Mississippi. Upon completing high school in 1964, he worked for a time as a cement finisher's apprentice with his dad. During that same period of time, he became very active in the Civil Rights Movement starting in Meridian, Mississippi working with the Council Of Federated Organizations, (COFO). In 1970, he joined the Nation of Islam under the Honorable Elijah Muhammed. He is now working in the Muslim American Society as an Imam under the leadership of Imam W. Deen Mohammed.

Bibliography

Alfahim, Abdul Rahim. *The 200 Hadith*. Makkah Printing and Information Est., 1988.

Bennett, Jr., Lerone. "Voices From The Past Speak To The Present." *Ebony Magazine, Vol. 40, Issue 4, February*, Johnson Publishing Company, 1985.

Boyles, John B., Editor. *Masters and Slaves in the House of the Lord, Race, and Religion in the American South (1540 -1870), Planters and Slaves Religion*. Blake Touchstone, The University Press of Kentucky, 1988.

DuBois, William Edward Burghart. *The Autobiography of W E. B. DuBois, A Soliloquy on Viewing My Life, from the Last Decade of Its First Century*. International Publisher's Co. Inc., 1968.

Gamble, Kenny, and Gilbert, Cary G., and Huff, Leon. *Livin' for the Weekend*. Philadelphia International, 1975.

Hart, Michael H. *The 100 -A Ranking of the Most Influential Persons in History*. Citadel Press, 1978.

Index to Muslim Journal. Library of Congress. https://lccn.loc.gov/94643141

Index to Muslim journal. Atlanta, GA : American Muslim Information Retrieval, Division of Capital Information Researches, 1993.

Jenkins, Timothy L., and Om-Ra-Seti. *Black Futurist In The Information Age*. KMT Publications, 1997.

Jackson, John G. *The Story of the Moors in Spain*. Black Classic Press, 1990.

Kunjufu, Jawanza. *Solutions for Economic and Community Empowerment*. Black Economics, African American Images, 1991.

King Jr., Dr. Martin Luther. *Strength to Love* ("The Measure of a Man"). Harper & Row, 1963.

Leadership Training and Development Study Guide, Muslim American Society. 2000.

Marable, Manning. *W E. B. DuBois, Black Radical Democrat*. Twayne Publishers, 1986.

Mohammed, Imam W. Deen. *Muslim Journal, Vol.25, No. 2, Pg. 11*.

--. *Muslim Journal, Vol. 28, No.4, p. 13*.

--. *IWDM Study Library*, Various lectures. Mubaashir Uqdah, http://www.iwdmstudylibrary.com/monthly-progress-archives .

--. *Imam W Deen Mohammed Publications, WdmPublications*, https://www.wdmpublications.com/

--. *W. Deen Mohammed Weekly Articles: Reprinted from Muslim Journal*. NewAfricaRadio.com, http://newafricaradio.com/articles/index.html .

Moore, Pete, and Robinson, William Smokey, and Tarplin, Marv, and White, Ronald. *Aint That Peculiar*. Tamla Records, 1965.

Muhammed, Amir Nashid Ali. *Muslims in America: Seven Centuries of History, (1312-1998): Collections and Stories of American Muslims.* Amana Publications, 1998.

Prothero, Steven R. "The Encyclopedia of American Religious History." *Proseworks Facts on File, Inc.,* 1996.

Robinson, Wilhelmina S. "Historical Afro-American Biographies." *International Library of Afro-American Life and History, The Association for the Study of Afro-American Life and History, The Publishers Agency, Inc.* Corn Wells Heights, PA, 1978.

Romeo, Patricia W. "I Too Am America." *International Library of Afro-American Life and History, The Association for the Study of Afro-American Life and History*, The Publishers Agency, Inc., Corn Wells Heights, PA, 1978.

Romero, Patricia W. "Afro-Americans in the Civil War." *International Library of Afro-American Life and History, The Association for the Study of Afro-American Life and History,* The Publishers Agency, Inc., Corn Wells Heights, PA, 1978.

"The New Encyclopedia." *Vol. 18, 15Th Ed., Encyclopedia Britannica Inc.,* 1998.

Washington, Booker T. *Up From Slavery.* Lancer Books Inc., 1968.

Wesley, Charles H. "In Freedom's Footsteps", *International Library of Afro-American Life and History, The Association for the Study of Afro-American Life and History*, The Publishers Agency, Inc., Corn Wells Heights, PA, 1978.

Wesley, Charles Harris. "The Quest for Equality." *International Library of Afro-American Life and History, The Association for the Study of Afro-American Life and History,* The Publishers Agency, Inc., Corn Wells Heights, PA, 1978.

Wilson, Jay Jay, and Ron Wallace. *Black Wall Street, A Lost Dream.* Limited Edition, Black Wall Street Publishing, Dularon Entertainment Inc., 1992.

www.ingramcontent.com/pod-product-compliance
Lightning Source LLC
LaVergne TN
LVHW091530060526
838200LV00036B/548